BOMBS GUNS AND KNIVES

VIOLENT CRIME IN AUSTRALIA

BOMBS GUNS AND KNIVES

VIOLENT CRIME IN AUSTRALIA

EDITED BY MALCOLM BROWN

NEW
HOLLAND

First published in Australia in 2000 by
New Holland Publishers (Australia) Pty Ltd
Sydney • Auckland • London • Cape Town

14 Aquatic Drive Frenchs Forest NSW 2086 Australia
218 Lake Road Northcote Auckland New Zealand
24 Nutford Place London W1H 5DQ United Kingdom
80 McKenzie Street Cape Town 8001 South Africa

National Library of Australia Cataloguing-in-Publication Data:

Bombs, guns and knives: violent crime in Australia.

Includes index:
ISBN 1 86436 668 0.

1. Motorcycle gangs — Australia. 2. Serial murders —
Australia — Case studies. 3. Murder — Australia — Case
studies. 4. Terrorism — Australia — Case studies. 5. Violent
crimes — Australia — Case studies. I. Brown, Malcolm, 1947-.

364.150994

Set in Jansen Text, Gills Sans and Times on QuarkXPress.

to Reg Mitchell PhD
medical statistician and chorister

contents

INTRODUCTION

Good and evil will grow up in this world together.

Dr Samuel Johnson

The little honeyeater sat in the boy's hands, silent, as all tiny birds and animals are when they go into shock. It had been downed from a tree by the repeated impacts of stones shot from shanghais by a group of boys in the central New South Wales bush in my distant youth. The boys were laughing as they fired at the bird, which sustained hit after hit while clinging to the tree without trying to escape.

I was with them, too young to stop it, but relieved that someone now had the bird in his hands and was cradling it. I was going to volunteer to take the bird and do what I could for it.

He tore its head off.

Human beings, or at least some of them, are cruel by nature. Violence and sadism can be seen in so many people, usually males.

Years later, at the Singleton army camp in the Hunter Valley – I was by this time a hapless second lieutenant – it was reported to me that some sergeants had been doing bayonet practice on a hessian bag filled with straw. When one of them had withdrawn his bayonet, he found blood on it. He then discovered a cat with a litter of kittens inside the bag, one of the animals was badly injured. The response of the sergeants was to engage in a bloodbath, plunging their bayonets repeatedly into the bag until all the cats were chopped to bits.

Of course, there was a war going on. The natural brutality that dwells in some of us was being harnessed, and disciplined, in the service of the nation. Those sergeants had seen action in Vietnam, confronting an enemy who had no qualms about treating them the same way they had treated those cats. The Singleton base was plagued by stray cats, the cats were to be got rid of anyway, and if such cruelty would scarcely have been condoned by senior officers, it was hardly a hanging offence. Some time later, I was conducting a range practice. A willy wagtail landed on a star picket in front of the mounds. One of my soldiers took aim and machine-gunned it.

I was never one for army life, and I was glad to complete my national service, opting for what I thought would be the more agreeable nerdy-nerdy realm of talk, talk, talk, talk and creative writing. Fat chance. I turned up at the door of *The Sydney Morning Herald* in December 1972, and after a brief assessment by the editor I was told, in effect, to 'get thee to the scullery', which meant the section of the newspaper dealing with police matters.

So along came the bodies.

I remember horrifying scenes in those early years: turning up one night on Sydney's north-side after two men had been involved in a knife fight, finding myself awkwardly placed in between them as they crouched, hiding behind cars, while the police tried to arrest them. On another occasion, I arrived at a scene where a man had caught another man with his wife. He had stabbed her first, then grabbed a rifle and chased his rival around and around a panel van until he cornered and shot him in the head. I saw bits of the dead man's brain scattered along the road.

They said 'I was not the personality to cover politics', so I have never moved far beyond reporting raw violence. Often that violence has been preceded by a build-up, the silent brooding of a disturbed person unable to compete in a fast-moving, intensely competitive world. Suddenly, they erupt. This eruption might or might not have a sexual component, which might be spontaneous and unplanned, or progressive and calculated.

Whatever the motivation or the method of the violence, people die, are ravaged, have their lives ruined or badly affected. Often, the victims are people who are totally innocent, or, if they have had some role to play in the life of the disturbed person, have never done anything to justify a death sentence. That includes police officers, judges, journalists, politicians and lawyers who, through the nature of their calling, have been bound to tread on the toes of disturbed people at some point.

For the perpetrators of the violent outrages, the lives of fellow human beings, their emotions, experience, spirituality, benevolence – all those things worth preserving – are brushed aside with the callousness of the boy in the bush who brushed aside the intrinsic right of the honeyeater to enjoy life in its own environment, or the sergeants who ignored the rights of the cats. And so much of this violence is shocking – a sudden intrusion of inhuman depravity that is traumatic, sometimes terminal, often without the slightest warning, on even the balmiest days or the most tranquil of nights.

David Morrison Howie, a lecturer at the Mitchell College of Advanced Education in Bathurst, central western New South Wales, was helping his wife wash the dishes and looking forward to the arrival of their new baby. He hardly expected to be in the sights of someone with homicidal intent. But on the night of 19 August 1981, Eric James Murray, an absconder from the nearby Kirkonnell Afforestation Camp, fired shots through the kitchen window with a single-barrel shotgun. Howie was killed. Murray then seized Anne Howie and her two infant sons with the probable intention of raping her. Anne managed to get a message to a service station operator along the way, and the police intervened to save her and her family and arrest Murray, who was later convicted. But her life and those of her family had been shattered. Today, a plaque may be found on the campus of Charles Sturt University, Bathurst, a tribute to an innocent family family destroyed by a capricious act.

On 2 March, 1997, 19-year-old Alison Lewis from Lithgow in the state's central west wandered down to the city's reserve in the early hours of the morning to join friends. A beauty queen and a talented pianist with a bright future, she had been partying and wanted to go for an early morning swim. She had no idea of what was waiting for her. The friends were not there because they had been attacked by a man lurking in the darkness. They had gone to the police who, busy with other matters, had not responded quickly. Alison's body was found some 12 hours later, naked, raped and strangled, buried in a long-jump sandpit.

As a newspaper reporter covering a country trip with the then One Nation Federal MP Pauline Hanson, I was called upon to visit Alison's parents. These type of assignments are the downside of the profession. It is usually a horrible job, known in the trade as the 'death knock'. You need a story and a photo, and you have to resist the impulse to leave people alone in their grief.

Alison's parents were cordial. They showed me her bedroom. The bed was still made for their child who would never come home, a teddy bear propped up on the pillow. Like thousands of other bereaved parents over decades and centuries, they struggled to comprehend how such a thing could happen, or why it should happen to them. There was not much else to report, save the emptiness and tears they felt. When I said I would send some flowers, they asked me to make a donation to the Lithgow Conservatorium of Music.

This book is about violence. Part One is about the bombs, the heavy artillery of the criminal world that shatters peace and individual lives, often indiscriminately. Like the shells that pounded the trenches in the First World War, they are the most brutal and terrifying of weapons. Bombs, with their incredible and random ability to cause destruction, crush the spirit.

Bombers have a variety of motives, but a common one is to inflict maximum pain and outrage. We deal with several of these motives in our chapter on South Australian crime: one bomb planted by a career criminal; one as part of a family relationship gone wrong; another to cover up a sexual crime that had become, as so many of them do, a murder. All bombings are cowardly, and as they say, the smaller the man the bigger the knife – or the bomb. For devastating periods, these little men grab centre stage and create absolute mayhem.

Part One also deals with violence that erupts not on a communal level but at a personal level, often within the intimacy of personal relationships – the 'crime of passion', the jilted lover, the man who loves someone so much he kills her (or him), or kills his children to stop his estranged spouse getting access to them. They are difficult crimes to encompass by legislation. The crazies among us see no reason, and our very efforts to create a humane, understanding structure in which to accommodate such a person can often succeed in turning the violence onto the institution itself. And sometimes the bombs go off again.

This book is also about firearms, which have been part of Australian society since the time Lieutenant James Cook, RN, landed at Botany Bay on his journey of discovery in 1770, and discharged a shot at an Aboriginal man challenging his arrival. And it is about knives, which have been with us much longer than all weapons, and are, when all else fails, the ultimate resort of a villain.

Another way a deranged individual can hit back is to take a rifle, a high-powered one, or several weapons, find a place crowded with people and start blazing away. Whether he knows the people or not is irrelevant. This is delt with in Part tTwo.

A variation of this type of attack was put into practice by truck driver Douglas John Edwin Crabbe. He was ejected from the Ayers Rock Inland Motel on 18 August, 1983. He retaliated by driving his prime mover at speed into the bar, killing five innocent people.

Sometimes, there are indications that a person is going over the edge. But what can authorities do? The law is very strict – it cannot, generally, lock people up for fear of what they might do. Normally, the system can come into operation only after something is done. And by then, it is too late. Josef Schwab took off with a rifle and a hired vehicle in 1987. He shot and killed five people in Western Australia and the Northern Territory. Paul Gerard Mason, going nowhere and mentally ill, took it out on two women he knew as girls, killed the baby of one and tried to kill the baby of the other.

The Backpacker Murderer, Ivan Milat, did not know his victims, but did know the killing ground.

Part Three looks at murders in the home territory. Many of these are crimes of passion, but not all of them. Sometimes, the murder occurs during a robbery, or because the killer has gone to where he can find his victim. Violence in the home transgresses the rights of the individual to the sanctity of his or her home. In 1989, Assistant Commissioner Colin Winchester went home as usual to relax and leave the problems of law enforcement – cracking down on marijuana-growing and whatever else – at the office. A killer was waiting there for him.

Lindsey Robert Rose, once an ambulance officer, became a hit-man. In three of the five brutal murders he was convicted of, he went to the homes of his victims. Young Victorian toddler, Jaidyn Leskie, had no option but to trust the adults under whose care he was given. In his case, the home didn't provide a sanctuary.

Part Four deals with gang violence. Australia has had its outlaw bikies for decades, dropouts from the mainstream who have split off from the rest of us and just like motorcycles. They have created their own subculture. Their saving grace is that most of the violence they are capable of is inflicted on other bikies. But sometimes, the innocent get caught up in it.

We deal with Brendon Abbott, who formed his own gangs but was primarily interested in banks. He was one of the more enterprising prison escapees. His escapade was, at least, a little more successful than that of John Killick, who was picked up in 1998 by helicopter, thoughtfully hijacked by his girlfriend, but who then drifted back to Sydney and was caught in a caravan park.

We have devoted a chapter to Asian crime. This is not to single out the Asian community for ethnic vilification. As is pointed out, progressive waves of migrants, who have collectively brought so much good to this country have also brought their criminals with them. With the recent surge in Asian migration, we must grapple with the crime which comes with that – crime which is not representative of the mainstream of the migrant group, but of the parasites who are part of any community.

At the time of writing, Sydney is preparing to host the Olympic Games. The nation is sprucing itself up to put on its best face, and at the same time it is organising its policing and anti-terrorism forces for worst-case scenarios. Munich was a disaster, and created the demand forever after for enhanced security. But the forces of terrorism, misanthropism or just criminal opportunism have a way of beating even the best-prepared defences, as we saw at Atlanta.

When the Olympic world last came to Australia, in 1956, we were, in relative terms, an innocent country, and even if the world at large was no stranger to violence, the era of terrorism had only just begun and not yet reached Australia. Now it has – the defining moment was undoubtedly the bomb blast that ripped through the entrance of the Sydney Hilton in 1978.

That blast brought international terrorism to our doorstep, provoked a comprehensive review of security, and ended forever a Federal Parliament which allowed people to enter unchallenged. It created a nightmare scenario for organisers of any event that brings the world to our doorstep. It is the ultimate nightmare for the organisers of the Sydney Olympics.

This book is dedicated in part to the victims of crime, and we start with two of the victims of the Hilton Hotel blast, Bill Farrell and Alex Carter, employees of Sydney City Council. As society saw them, these two men were doing menial but vital jobs – collecting garbage – which required sturdy, reliable men, men who would turn up day after day, night after night, year after year, seeking nothing more than their pay and entitlements. These men, doing their duty that night, and others like them are totally undeserving of the evil that is brought upon them.

Malcolm Brown
July 2000

part one

THE
BOMBS

the Hilton Hotel bombing

Family Court violence

mayhem in South Australia

THE HILTON HOTEL
BOMBING

After each war there is a little less democracy to save.

Brooks Atkinson
American journalist

There was nothing alarming about the scene outside Sydney's Hilton Hotel on the night of Sunday, 12 February 1978. The leaders of 12 countries had arrived for the Commonwealth Heads of Government Meeting (CHOGM), they were met by Prime Minister Malcolm Fraser and, amid security thought to be the tightest available, they settled down to a talkfest. There were protesters about one cause or another: against New Zealand Prime Minister Robert 'Piggy' Muldoon for his strong anti-abortion stand, against Malaysian and Singaporean national leaders for anti-democratic practices. The Malaysian Prime Minister, Datuk Hussein bin Onn, had also been the subject of a kidnap threat.

Another target was Indian Prime Minister Moraji Desai. His government had in custody one Prabham Ranjat Sarkar, also known as Shrii Anandamurti or 'Baba', founder of the Ananda Marga ('Path of Bliss') movement. Sarkar, convicted of conspiracy, abetment and murder of six of his followers, had been locked up for life.

It is necessary at the outset of this saga to look closely at these events, and at the reaction of the Ananda Marga cult members.

They provided the background for inquiries New South Wales police were to make, and provided a logic of their own.

Sarkar, originally a journalist, later a clerical employee on the Indian railways, claimed to have had a series of visions and a revelation that he had divine status. In 1955, at the age of 34, he had founded his movement on the three ingredients of personal tranquillity, meditation and social conscience. The movement, based at Purilia in West Bengal, spread its message nationally and internationally, formed a political wing, the Universal Proutish Revolutionary Group, and a military wing, Vishna Shanti Sena (VSS). During the 1960s, Sarkar advocated action against social injustice, and told his followers: 'Struggle is the essence of life. Yours should be a pauseless struggle against corruption, hypocrisy and animalism.'

Violence followed, possibly perpetrated by opponents, or by factions within the movement. In 1967, a bomb killed five of the cult's followers; another in 1969 killed one follower and injured several others. In 1970, the bodies of six murdered cult defectors were discovered in the town of Ranchi. In June 1971, Indian police raided Ananda Marga headquarters, seizing an arsenal of weapons and several skulls. The VSS commander confessed to his involvement in 17 murders and 50 attempted murders, but said he had been carrying out Sarkar's commands. In December that year, police arrested Sarkar, charged him with conspiracy to murder and put him into custody, pending trial.

In Australia, where the Ananda Marga had established itself in 1973, Timothy Edward Anderson, army officer's son and one-time Melbourne University student, became an early recruit. He visited Sarkar in prison in 1975. That same year, the government of Indira Gandhi declared a state of emergency and banned Ananda Marga, jailing 2000 *avdhoots* (full-time cult workers), who refused to disband. These included at least two members from Australia. In what was a virtual civil war, Sarkar's followers bombed power and radio stations and heavy water plants, and derailed and sabotaged trains. A hand grenade killed the Indian Railways Minister, Mr J.N. Mishra. In 1976, Sarkar was brought to trial and, along with four co-accused, convicted and sentenced to life imprisonment. His followers claimed a conspiracy, that he had been set up.

Violence spread internationally. Around the world in 1976 and 1977, there were more than 40 violent incidents linked with the cult and aimed, for the most part, at the Government of India, including knife attacks on Indian diplomatic staff in London, Washington, Los Angeles and Manila, Molotov cocktails in Kathmandu and Ottawa and an attempted aircraft hijacking in Stockholm. In New Zealand in 1976, an incident occurred which had profound significance for Australian security authorities. Four Ananda Marga members kidnapped a police officer and attempted to steal explosives. One of those arrested was an Australian. In 1977, the British Government banned the cult, the then Home Secretary, Merlyn Rees, declaring: 'There is a violent wing in this organisation, and I do not believe this country should be haven for people who have engaged in violence of this nature.'

In Sydney, the graffiti 'Free Baba' became common. In August 1977, a cult follower left a pig's head on the counter of Air India's booking office in Sydney. A parcel containing another was placed at the reception desk of the Indian Consulate-General. In Melbourne, an Air India employee was stabbed at his counter. In Canberra, an Indian military attache, Colonel Iqbal Singh, was stabbed as he lay in his bed. Then, along with his wife, he was kidnapped. The man, who was convicted, had wanted Sarkar freed.

Tim Anderson, who had moved to Sydney in 1976, had become Ananda Marga's public relations officer. He operated out of cult headquarters in Queen Street, Newtown, in Sydney's inner suburbs. He announced that Ananda Marga was not associated with the violence, which in his view was created by various intelligence agencies and police forces to discredit the cult. As the cult's public face, he was well presented and articulate. He was also known to the media, and to the Australian Security Intelligence Organisation (ASIO) and police special branches, which were by then actively spying on the Ananda Marga cult.

From the time of their creation in 1948, ASIO and special branches, working cooperatively and sharing information, had kept tabs on extremist groups. Formally, they were working together for the preservation of Australian security. Over time, operating under the cloak of secrecy, they might have developed their own agendas. They had many critics, but the logic of having agencies keep watch on potentially antisocial elements within society was compelling.

Ananda Marga was assessed as a legitimate target for ASIO intelligence gathering and what went with it: telephone taps, opening of mail, physical surveillance and use of informants. The identities of various cult members were noted. In Brisbane, the cult's one full-time worker, Evan Dunstan Pederick, came to notice because of his participation in street marches and other protests, and his writings to the *Courier-Mail*.

In the months prior to the CHOGM meeting, word was getting back to intelligence services that Ananda Marga members were talking about violence, that there was a secret training camp at Stanhope, Queensland, and that plans had been hatched to bomb the Indian High Commission. In early 1978, Commonwealth Police passed onto ASIO intelligence relating to Pederick. A disenchanted sect member claimed Pederick had said: 'Do not worry about killing people; you kill flies and ants and cockroaches, so don't worry about people.' Sydney artist and writer David Wansbrough said later that while working with Ananda Marga, he concluded that members were extreme and that some had been making threats against Desai several days before his arrival. He had been assured there was 'plenty of security' for the visitors.

At about 1 am on Sunday 12 February, a taxi driver, Robert Trotter, saw another taxi stopped at the corner of Market and George streets close to the Hilton Hotel, according to his later account. His attention was attracted to that taxi because there appeared to be a passenger inside and the 'for hire' sign was illuminated, against regulations if a passenger were aboard. Trotter did not get a good look at the passenger, but he noticed the driver. It was, he said later, Tim Anderson.

Later that day, ASIO telephone taps on Ananda Marga's headquarters picked up a call involving Tim Anderson discussing with another cult member about what they should do during

Desai's visit – whether there should be a demonstration at the airport or outside the hotel.

Desai and the Australian security agencies were aware of the security risk. For that reason Desai was not brought to the Hilton Hotel by its main entrance in George Street on the Sunday afternoon but to the back entrance, in Pitt Street, where Fraser met him. At about 5.10 pm, Desai left the Hilton by the George Street entrance for a reception hosted by Fraser at Kirribilli House.

Shortly after midnight on Monday 13 February, *The Sydney Morning Herald* received an anonymous telephone call. The person said: 'You'll be interested in what the police are going to be doing down at the Hilton Hotel.' At 12.35 am, the switchboard operator at Sydney Police Headquarters, Suzanne Jones, received a call from a man whom she said had a foreign accent, asking to be put through to Special Branch. Nobody from Special Branch was available at that time, so the call was put through to the duty officer at the Criminal Investigation Branch, Cec Streatfield. The caller told Streatfield there was a bomb outside the Hilton Hotel. Streatfield picked up the phone to ring Central Police Station, the closest police centre to the Hilton. But there was scarcely time to put into effect a plan of action.

At 12.38 am, a Sydney City Council garbage truck stopped to pick up the contents of a rubbish bin outside the Hilton Hotel's George Street entrance. Driver William Ebb was watching his co-workers, William Arthur Farrell and Alex Raymond Carter, behind the truck to ensure that he did not drive off too early. He saw Carter carrying the bin. He heard the clunk as he banged it against the side of the truck, an action necessary to loosen sticky rubbish. Then Ebb felt a puff of wind, saw an orange flash and heard a thunderous explosion. A third garbage collector, John Watson, who had gone ahead to pick up another bin, started running, and Ebb, leaving the truck, went after him.

Returning, Ebb and Watson found a torso with its limbs blown off. They thought it was Carter, but in fact it was Farrell. The biggest part of Carter ever found was a foot, hurled through a Fletcher Jones store window across the street, in the Queen

Victoria Building. Constable Paul Burmistriew, on duty nearby, was mortally wounded. Eight others were injured.

The eventual police theory was that the banging of the bin on the side of the truck had brought together two metal contacts which were meant to be operated by remote control. Once they connected, the bomb went off. That never properly accounted for the warning telephone calls. The caller, or callers, might have meant the bomb to have been found, which would have created a security scare and delivered some sort of message. In this scenario, the garbage truck's arrival might have been a ghastly coincidence.

The event stunned the heads of government, as it did the New South Wales and Federal governments, and the public. Desai, who was back in the hotel at the time of the explosion, described the bombing as 'a mad act of terrorism', pointing the accusing finger at Ananda Marga though conceding he had no evidence. No group claimed responsibility.

At dawn on the Monday, Anderson was asleep in his home in Queen Street, Newtown, two doors from Ananda Marga headquarters. He was woken by an early morning call from a reporter from the Sydney *Sun*. Many media calls followed. At 3 pm, he issued a press release, stating: 'Suggestions that Ananda Marga is in any way connected with the incident are simply unthinkable.' He suggested the KGB had done it, or India's Central Bureau of Intelligence, to discredit his cult. Three hours later, police, armed with a search warrant, went through his home without result.

Days passed and forensic examination had not even been able to detect what type of explosive had been used. According to Aarne Tees, a senior detective assigned to investigate the outrage, police examining the debris of the bomb had found what appeared to be parts of a toy car, but because there was a toy shop nearby, they thought it was just a bit of rubbish thrown away. A team of 55 detectives, commanded by Detective-Inspector Norman Sheather, went on to interview some 1500 people, including students from Malaysia and Singapore, and people who were involved in the Muldoon protests, including a young New Zealand woman whose hostile statements about Muldoon had been noted.

On 15 February, the then New South Wales Premier, Neville Wran, announced a $100,000 reward for information leading to the conviction of the person or persons responsible for the bombing. Inevitably, suspicion centred on Ananda Marga. Three days after the Hilton Hotel bombing, three members of Ananda Marga, two of them Australian, were caught in Bangkok in possession of explosives. On 28 March that year, an unexploded bomb was found on the grounds of the Indian High Commission in Canberra. But all this was circumstantial. Commonwealth Police did have a photograph of people outside the Hilton Hotel on the Sunday during a protest against Muldoon, and Anderson was in it. Anderson was also photographed at Sydney Airport that day, but it was appreciated that Anderson had an interest in the visit and a right to stage a lawful protest. After several weeks, police felt they might have reached an impasse.

In June 1978, less than four months after the Hilton Hotel blast, Robert John Cameron publicly announced he had established the National Front, modelled on the British extremist organisation, in Australia. Formerly a Swastika-wearing member of the Australian Nazi Party, he was interviewed in Sydney by reporters, including this writer who wrote an article for *The Sydney Morning Herald*, which appeared on 8 June. His message was typical extremist fare – intolerance of Asian migration, suspicions of the concept of 'world government', a touch of anti-Semitism.

Cameron claimed to have established the Front 12 months previously, but nobody had heard of him. Of particular interest to Special Branch was the possibility of 'Nazi' strongarm man, Ross 'the Skull' May, teaching martial arts to members of the organisation. Several days later, a member of Special Branch rang this writer at *The Sydney Morning Herald* asking to be put in touch with Cameron. Cameron had committed no offence and was not on the run so this writer arranged it. There was nothing unusual about police wanting to talk to members of such a group.

There is no necessary relationship between the police contacting Cameron and their liaison with a mysterious and disturbed individual, Richard John Seary. But at some time after the bombing, Seary offered his services to New South Wales Police as an agent, to infiltrate an Indian group – he initially suggested Hari Krishna – to find out whether such a group had anything to do with the bombing.

Special Branch accepted his offer and directed him towards Ananda Marga. The use of Seary, a man with a patchy past, was to be questioned. Known to have used narcotics, including cocaine, LSD, heroin, opium and amphetamines, he had adopted a nomadic lifestyle. Diagnosed later as having a personality disorder, with schizoid traits, he was apparently not given a proper assessment by Special Branch. But what of it? Police informants can come from any background. The informant likely to raise the most suspicion is someone who is clean-living and upright, as they might be 'bunging on an act' to curry favour.

Though Cameron was later to say he had never had anything to do with Ananda Marga, it is possible he put his own party's literature – the contents of which were anathema to Ananda Marga – in the cult's doorway. According to Seary in his later information to police, Ananda Marga decided on 15 April 1978 to teach Cameron a lesson. Cult members, Paul Alister, 24, and Ross Dunn, 22, both unemployed, were later to say that by that they only meant they were going to paint slogans on his house. Seary maintained they planned to bomb his home.

That evening, after consulting with Special Branch, Seary drove to Carillon Avenue, Newtown, picked up Alister and Dunn, and headed towards an address in Yagoona in Sydney's south-west, where it was understood Cameron lived. In the car were sticks of gelignite and detonating equipment. In fact, they were heading for the wrong address. Cameron had moved from there 15 months previously. But the car never got there. Police, having been alerted by Seary, stopped it and arrested Alister and Dunn.

Alister and Dunn were charged with conspiracy to murder Cameron. The arresting detectives, John Burke, Dennis Gilligan, Robert Godden and Barry Summerfield, claimed there had been an attempt to detonate the bomb as they made the arrests. Alister and Dunn were charged with conspiring to murder Cameron and with the attempted murder of the police officers. Next morning, police arrested Anderson, who, on Seary's information, had masterminded the bombing attempt.

On 24 July, Seary told Central Court of Petty Sessions that in March 1978, he had been appointed second-in-command of the cult's military wing, under Alister. On the afternoon of 15 June, he had discussed with the three the proposed bombing of Cameron's house. Anderson's plan had been to remain at headquarters, waiting for word that the bomb had gone off, then to distribute press releases claiming responsibility. Seary said Alister had told him that Anderson had sent letters to three Sydney newspapers one week earlier, condemning the National Front in the name of the 'One World Revolutionary Army'. Alister had said: 'We want them to know there is a revolutionary army of moralists who will avenge immoral acts.'

On Seary's later account, Alister and Dunn had both made admissions about involvement in the Hilton bombing. Seary had asked: 'Did you blokes do the Hilton?' Alister had replied that he, Dunn, Anderson and a friend had 'fixed it'. Dunn had said that after another cult member had checked everything was safe, he had placed the bomb, wrapped in a newspaper, into the rubbish bin by 'pushing it down the side'. Alister, Dunn and Anderson were tried twice. The first trial, in February 1979, resulted in a hung jury. At the second, in July 1979, they were convicted of conspiracy to murder Cameron and sentenced to 16 years' imprisonment. The charge of attempted murder of the police officers was not proceeded with. With the three locked up, the police could take their time with the rest of Seary's evidence.

But there was general unease among onlookers. Even if Alister and Dunn had said what was attributed to them, need they have been telling the truth? Might they have been big-noting themselves, or having a lend of Seary? The police operation smacked of a frame-up. To critics, there was a suspicion that Seary had taken the bomb equipment himself, and that the arresting police were making a de facto arrest for the Hilton bombing. On the other hand, from the police point of view, if the trio had in fact been party to an attempted bombing of Cameron's home, and their names were out, it was at least possible that more evidence would fall into place. Perhaps the entire concept of police operating in this murky area of fringe politics was altogether too irregular. Questions had been raised nationally.

In South Australia in November 1977, the Dunstan Labor Government decided to initiate an inquiry into the operation of the South Australia Police Special Branch. The report, by Acting Justice White, was damning. In the month preceding the Hilton bombing, the then New South Wales Premier, Neville Wran, had instructed the state's Privacy Committee to look at the record-keeping practices of the state's Special Branch. The committee was to find a strong ASIO influence on the branch's operations.

Leaving that aside, what was the probability of the trio actually having embarked on this bombing escapade? It was a serious thing to attempt, with the prospect of bringing them long gaol sentences. All this for the sake of a petty fringe agitator who had only just announced himself, had made no impact, and would, in time, be attended to by Special Branch?

Bombing someone's home would normally take extensive planning and reconnaissance. Alister and Dunn had not even been going to the right address. And why, but why, would Ananda Marga, knowing it was under investigation for possible involvement in the Hilton bombing, have contemplated another one? And why would they, as Seary alleged, have made plans to publicise their responsibility for it?

Tom Molomby, then a journalist, attacked the Crown case and became a steadfast supporter of the convicted trio. Marcus Einfeld QC, then a member of the trio's defence team, said: 'If Tim Anderson is the Hilton bomber, I am the man on the moon.' Documentaries were publicly screened. A group of academic lawyers formed itself into a group called 'Academics for Justice'. On 18 June 1981, the then radical Labor Member for Illawarra, George Peterson, claimed Alister, Dunn and Anderson had been 'framed' and had become 'victims of the greatest miscarriage of justice in Australian history'.

In July 1981, a bag containing a bundle of 52 sticks of gelignite, which had been emptied by a caretaker a year earlier from No. 2 locker at the Roundhouse at the University of New South Wales – part of a process of clearing out unused lockers – was discovered. The wrapping for the gelignite was saturated with material that had seeped from the gelignite, so it had wiped out the fingerprints.

Tees said later that the wrapping had printing on it containing a flaw, and that the same flawed printing had been found around the gelignite used in the alleged Cameron bombing attempt. Wrapped around all of it was a copy of *The Sydney Morning Herald* dated 11 February 1978. Police traced the lease of the locker to an M.G. Melton. They found a New South Wales University student named John J. Melton, whose father had the initials M.G. The younger Melton was a weapons trainee with the Royal Australian Navy. He denied putting gelignite in the locker.

In October 1982, the then State Coroner, Norman Walsh, conducted an inquest into the Hilton bombing and the three deaths. Seary repeated what he claimed were Alister and Dunn's admissions. He said that Dunn had said he knew 'what 12 sticks of gelignite could do'. He said he believed the two were genuine because they had had an ideal – 'stamping out corruption'. On 13 October, Walsh found that a *prima facie* case had been established against Alister and Dunn and, in accordance with procedure, terminated the inquest and sent papers to the New South Wales Attorney-General. But things were not going at all smoothly from a police point of view.

In May 1985, Supreme Court judge James Wood, inquiring into the convictions of Alister, Dunn and Anderson, found Seary, the key witness, could not be relied upon and recommended the three be pardoned. Leading silk Chester Porter QC was asked to provide an opinion on whether the three were entitled to compensation. He said that in his view they were not entitled to it but that an ex gratia payment might be considered. The three each received $100,000. Wood's finding ruled out the use of Seary in a prosecution of Alister and Dunn for the Hilton bombing. Critics of the police operation were crowing that they had been totally vindicated. By then Labor governments in Western Australia, South Australia and Victoria had abolished their Special Branches.

In February 1989, Raymond John Denning, an inmate of Pentridge Gaol in Melbourne, sent a message to Tees, who had charged him in 1981 with armed robbery offences, that he had some information. Tees, 26 years a police officer, a detective of the old school used to mixing with the criminal element to get information, knew the benefits that flowed when a criminal was ready to 'sing'.

It was a difficult area in which to operate, and difficult to regulate. Informants could turn out to be liars, or be so shonky in other ways that they had no credibility. Eric Heuston, alias Eric Grant, a criminal who had spent much of his life in institutions or gaols, was an informant dismissed out-of-hand by Victorian QC Barry Beach in his report on police corruption. Another, in New South Wales, was Fred Many, convicted of rape and attempted murder, whose information was used to pin serious crimes on Sydney criminal Tom Domican. Domican beat the charges and Many was totally discredited.

Some notorious characters had seen the value, to themselves, of exploiting the attitude of social conscience activists. New South Wales had had a string of them, including Darcy Dugan and James Edward 'Jockey' Smith. In Brisbane, Whisky au Go Go bomber James Edward Finch persuaded supporters he had been 'verballed', and actually persuaded one hapless young woman who supported his cause to become his wife, at least for the brief time it took her to realise her folly.

Denning was the product of a wretched upbringing, a juvenile offender who went into major crime. In an escape attempt from Parramatta Gaol in 1974, he had, on later court evidence, belted a prison officer, Willy Karl Faber, with a claw hammer, inflicting fatal injuries. For that, he received a life sentence on March 1976. Denning had undoubtedly been dealt with harshly by the system, spending 22 months in the 'electronic zoo', Katingal, at Long Bay.

Denning escaped from Maitland Gaol in 1977, spent 19 months on the run, taunting police, sending audio tapes to Radio 2JJJ,

THE HILTON HOTEL BOMBING

appearing on the television program '60 Minutes', and leaving a note in front of the CIB. Recaptured and in the Metropolitan Remand Centre in 1979, he became acquainted with Anderson, then awaiting trial on the murder conspiracy charge.

In 1980, Denning escaped from Grafton Gaol, went to Queensland and, together with another escapee, Russell Cox, committed an armed robbery netting $322,622. Recaptured and brought to court in February 1983, he pleaded guilty to escaping, armed robbery and firearms offences. Judge Alf Goran, sentencing him to ten years' imprisonment, said: 'It appears to me you attempted to become some sort of folk hero. The reality is you continued your pattern of crime.'

Denning escaped from Goulburn Gaol on 15 July, 1988, with fellow prisoner Raymond Carrion, and together they committed an armed robbery in Brisbane which netted $44,474. In Brisbane, Denning got a telephone number for Russell Cox and arranged to meet him in Melbourne. They met at the Doncaster Shopping Centre on 22 July, but armoured car security guards became suspicious and alerted police, who moved in and arrested Denning and Cox. They were charged with conspiracy to rob an armoured car, using a firearm to resist arrest, and being equipped to steal.

In Pentridge, Denning and Cox had a falling out because Cox kept gloating that the wrong man, Graham Jensen, had been blamed for the murder of a security guard, Dominic Hefti, during an armed robbery on the Brunswick Shopping Centre on 11 July 1988. Jensen had been shot dead during an arrest attempt. Denning, who claimed to have been verballed and framed over the lethal assault on prison officer Faber, apparently decided the issue of verballing overrode all other considerations, and on one interpretation of events decided to turn over a new leaf and help bring out the full facts. He knew Tees from their earlier encounter, and regarded him as 'a straight cop' who would keep his word. He got in touch with him.

Another view is that Denning, committed to stand trial for conspiracy to rob the armoured car, facing escape charges in New South Wales and possible charges over the armed robberies in

Queensland, tired of prison life and taken with the idea of getting a reward, decided to play the system for all it was worth. Whatever the truth of that, Tees interviewed Denning in Victoria. Denning said Anderson had indicated to him that he had been involved in the Hilton bombing.

Tees wanted Denning transferred to New South Wales. Denning had appeared in Melbourne Magistrate's Court charged with using a firearm to avoid arrest, and being equipped to steal, and had been given seven years' imprisonment. The conspiracy to rob charge had not been strong and had been withdrawn by the Crown. At Malabar Detention Centre in Sydney, Denning made a formal statement on 1 March. He made another, with more precise – or amended – detail, on 22 May.

Denning said he had known Anderson in jail between 1979 and 1984, and during that time had had scores of conversations with him. On Denning's account, Anderson, over a prison 'phone' system (using the gaol plumbing system which was capable of conveying sound) had said: 'The main thing is I won't go down on the Hilton... me and some other done it but one of them's got an alibi.' He further claimed, that when they were together at Parklea Prison, Anderson had said on 28 June 1984: 'See, what I told you years ago was right... we've still got no problems with the Hilton.'

Denning did get some favourable treatment in return for his cooperation. He was indemnified from prosecution for the armed robberies in Queensland. When he faced court in New South Wales charged with escaping from custody, he benefited from favourable testimony from police, who did not mention the Queensland armed holdups.

On 30 May 1989, police raided Anderson's home in Glebe, arrested and charged him with setting an explosive with intent to cause grievous bodily harm. Anderson, then a student at Macquarie University studying for a PhD in political economy, appeared at Central Local Court and was released on $60,000 bail. The arrest was sensational, but created an instant outcry from his supporters.

Whether, ultimately, Denning's evidence would ever have been enough to convict Anderson is a moot point. There were immediate difficulties from a prosecution point of view. What was the probability of Anderson having blurted that out, especially over the gaol plumbing, which was a virtual party-line? What would it have gained him to have said that? Surely he would have suspected that Denning would repeat it. Would he have been telling the truth anyway? Anderson would still have faced arrest even though a co-accused had an alibi. And gaol records did not place Denning and Anderson together in gaol after 1979.

But something else did fall into place. Evan Dunstan Pederick, son of a Methodist minister, had once studied mathematics at the University of Western Australia. He had been involved in a serious car accident in which the life of a pregnant woman had been endangered, had dropped out of university and had travelled in Southeast Asia. In 1976, he had settled in Hobart, where a flatmate had introduced him to Ananda Marga, which he had joined.

After intensive training with the sect in 1977, he had begun to believe that Sarkar was 'nothing less than God'. On his later account, Pederick had met Anderson in January, 1978, at an Ananda Marga retreat in Galston in Sydney's north. Anderson had told Pederick he was impressed by his commitment, and that Desai's visit to Sydney would be a good opportunity to deliver a sharp message to the Indian Government. Pederick had asked whether Ananda Marga was going to make some sort of threat while Desai was in Sydney. Anderson had replied: 'No, I mean we are going to kill the guy.' Pederick had said: 'Isn't that a bit drastic?' Anderson had replied: 'It would be a great sin for us not to do the one thing that would assist Baba in his mission.'

Anderson had said members of Ananda Marga already had explosives and detonators but needed someone to plant the bomb, that Pederick would be perfect for the job because he was unknown locally, that to carry out his task, he would have to distance himself from Ananda Marga, and that if caught he would be disowned. Pederick had agreed to participate, had found cheap lodgings, and had studied bomb-making in a public library.

In early February, Anderson had given him 200 sticks of gelignite and the key to a locker at 'Macquarie University' (the location initially stated by Pederick, later changed to the University of New South Wales) and had told him to place surplus gelignite there. Pederick had built a remote-control detonating device from the parts of an electrically controlled small car and had tested it at Narrabeen in Sydney's northern suburbs. Nervous, he had, against instructions, gone to the sect's headquarters in Newtown, surprising Anderson, who had admonished him and then taken him outside to talk, to escape any ASIO listening devices.

On the evening of Saturday, 11 February, Anderson had picked Pederick up in a taxi he was driving and dropped him at the corner of Market and George streets. Pederick said that, dressed shabbily and wearing a false moustache, he had shuffled along George Street, carrying 50 sticks of gelignite wrapped in newspaper. A bystander had pointed out he was wearing a false moustache. At about 6 pm, he shoved the bomb into the bin outside the Hilton.

When the interviewing police had put to him that 50 sticks of gelignite would not have fitted into the bin, Pederick amended the number, initially to 15, and then 30. Police pointed out that taxi driver Trotter had put Anderson and a passenger in a cab near the Hilton hotel at about 1 am on the Sunday morning. Pederick changed his time for planting the bomb to correspond with that.

Pederick said that at 5.30 am on the Sunday morning, he had returned with the detonator and a remote control device. He had placed the detonator, attached to a single stick of gelignite, in the same rubbish bin, and had kept the transmitter in an airline bag. Anderson had relieved him at 1.40 pm on the Sunday, telling him Desai would not be arriving until later in the afternoon. Resuming his watch, on the other side of George Street, Pederick had seen a 'small brown man' arrive at the main entrance to the Hilton, and be greeted by Malcolm Fraser at about 4 pm.

Pederick had twice attempted to detonate the bomb, and when nothing happened he walked away, attributing the failure to the divine intervention of Sarkar. He then walked to Town Hall station, collected his rucksack from a locker and posted the key to the university locker to Anderson. He caught a train to Hornsby and hitchhiked to Brisbane, disposing of the remote control on the way.

Pederick's interest in Ananda Marga had declined, and he had left the cult in 1980. He had joined the Commonwealth Department of Social Security, married Carmel Cross, produced twin sons and lived in the Brisbane suburb of Auchenflower. In 1982, he had joined the Anglican Church but was troubled by his conscience. In a later newspaper interview he was quoted as saying: 'I couldn't equate something which sounded so good with something that resulted in such wicked actions. The end never justifies the means. I had begun to join the real world.'

On 31 May 1989, aged 33, having heard news of Anderson's arrest, Pederick had, on his own account, decided to make a clean breast of it, confessing to his wife's Catholic priest, Fr James Brown. Brown was somewhat sceptical, but contacted Brisbane police, who shared the scepticism and drove Pederick home. But they contacted New South Wales Police and Tees, with Bob Godden, went to Brisbane to interviewed him. He had him charged with having feloniously and maliciously murdered three people.

Pederick was extradited to Sydney on 2 June 1989. Two days later, he went with police to the scene of the bombing and pointed out locations. According to Tees, Pederick's description of the layout of the building at the University of New South Wales where he deposited the gelignite corresponded with the way the building was at the time.

Pederick and Anderson appeared in different courts on 6 January. Tees gave details of Pederick's confession in the Glebe Local Court. Magistrate Kevin Waller refused bail. Anderson told magistrate Derrick Hand that the information against him was 'absolute nonsense'. Tees said Anderson had made confessional statements to Denning, had been implicated by Pederick, and on the morning after the blast, Anderson had gone into a newsagency in Newtown, looked at a headline in *The Sydney Morning Herald*, and said: 'We only got three.'

In the Supreme Court of New South Wales on 29 August 1989, Pederick offered to plead guilty to three counts of manslaughter, and to conspiring with Anderson to murder Desai between 1 January and 13 February 1978. Mark Tedeschi QC for the Crown told the court that the Crown was pressing to have Pederick convicted of three counts of murder, and conspiracy. Pederick said that Anderson had told him that if he, Anderson, had not heard anything by early Sunday evening, he would assume the plan had failed and would telephone the police to alert them about the bomb, explaining that discovery of the bomb would be 'the next best thing to causing the explosion', and would convey a strong message to the Indian Government.

Pederick said he had not known which entrance Desai would choose but the one in George Street had been his 'best guess'. When Desai arrived, he had seen hundreds of people outside the hotel and though distraught at the thought of the carnage, had been prepared to cause it. When he heard later of an explosion, he had thought it must have been another bomb. 'But then, of course, I realised that… it was my bomb,' he said. As a result, he had 'lived with a sense of remorse and a sense of shame for at least ten of the last 11 years', and had become 'more and more torn by guilt'.

Psychiatrists said Pederick had been an emotionally confused young man, that he had been indoctrinated and dominated by Anderson. Pederick's counsel, Michael Maurice QC, pleaded that Pederick had not acted with 'reckless indifference to human life' because he had left the scene convinced that the bomb would not go off. On 14 September 1989, the jury found Pederick guilty of three counts of murder. Justice McInerney said he had been convicted of a 'terrible crime' but he accepted there were mitigating circumstances and sentenced Pederick to 20 years gaol on each of the murder charges and 18 on the conspiracy to murder charge, the sentences to be served concurrently, and with a non-parole period of 13 years.

Anderson stood trial in the Supreme Court of New South Wales in 1990 before Justice Michael Grove. Denning repeated the accounts of Anderson's self-incriminating statements. Pederick gave the account he had told police, but his evidence was now being strongly attacked. He could not have seen Desai arrive at the George Street entrance of the Hilton. Nor could he have mistaken Sri Lankan President, Junis Richard Jayawardene, for Desai on the

Sunday afternoon. Later in the trial, the Crown put to the jury that Pederick had in fact seen Desai, but at the time when Desai was departing the Hilton late in the afternoon, and that the recollection of Pederick, who had by then completed his evidence, had become clouded. The scenario became known as the Departure Theory.

There was at least some evidence to actually place Pederick outside the hotel where he said he was. That included taxi-driver Trotter's evidence and that of one James Mumme who said that he had been in the Queen Victoria Building on the weekend and had seen a very odd-looking man wearing a false moustache. Mumme was able to pick out Pederick, in a false moustache, from a series of photographs shown to him by police.

About the time Desai left the Hilton, late on the Saturday afternoon, an amateur photographer, Anthony Cuthbertson, had taken a photograph in which a shadowy figure, possibly of a man standing with a hand on his hip, could be seen at the place where Pederick said he stood to detonate the bomb. But Cuthbertson's evidence had problems. The Crown had long been aware of the photograph. The person in the picture had shoulder-length hair, whereas Pederick had had short hair. In 1989, a Crown solicitor, during a conference, had made a written remark about the pose of the figure, saying it was 'not one of his [Pederick's] poses', although, according to Tees, there was confusion about what picture was being referred to.

Another piece of evidence was more substantial. Pederick said he had assumed the name 'Peter Low', and had put the name, together with the address, 'c/- PO West End Qld', in Anderson's address book, for post-bombing contact. That name was found in Anderson's address book, apparently in Pederick's handwriting. Tedeschi put to the jury that Anderson had not been able to properly explain the entry at first, and that he had come up with a belated explanation which was unsatisfactory and smacked of recent invention.

Anderson's counsel, Peter Hidden QC, pointed out that the conflicts between Pederick's account of events and the objectively verifiable facts created a barrier to accepting anything Pederick said. He argued that just because Pederick had gone to gaol for 20 years, this did not necessarily mean he was telling the truth, and he should not be seen as 'a gold-plated witness'. He asked: 'How could Pederick have got it so wrong unless he really wasn't there?' Was Pederick the full quid? In his summing up, Justice Grove instructed the jury there was no evidence before them that Pederick suffered an abnormality of the mind, so he must be presumed to be sane.

On 25 October 1990, after a 51-day trial, the jury found Anderson guilty as charged. The packed public gallery burst into cries of derision and Justice Grove ordered the gallery cleared. On 12 November, taking into account that Anderson had already served seven years for a crime he had not committed, and saying he did not want to offer Anderson a 'martyr's crown' by giving him life, he sentenced Anderson to 14 years imprisonment, with a minimum period of 11 years.

In April 1991, Justice Wood, in a sentence redetermination hearing, decided that Denning should be released on 25 November that year instead of serving the remainder of his life sentence. It was a sore point for Anderson's supporters, and was questioned by the then shadow Attorney-General for New South Wales, Paul Whelan. From the police viewpoint, Denning had caused the arrest to be made and triggered Pederick's decision to come forward, allowing them to wrap up the case.

Anderson became a *cause célèbre* in sections of academia, politics, the arts, journalism and prison activism, including with former New Zealander Brett Collins, a vocal prison activist who had met Anderson in gaol. Books were written, documentaries produced, bumper stickers such as 'Hands Off Tim Anderson' were made, and T-shirts screamed the words 'Frame-Up'. But Anderson was refused bail pending his appeal against his convictions.

Anderson's case went before the Chief Justice, Murray Gleeson, and Justices Finlay and Slattery in the New South Wales Court of Criminal Appeal. His counsel, Ian Barker QC, submitted that Grove had been wrong in his direction to the jury on the issue of Pederick's sanity saying that the question should have been left to the jury which, in view of the inconsistencies in Pederick's evidence, might have concluded he had been suffering from 'some abnormality of the mind'. It was 'highly dangerous', Barker argued, to tell the jury that there was a presumption of sanity.

The Crown, represented again by Tedeschi, said there had been evidence available that Pederick was not suffering from any such abnormality. Two psychiatrists had been ready to testify to that, but Grove had not allowed that evidence to go to the jury. Tedeschi said Anderson's own counsel, Peter Hidden, had not suggested Pederick was 'mentally disturbed, mad, or suffers from any psychosis'. For the jury to have concluded that Pederick was not sane would have been contrary to the evidence. And there was 'a wealth of evidence' against Anderson. If some of Pederick's evidence did not stand up, it was still up to the jury to conclude that he was 'a witness of truth'. Anderson's lawyers had not been able to advance any explanation as to why Pederick would seek to falsely implicate either Anderson or himself.

Barker's argument was that there were such serious discrepancies between Pederick's accounts and the verifiable objective facts that his accounts were unacceptable. The Departure Theory, brought in after the Desai/Jayawardene scenarios had proved untenable, had taken the defence by surprise. The defence had not had proper time to consider it. That scenario had either not been properly investigated or the police and Director of Public Prosecutions had overlooked vital clues to indicate that this evidence did not stand up. Grove, he submitted, should have directed the jury to ignore it.

Barker called a former prison colleague of Denning's, Geoffrey Fletcher, to give evidence that Denning had once told him: 'If you're prepared to say Tim Anderson told you he bombed the Hilton Hotel, you could get the reward money and that would be the end of your money worries and you could help get me out.' Fletcher said he had questioned whether Denning was serious. Denning had said he was only joking, but had added: 'Tim Anderson is a prick. He treated crims like dirt when he was in prison.' Denning had also said: 'Mate, $100,000 [the then reward]… it's lot of money.'

Tedeschi claimed the Crown had offered the defence an opportunity to have Pederick recalled so he could be tested on the Departure Theory, but the defence had declined the offer, and even at the appeal hearing, the defence had produced nothing to rebut it. He called fresh evidence which supported Pederick's account. A member of the public, Nicholas Tsambouris, reading a news report of the case, had come forward as being the stranger mentioned by Pederick as having commented on Pederick's false moustache.

Another piece of evidence confirming Pederick's account was Cuthbertson's photograph, but this was attacked by Barker, who said it was vague and had been presented to the jury after Pederick had concluded his evidence. Allowing the jury to speculate upon it, he submitted, would have been devastating to his client.

Gleeson, in a 72-page judgement delivered on 6 June 1991, said there had been 'an inappropriate and unfair attempt by the Crown to persuade the jury to draw inferences of fact, and accept argumentative suggestions, that were not properly open on the evidence, and that were in some respects contrary to the evidence'. One was Denning's evidence of a conversation he said he had had with Anderson at Parklea Gaol in 1984. Prison records had not placed them together at Parklea at that time and the Crown's suggestion that prison records were erroneous amounted to a search for 'an hypothesis consistent with guilt'.

Gleeson was scathingly critical of the Departure Theory. Tedeschi, he said, had put to the jury that Pederick had actually been misled by the police and prosecutors when they had questioned him about Desai, or Jayawardene, arriving at the hotel's George Street entrance on the Sunday afternoon. 'Pederick was said to have made a mistake, but it was not his fault, it was the fault of the prosecuting authorities,' he said.

Pederick had given detail in his account to police which was 'difficult to reconcile with objective facts', Gleeson said. He had been 'incapable of giving a description which does not involve serious error'. Gleeson said he 'seems to have been a person whose reasoning processes were somewhat unorthodox', his account of the attempted assassination was 'clearly unreliable', and the question of Pederick's sanity was an issue the jury should have been directed to consider. For Grove to have said Pederick could be presumed to be sane carried a serious risk of confusing the jury.

Gleeson was dismissive of Denning's contribution, which comprised evidence that was 'fragile'. 'I consider that a jury, acting reasonably, would give Denning's evidence little or no weight,' he said. The evidence against Anderson had not been properly investigated, and that included the arrival of Jayawardene at 8 am on the Saturday, a fact officially recorded but left to the jury to produce. The deficiencies in the investigation had been compounded by 'inappropriate and unfair actions' by Tedeschi.

Gleeson said that had the case been conducted properly, there was 'strong likelihood' that Anderson would have been acquitted of any involvement. But it was not a case where he would say the jury was not entitled to convict. It was a matter of the court's discretion whether a retrial should be ordered, and he had decided that option should not be taken. 'I do not consider that in these circumstances, the Crown should be given an opportunity to patch up its case,' he said. With the concurrence of Finlay and Slattery, he quashed the conviction and entered a verdict of acquittal.

In the sour aftermath, Anderson returned to private life, later to pop up as secretary of the New South Wales Council for Civil Liberties. Seary disappeared from the public arena, emerging briefly in 1999 in an unsuccessful action for defamation against Tom Molomby. Tees became a barrister, Tedeschi the Senior Crown Prosecutor for New South Wales. Elsewhere, there were dark suggestions of conspiracy, claims that ASIO had set the bomb to boost a case for greater resources. There were persistent calls in political circles for a joint Commonwealth–State inquiry into the case, and claims that this had been resisted by governments for fear of what might come out. No inquiry was ever held.

Denning, released from gaol, was initially kept on a witness protection program but was dropped from it. On 11 June 1993, he died of a heroin overdose.

Pederick continued his gaol term but finally, appreciating that he was in gaol on the basis of a confession that had been utterly discredited, applied for a review of his conviction. In 1996, the New South Wales Government asked a retired Supreme Court judge, Ken Carruthers QC, to examine the case. Carruthers told the government that the case did need examination. The matter was referred to the New South Wales Court of Criminal Appeal as an appeal, and on 21 May 1997, Justice David Hunt turned the appeal down on the grounds that Pederick had never explained how he came to make the 'false' confession.

In 1997, following an adverse assessment of the New South Wales Special Branch by the Police Royal Commissioner, Justice Wood, the branch was wound up and replaced by another body. On 27 November that year, Pederick, then aged 41, was released on parole, after an incarceration of eight years, three months and 27 days. He remained, in formal terms, convicted. The case had been 'solved' but in reality it was a wretched, unresolved mess, destined to drift into history as something nobody wanted to know about.

Were the police seriously at fault? Did the police have any option but to try to break through the formidable barriers by unconventional means? The use of Seary was undoubtedly a gamble, as was the use of Denning. The gamble appeared to have paid off with Denning. Had Pederick been accurate in his account, the conviction of Anderson is likely to have stood. The investigation and prosecution would have been seen in history as a triumph for the forces of law and order. But in the event, nobody won. There had been many casualties, and a man had been gaoled on the strength of a confession which was vigorously demolished to establish someone else's innocence. It might be seen as an insanity that flowed from the perpetrators of the outrage and permeated the whole investigative and judicial process, leaving the institutions slightly diminished.

FAMILY COURT VIOLENCE

I kiss'd thee ere I kill'd thee...

William Shakespeare
Othello

The two men waited in the darkness, dressed in military fatigues, their faces blackened, clutching firearms, hearts beating. They were frightened; they had never done anything like this before, but they felt compelled. Their eyes were fixed on the house at Warnervale on the New South Wales central coast, where Christine Hicks, the estranged wife of central coast boxing trainer Cec Waters, was living with horse trainer Allen Henry Hall.

Hicks and Hall were living in some apprehension. On 24 February 1988, their former home at Jilliby, also on the central coast, had been burned down. They had received a note: 'More is to come.' They had little doubt who had been behind that. It was Cec. Christine Hicks had voiced her fears to police. But nobody could prove anything. It was now June. While Hicks and Hall were watching television, the dogs outside sniffed out the men in the bushes and started barking furiously. Hall came out of the house to find out what was happening. As he stood there, silhouetted, the men fired. Hall fell, mortally wounded. Hicks ran out, found Hall on the ground, and heard the car screeching away.

The Waters family, and the murder case that dragged on for years, captured the public's imagination. The drama was played out against a backdrop of professional sporting promotions and boxing championships. When all the facts came out, the men in the bushes were identified as Australian heavyweight boxing champion Dean Waters, the eldest son of Cec, and a motor mechanic who had trained with him, Damon Ashley Cooper. Both had been acting on the orders of Cec.

It was a case that had been crying out for intervention by the State, whether by use of Apprehended Violence Orders (AVOs) or adjudication. But any such intervention needs flexibility and a high degree of understanding. Proactive policing of family matters had found its expression in Australia in the institution of protection orders, aimed at preventing a nominated individual from approaching one or more nominated individuals. Domestic assaults, normally by men on their wives or de facto partners, had been largely ignored until the 1970s when, as an issue brought to public awareness by the women's movement, they came to be recognised for what they were – tangible symptoms of a vast ocean of suffering.

Adjudication by the Family Court was meant to have been a mechanism to deal with situations that had gotten, or were in danger of getting, out of control, sometimes with deadly consequences for individuals. In the end, no institution or law can restrain individuals intent on seeking their own vengeance. But the State had to try, and accept along with it, the deadly risks of the best-intended moves backfiring and of the violence being turned onto the institution of State itself, and its servants.

Cec Waters, born in England in 1926 and married to Christine Hicks, more than 20 years his junior, had run the family home at Kulnura, in the central coast hinterland of New South Wales, as an obsessive, heartless autocrat. He had bullied his family to an intolerable degree. He had decided that his three sons, Dean, Guy and Troy, all by a previous marriage, should become champion boxers, and after virtually strapping on the gloves in the cradle, had trained them to a high degree of pugilistic prowess and put them into the ring. Guy and Troy had taken Commonwealth titles, Dean an Australian one, and both Guy and Troy would fight for world titles. Anyone who had been inside the Waters' family establishment – as this writer had – would appreciate Cec Waters' mesmerising impact. The boys were essentially decent, and brought up in a different environment would probably not have become pugilists at all. They did not deserve their father.

Cec Waters, used to having his own way, was more than a little miffed in December, 1987, when Christine moved out and took up with Hall. Hall, 39, had a long criminal record, including convictions for homosexual assaults on men. He was not much chop, but was at least better than Cec. Cec Waters decided that his wife and Hall had besmirched the family name and humiliated him. He told Dean his stepmother was a 'hobo', 'tramp' and 'whore', that Hall was a no-good, alcoholic druggie, who bashed women and molested children, and both had to die. In May 1988, Cec Waters took Dean into the Ourimbah State Forest, where they dug graves. In a later interview with police, Dean Waters said: 'I feel ashamed now and I can't understand how it happened, but I found myself deep in the bush digging a grave which was supposed to be for my mother.' He had felt disgusted, he said, and had walked away. His father had sneered at him, calling him a coward.

On 29 June, Dean Waters, according to his own account, succumbed to his father's demands and went out with Cooper, who also claimed later to have been a slave to Cec Waters' will. The two armed themselves with a 12-gauge shotgun and a .22 calibre rifle. After the shooting, Cec Waters praised his son for the killing of Hall but chastised him for sparing Hicks. Investigating police found a footprint, which appeared to match Dean Waters' running shoes, and a tyre print.

On 11 August 1988, police charged Dean and Cec Waters with conspiring between themselves and another to kill Hall. On 31 October, Dean Waters, aged in his mid-twenties, was charged with the murder of Hall, Cec Waters as an accessory. In July 1989, magistrate Bill Pierce dismissed the information against Dean Waters on the grounds that no properly instructed jury, on the evidence available, would be likely to convict. The charge against Cec Waters went no further.

On 8 February 1997, Dean Waters – who had been confronted by a patient, dogged detective, Dennis O'Toole – went to Wyong police station and confessed. 'It was on that day, 29 June 1988, that I guess I surrendered to his will,' he said. He named Cooper as his accomplice. Charged, along with Cooper, with murder and arson, Waters was committed for trial. Cec Waters, also charged with murder, said he would deny everything, and on 4 April 1997, died of a heart attack. Cooper was convicted in the Newcastle Supreme Court in May and sentenced to 18 years gaol, with a minimum of 12 years to serve.

Dean Waters' turn before a jury came in July 1997. Waters said he was pleading not guilty to murder on the grounds of diminished responsibility, but would be prepared to plead guilty to manslaughter. The Crown prosecutor, Paul Lynch, pushed for a murder conviction. Evidence was presented illustrating Cec Waters' brutality. The jury was told that Cec Waters had told Troy that if any of the boys tried to escape from the family, he would find them and kill them. Psychiatrist Rob McMurdoe, for the defence, spoke of 'emotional and physical brutalising and someone exposed to excessive and inappropriate punishment… I understand he [Dean Waters], was forced to do literally ludicrous and revolting things'. Lynch pointed out that the killing had been a deliberate act, meticulously planned. On 31 July, the jury found Waters not guilty on all charges. Dean Waters sat weeping in the dock, until reminded by the judge that there was no reason for him to stay there any longer. There were some public expressions of surprise at the acquittal. Cooper's appeal against his conviction and sentence was spurred on by the Waters verdict, but on 24 February 1998, it was dismissed.

The reappraisal of the law in relation to marriage came with the scrapping of the *Matrimonial Causes Act* (Cth), with its burden of proof and formalised processes, and the passage, in 1975, of the *Family Law Act*. This Act had only one ground for divorce: the irretrievable breakdown of marriage, proof of which was a year's separation. The *Family Law Act*, over the next quarter-century, was a success, at least in terms of the sheer numbers of marriages that were dissolved, and sometimes saved, without serious incident. The extraordinary rise in the number of AVO applications indicated that there was, and had always been, a need for such mechanisms. But right from the Act's inception, it was obvious that situations would arise where the degree of obsession, mania, whatever, was so extreme that no law could ever contain it, and it is these situations which remain at the cutting edge of all legislative reviews.

Wednesday morning, 20 November 1974, was just another day in political life. The *Family Law Act* was going through its legislative process, amid controversy. This writer, then a reporter in Brisbane, had emblazoned on his consciousness the type of situation which, one way or another, proactive intervention by the state was meant to address. The question was: how could it do so?

On that morning, Pauline Joy Winchester, aged 17, a picture of happiness, an engagement ring on her finger, was waved off by her beaming mother, Dorothy, who then went back into her home in Sandgate, suburban Brisbane, to prepare for the engagement party planned for Saturday night. Pauline worked in a legal office in Queen Street, in Brisbane's Central Business District. She was known to have been well brought up. She had done Junior Level at high school and then trained in office work. That day, she would be getting good cheer, best wishes, a bit of ribbing, perhaps. She would see her fiancee, 18-year-old fitter and turner Robert Boyle.

There was one cloud over her life. Another man, John Campbell Edwards, 23, Bachelor of Laws, due in six months to be admitted as a solicitor of the Supreme Court of Queensland, had spotted her in early 1974 when he was an articled clerk. He had fallen for her, and despite total lack of encouragement from her, had become obsessed. American-born, Edwards had arrived in Australia as a child. His mother had worked to put him through law school, a commitment which he had repaid by devotion to her and attention to his studies. He was writing a thesis on constitutional law, owned a motorbike and had a rifle, apparently for recreational shooting. He was, his mother said later, 'a gentle, beautiful man'.

Pauline refused Edwards' entreaties to go out with him. In May, when his persistence became too much, she moved to another legal office. Edwards kept ringing her, and they kept meeting in the street. In early November, when Edwards showed no signs of letting go, she told him she had become engaged. Edwards disappeared from her life, or so she thought. But he had not disappeared. The rebuff had driven him over the edge. Edwards, Brisbane *Courier-Mail* reporter Peter Hansen theorised later, had been miffed by the fact that he, with all his qualifications and prospects, had been dumped for someone far humbler in the social spectrum. On the Tuesday night, 19 November, she had been out with Boyle and had told him about 'this other chap'. She had seemed frightened, Boyle recalled later. Edwards was at that moment at home watching TV, but had apparently decided that if he could not have Pauline, nobody would.

On the Wednesday morning, Edwards told his mother he would not be going into town with her, he would take his motorbike. At 8.30 am, Pauline Winchester, as was her normal practice, walked up Isles Lane, Brisbane, apparently perfectly safe among office workers and early shoppers. As she walked past a florist shop, Edwards stepped out, holding a sawn-off .22 calibre rifle. He opened fire, pumping six bullets into her, then put the muzzle of the rifle into his mouth, pulled the trigger and fell beside her – the shocking climax, Hansen wrote the next day, 'of the most tragic one-sided love affairs that ever went wrong'.

The *Family Law Act* was to be administered by a dedicated institution, the Family Court, which would strip away the formal trappings of ordinary courts and have counselling processes. Established with such high hopes, it was to be presided over by Elizabeth Evatt, one of the brilliant Evatt clan, and it was hoped the new system would bring humanity as well as justice to an area where the harsh grating of the traditional legal system caused much injury. Then it started making decisions, and dealing with subjects the custody of children, based on the principal that the children's welfare had priority. Often, for many reasons, the children went to the mother, as the person best placed to attend to their total needs.

From the outset, many people, particularly men, felt the rulings harsh and unconscionable. No more could fault be brought up as a factor, as it had been under the *Matrimonial Causes Act*, where in the past warring couples had taken to the courtroom to thrash out issues such as cruelty and adultery. People feeling aggrieved – in most cases men – started getting together and forming organisations, ostensibly aimed at bringing about changes in the *Family Law Act*. The people joining such groups varied. Many were rational and sensible, others not. The irrational tended to single out the Family Court and its judges as targets for their rage and frustration. All this was not lost on the Family Court. Elizabeth Evatt said: 'I don't believe any security arrangements can give a watertight guarantee, but I would like to see improvements. We have sought to deformalise, demystify and reduce the level of trauma associated with the breakup of a marriage. But under any system dealing with matters so close to families, so close to people's hearts, some people are going to get distraught and things will happen, such as the murder of whole families. The feelings of anger are usually directed against the family, but sometimes it is against the person in authority.'

Dr Silvano Mariti, born in Italy in 1922, a migrant to Australia in 1952, and married to a woman 19 years younger than himself in 1969, became one of the Family Court's early and most trenchant critics. The couple had a boy and two girls and might have been happy, but things started to go wrong. In early 1978, Mariti's wife was admitted to Hornsby District Hospital. She applied for custody of her children. If all the facts were publicised, they suggested a serious enough situation. On 28 February that year, Justice Yuill in the Family Court ordered Mariti to surrender his passport and not to take the children outside the metropolitan area. The next month, following further action by Mrs Mariti, Justice David Opas awarded custody to her. Mariti, claiming not to have heard of the hearing of her affidavit, was devastated.

After further litigation, the order was varied to give Mariti access to his children, subject to qualifications. In August 1978, with Justice Ray Watson then in charge of the case, Mariti took the children out on an access visit and did not return with them. Instead, he took them to Perth and attempted to stow away on a ship bound for Singapore. From there he planned to fly to Rome. Apprehended on board and returned to Australia, Mariti appeared before Watson and was jailed for 12 months for contempt of court.

On 23 June 1980, Opas completed his hearings at the Family Court at Parramatta, talked with colleagues and studied papers until 5.30 pm, then was taken by a Commonwealth car to his home in Edgecliff Road, Woollahra, in Sydney's east. He was about to have dinner with his wife and two children when the bell sounded at the garden gate. He went to answer it and was shot dead.

Known as a reasonable and fair judge, Opas, 43, had been a Family Court judge since 1977. Inclined to award custody more often to the mother than to the father, he was, like other Family Court judges, aware of the bitterness. Journalist Sue Arnold wrote in the Sydney *Sun*: 'Parramatta Court, where Justice Opas sat, has been the scene of some angry demonstrations by various men who flouted the law and abducted their children.' It was quite obvious to investigating police that there were plenty of potential candidates. The then acting chief of the New South Wales Criminal Investigation Branch, Detective Superintendent Barney Ross, said: 'Justice Opas had 40 cases yesterday and was scheduled to hear 40 today, so you can see the size of the task.'

In July 1980, Justice Baker in the Family Court realised Mariti was totally obsessed and refused him general access to his children. In 1981, with his children gone, Mariti published a pamphlet, *Is Love a Crime?*, and in 1983 another, *Legal Obscenity*. He said he would take his case to Amnesty International and the International Court of Justice. In February 1984, Justice Richard Gee heard a further application by Mariti for access and dismissed it. On 26 March, Justice Renaud stood over Mariti's claim for continued access. Mariti, damning not only the Family Court but the whole of Australian society, had supporters, including a self-styled 'Family Law Action Group' (FLAG), one of whose members had also been gaoled for contempt, and had been nicknamed 'The Crusher' because every time he spoke he said: 'Crush the Family Court.'

In the early hours of 6 March 1984, Gee and his two children were asleep in their home at Belrose, in Sydney's northern suburbs. Mrs Gee was in hospital having an operation. Gee had been threatened with violence but he said later he had not taken such threats seriously, because it was part of the job. At 1.45 am, the house was hit by a huge explosion, in which 50 sticks of gelignite were used. The children were uninjured but Gee received lacerations to his legs, left arm and face.

Again there was public soul-searching. There were, Evatt said, people in the community who were of 'a criminally dangerous disposition'. 'They, like everyone else, can be involved in matrimonial cases and when such people are involved, you don't know quite what to expect,' she said. The Family Court's then director of counselling, Don McKenzie, said: 'We are in an area of intense emotion, and a large number of people are bitter. It is fairly difficult to predict whether anyone will become murderous.' He said that of 40,000 marriage dissolutions in Australia each year, 85 per cent were settled out of court. The remaining 15 per cent were fought out in court. 'People going through the courts are in a changed state of consciousness,' he said. 'Often people don't understand what is being said to them. They get into a situation where they can get themselves into trouble very quickly.'

At 10.20 pm on 15 April 1984, a bomb exploded outside the Family Court Registry in Phillip Street, Parramatta, causing extensive damage, hurling bricks and debris 70 metres. Nobody was injured, but it was ominous. The following month – and this is not to suggest a necessary connection – Mariti sent a copy of a pamphlet, *Evil Scum*, to Justice Renaud at the Family Court's Parramatta Registry. It portrayed several Family Court judges, including Elizabeth Evatt, unfavourably. A rational view of the pamphlet might see that it was the ravings of an obsessed individual. A note attached to the pamphlet said: 'Please order the mother to give the children back, for everyone's sake.' Police interviewed Mariti at his home at Double Bay, in Sydney's eastern suburbs. Mariti denied threatening anybody or trying to influence Renaud. He said he was just asking Renaud to help him. The then

Detective Sergeant Frank Mellis searched the house and found a large number of pamphlets, as well as sealed envelopes addressed to foreign consulates and embassies, and Australian radio stations.

At 8.15 am on 4 July 1984, Justice Ray Watson was about to leave his home unit in Greenwich on Sydney's lower north shore, for work at Family Court at Parramatta. There were five other units in the block, and no special security devices. Watson's wife of 14 years, Pearl, 55, worried about security but Ray Watson did not want it. He did not feel that judges should live locked in cages. Sometimes, his Commonwealth car driver would come up and knock on the door. This time, the driver waited in the street. At 8.15 am, Pearl Watson went to open the door. A bomb was leaning against it, or wired to it. There was a massive explosion. She was dismembered and blown through a wall. Ray Watson, briefly knocked unconscious, came to and then staggered onto the street calling out for help.

In the aftermath, as police did a survey of the number of injured and the wreckage of the unit block, the late John O'Gready, a veteran photographer on the Sydney *Sun*, also looked at the carnage. He said later: 'I've seen gas explosions and bomb explosions before, and I don't know how the block of units is still standing.' Police interviewed Mariti and searched his home and car. They found news clippings relating to the Family Court violence, but Mariti said he had not had anything to do with it. That night, on his later account, he attended a meeting of FLAG. He had heard one of the group say, 'Everyone knows who the bomber is', and the group had become very angry. It occurred to him he was being singled out and might be 'framed'.

Media, police and politicians began intensive reporting on the background of despair that might have lain behind such actions. On 8 July 1984, the Sydney *Sun-Herald* published a photocopy of *Evil Scum*. Evatt, who by then had seen the murder of one her judges, and of the wife of another, and injuries to two more judges, was at the end of her tether. To be singled out, photographed and named in a disparaging way was too much. She sued for defamation and tearfully gave evidence. The Fairfax group wanted to call

Mariti to give evidence. He came of his own accord, sitting briefly in the courtroom until New South Wales Police Special Branch asked him to go outside. Hearing from this writer that Fairfax needed him to give evidence, he laughed sarcastically, again condemning *The Sydney Morning Herald* for not acceding to his request to publish an appeal for the return of his children, and walked away. How much impact Mariti's evidence would have had is questionable, but Evatt won the action.

Police placed FLAG under surveillance. This writer spent some time with a leader of the group, John William Louden, a rational though bitter man who had had three marriages. I found myself under surveillance and was later called to give evidence at the coroner's inquest into the death of Pearl Watson.

In August 1984, Mariti was summonsed to appear before Justice Elliott in the Federal Court, following an application by the Federal Attorney-General that he be imprisoned for contempt over his message to Justice Renaud. Elliott found a *prima facie* case proven and invited Mariti to make submissions. Mariti said: 'I have not seen my children for six years. I feel I have been unjustly treated. It is still a matter of the heart, never of criminality.' He said the late Morris Revelman, a bitter critic of the Family Court system, had advised him to 'use the worst language because these people have the hide of an elephant'. Elliott said Mariti had spoken of his former wife as 'an insult to motherhood' and as 'a gangster's moll', which was a contempt, because she was party to a Family Court action. The choice, he said, was to deal with such matters 'either by the democracy of the law courts or… with violence and intimidation'. Mariti refused to apologise to his wife. Elliott convicted and sentenced him to three months' gaol, suspended on an undertaking by Mariti that he would not distribute any other material insulting to the Family Court.

If police thought Mariti had a hand in anything more violent than distributing literature, they had no proof. In the meantime, violence definitely not connected with Mariti, continued. In February 1985, a Torana sedan was parked outside a house in Kira Avenue, Northmead, in Sydney's north-west. Its owner, Peter

Raymond Tall, was about to get in but by chance opened the bonnet to carry out repairs. Under the bonnet, wired to the ignition, was a bomb, powerful enough to have killed anyone attempting to start the car and to wreck both car and house. It turned out that the house had been formerly occupied by a solicitor, Gary Allan Watts, who had appeared in a Family Court action relating to Andrea Margaret Warwick, estranged wife of a fireman, Leonard John Warwick. Police believed the bomb had been placed in the car in the mistaken belief that it was Watts' car. Watts had shifted from his then address to another and hired an armed guard. At 9.25 pm on the night of 21 February, the guard saw an intruder and fired, apparently without hitting anyone.

On 21 July that year, another outrage. At a Jehovah's Witnesses hall near Liverpool in Sydney's south-west, a service was in progress when a bomb, placed under the speaker's platform, exploded at 10 am. It ripped off the roof of the building, blew walls apart, smashed windows, spread debris for hundreds of metres, and killed a father of three, Graham Wykes, 37, and badly injured 14 others, including his wife and two daughters. Of 107 people who were at the meeting that day, 79 were hurt. Later evidence before the New South Wales Coroner's Court suggested there might have been a Family Court connection.

On 10 February 1987, the then New South Wales State Coroner, Kevin Waller, began an inquest into Pearl Watson's death. He said at the outset that he would take in evidence relating to the other Family Court outrages because they had common features. The inquiry soon centred on Leonard Warwick. There was another incident associated with him: the death of his brother-in-law, Stephen John Blanshard, whose body had been found in Cowan Creek in Sydney's north, in February 1980. Blanshard had been shot in the head and his body weighed down by bricks. John Keily, for Warwick, submitted at the inquest that Blanshard's death, and the shooting of Warwick, were irrelevant. Waller said there were 'extraordinary connections' between the various incidents, though he was careful to say that there was no *prima facie* evidence linking Warwick to any of them.

The then Detective-Sergeant John Zimmer said Warwick's home at Casula had been searched, as well as his car and his room at Liverpool fire station, but nothing of significance had been found. When the court came to consider the evidence of the bomb found in Tall's car, a scientific expert, Robert Barnes, said he was very confident that there were similarities between the bomb found in the car and the bomb that had exploded in the Jehovah's Witnesses hall. Barnes said the bombs had used molignite, which was an Australian-made explosive. He said the person or persons who had been involved in the Family Court bombings had had knowledge of explosives and that the explosives had been tailored to hit a particular target. The bomb that had destroyed Richard Gee's home had been 'simple, innovative and impossible to detect by those inside the building'.

A number of disgruntled former Family Court litigants were questioned. One was Shoutak Michael Abroo who, according to his estranged wife, had said he would pay somebody to make a bomb. Abroo denied saying such a thing. He said he had been given 'a rough time' by the Family Court at Parramatta and was still upset by some of the judges, including Gee, who had 'made me and my barrister very small'. Edwin Collin Archibald, secretary of a group called Families Against Unnecessary Legal Trauma (FAULT), said Warwick had told him that the Jehovah's Witnesses church had been hiding his wife and child. Archibald said he believed that Warwick had been referring to the church that had been bombed. When Warwick appeared on 12 February, he took advantage of his rights under the *Coroner's Act* and said that he would not answer any questions on the grounds that they might tend to incriminate him.

The following day, Mariti was summonsed to give evidence. He told Waller: 'I have more right to my children than any man in the world, judge or no judge, prime minister or no prime minister. When a judge is inhumane and a crook, I cannot obey him.' Mariti said he had had nothing to do with any of the bombings. He agreed he had said he would like to kill Justices Watson and Opas, but they were only expressions that 'sounded like threats', and did not translate into violence. He denied saying to a journalist, 'If the Family Court was in Italy, it would be blown up in a week,' or 'If judges in Italy behaved like their colleagues here, there would be a funeral every week.' But he said that if the court system in Australia had been 'fairer', Opas and Watson would be alive. He admitted saying to the then Registrar of the Family Court, Philippa Lynch: 'So you know how I feel now, you talk to those judges every day, you tell them Mariti wants to see his children. I must see them before Christmas, or I will go on hurting more people.' But by 'hurting', he only meant 'attacking by the use of more writings'.

On 22 May 1987, Waller said that 'with a sense of disappointment and frustration', he was recording an open verdict on Pearl Watson. He said there was insufficient evidence to say at whose instigation the bomb had been planted and by whom it had been planted, yet there was no shortage of suspects. A number of people had been named as possible suspects, but there was insufficient evidence against any of them. He said: 'Where is the justice, when an innocent person can be wiped out with apparent impunity? Realistically, it would seem that it will only be when someone close to the killer or killers presents first-hand evidence of his or her words and activities that the cases will ultimately be solved.' With Warwick, he said, there was both motive and opportunity. 'Mr Warwick could be said to have had a personal grudge against all the individuals or organisations involved, and his work shifts as a fireman allowed him the opportunity to commit all the acts under investigation.

'In this case, the coincidence of motive and opportunity as regards all the events is quite extraordinary. On the other hand, there is no evidence that Mr Warwick has ever possessed an explosive, knew how to construct a bomb, or has ever been seen at the site of any of the crimes.'

Who killed Ray Opas, Pearl Watson and Graham Wykes, and carried out other bombings associated with the series of incidents, went into the 'unsolved' file. But, from a departmental perspective, there was not much time for reflecting on such matters. There were plenty of other instances of people going over the edge.

By the early 1980s, the push for a system of recognising and dealing with domestic violence had borne fruit. In New South Wales, an Apprehended Domestic Violence Order system was introduced in 1983, offering protection to spouses and former spouses. But it was far from a perfect solution, as events elsewhere demonstrated. In October 1995, a divorced man in Western Australia, Norman Drummond, decided that if he could not have custody of his children, his wife would not either. During an access visit, he took the children into bushland and gassed himself and the children with exhaust fumes. Three years later to the month, the tragedy was repeated. Ronald Jonker, 32, of Perth, separated from his wife in early 1988 and engaged in a bitter custody dispute over their three children, became involved in an altercation on 19 October, that required police intervention. Two days later, the Family Court ruled that Jonker could have access to his children on only two weekends out of every three. He reacted by driving them onto a lonely road 130 kilometres north of Perth, and gassing himself and his children.

The tragedies were to keep occurring. In July 1999, Western Australia was rocked by two further murder-suicides in which children had died. On 3 July, Perth mother Barbara Ann Wyrzykowski jotted down a farewell note, loaded her five young children into her Toyota Tarago van and headed for the bush. With her children – aged between one and eight – watching from inside the van, she left the vehicle running, hooked a rubber hose to the exhaust pipe, climbed into the front seat and died with them. Then Mark Heath, 31, an unemployed man who had split with the children's mother two years before, worried about complications that had set in with his family, did something similar. He drove to a spot 250 km south of Perth with his two sons and two daughters – aged between two and eight years – and gassed them and himself.

Peter Vogel, writing in *Certified Male*, a journal on men's issues, in November 1998, said that the key to so many tragedies lay in the continuing practice, despite legislative changes, of Family Court judges awarding custody to mothers. He said that for an Australian man marrying at that time, there was a one-in-three risk that his marriage would end before his children had been reared. 'He faces a one-in-ten risk that he will have no contact at all with his children by the time they are adult,' he said. 'This means his risk of losing contact with his children is not mere paranoia; it's twice the risk of contracting lung cancer.' Every day, 77 fathers separated from their child's mother, and 71 of those fathers would not be living with their children five years later, he said. There were 558,000 separated fathers denied as much contact with their children as they would like. Unemployment among men registered with the Child Support Agency, the government agency established to regulate our equivalent of maintenance payments, was 30 per cent. On average, at least one non-custodial father committed suicide every day. In the previous four months in Queensland alone, three Queensland fathers had killed themselves and their children.

By the late 1980s, once AVOs had been accepted and the public in general had been educated to appreciate them, the number of applications skyrocketed. In 1989, 77 per cent of women seeking a protection order against a spouse or de facto spouse cited at least one alleged physical assault. In addition, 23 per cent alleged that they had received at least one death or shooting threat from a spouse. Other abuses were injury to the children or threats to harm themselves or other relatives, property damage, verbal abuse, and harassment such as persistent phone calls late at night. The protection system was broadened to include other relatives and those involved in 'intimate personal relationships'. In 1990, this was broadened again to take in anyone fearing violence from another. The AVOs were designated either 'domestic' or 'personal'.

A correlation has been found between unemployment, and other social stress, and violence. In 1988, in Campbelltown in Sydney's south-west, there were 204 protection orders sought per 100,000 residents compared with eight per 100,000 in leafy, well-off Ku-ring-gai in the city's north, although that might be qualified by the unwillingness of people in the latter socio-economic group to report domestic violence. When it comes to lethal violence, women, no matter what their class, are usually the victims. Between 1968 and 1988 in New South Wales, 48 per cent of women killed in homicidal assaults were killed by their spouse or de facto spouse. Conversely, the figure for men was only nine per cent. And when it comes to the crunch with homicides, the deciding factor is not social or economic circumstances but some psychiatric factor, even if, in strictly legal terms, the offender is not mad.

In 1991, Margaret Case, aged 45, had divorced her husband, a Darwin mathematics teacher, Colin Arthur Case, 52. Case would not leave her alone. In fact, she endured months of terror. She moved to Adelaide where, in August 1991, she found a job as electorate secretary of South Australian senator, John Olsen. Ms Case applied to the Family Court for protection orders against her former husband. The Family Court issued an injunction against Case approaching or molesting his wife. Margaret Case kept in daily contact with the Australian Federal Police. Case pursued his former wife relentlessly, warning her in advance that he was on his way, with a rifle. Sometimes when he rang, he disguised his voice. Ms Case alerted Senator Olsen and police. On Monday night, 23 March 1992, she caught a taxi to visit her lawyer. A shot rang out outside the house and she fell dead. Case, who was arrested two days later lying beside a dirt track, suffering dehydration, was tried and convicted. During sentencing submissions, it was stated that when Case bought the weapon he used, he had asked for one 'suitable for killing pigs'. He was sentenced in July, 1993, to life imprisonment with a 20-year, non-parole period.

Margaret Case really had had no choice but to leave the country and trust that she left no trail for him to follow. The only way she could have lived within Australia was for police to have enforced the orders of the Family Court and locked Case up for contempt of court. Linda Matthews, a South Australian member of the National Committee on Violence, said police had to be trained to take women's complaints against men seriously. 'This case is not isolated,' she said. 'It's all too common for women to tell police their husband has threatened to kill them, and get the reply, "They usually don't do it." '

The potential lethal violence the institutions of the state have tried to grapple with could occur in any relationship. Sometimes, a third party becomes a victim. The most horrifying prospect for a police officer is to be called to a domestic dispute as a person sworn to uphold the law and protect the community, and to become a target of pent-up rage, frustration, insanity, whatever it might be. On a Saturday night, 8 July 1995, a 35-year-old electrical worker, John McGowan, had been drinking at the Crescent Head Country Club on the New South Wales north coast, and at some time had consumed cannabis. He made a threatening phone call to his former girlfriend, Debra Minett. Afflicted with serious psychiatric disorders, which had him, among other things, dressing as a soldier and engaging in military fantasies, he was not to be taken lightly.

McGowan and Minett had had a tempestuous relationship, lasting from early 1993 until August 1994. According to her later account, he threatened her, was violent and said the Devil had sent him to kill her. 'He would put me on the ground and hit my head against the floor... hold me by the throat against walls and try to strangle me,' she said. Psychiatrist Rod Milton was to say that it was a confused relationship and that Ms Minett, 'an insecure and troubled person herself', had become 'disastrously attached' to McGowan. Though she had been unable to commit herself to him, she had been unable to let him go.

On the night in question, McGowan vandalised Minett's car with paint. At some time after 1 am, she called police. Constables Peter Addison and Robert Spears went to her home and spoke to her, then turned up at McGowan's house. Dressed in military fatigues and wearing a balaclava, McGowan was at that moment around the twist. Seeing them, he opened fire with a .223 Ruger Mini 14 rifle, hitting Spears in the head and killing him instantly. Addison ran down the side of the house, turned and returned fire but was fatally wounded. McGowan then shot himself in the head.

On 13 October 1995, coroner Derrick Hand was critical of Minett for not telling the police that McGowan had a rifle. He attributed the failure to do so as a desire she had, despite a past abusive relationship, to protect him. Minett denied outside the court house that she had known McGowan had a firearm. Be that as it may, the State, through its police force, was trying to intervene in an essentially proactive way and had had the violence turned onto its own agents.

That year, in its relentless twisting and turning, fine-tuning and reviewing, trying to juggle the apparatus of state that would produce the best result, the Federal Government amended the *Family Law Act* to try to eliminate violence. The amended legislation emphasised that both parents in a failed relationship had the rights of access to children. It was a move that many of the Family Court's critics thought long overdue, and it seemed to have given some sort of guarantee to a multitude of angry men.

But how was that going to cope with the case of Brisbane's Peter May (formerly Majstorovic) who for years had subjected his wife, Helen, and their three children to terror? In late 1995, May was gambling heavily. He assaulted his wife and children, at one point slashing his wife's wrists with a knife and throwing boiling water over his seven-year-old son. His mood was not helped by the fact that he was facing fraud charges. On 16 November, with the help of her parents, Helen May moved to a secret address in Brisbane and on 28 November took out an interim DVO against him. Police seized May's .22 calibre rifle and shooter's licence. May went to a support group, Men's Rights, made up of individuals who had been involved in Family Court actions. He became convinced that the system was stacked against him and that he would lose his family. Men's Rights said through a spokesman later that the group did not advocate violence. Certainly, a group cannot at a *prima facie* level be held responsible for the extreme acts of individuals associated with it. The Brisbane *Courier-Mail* found that Men's Rights had a practice of tracking down women who had fled to shelters and had taken out DVOs. May had reportedly sought help from the group in finding his wife, and although Men's Rights cannot in anyway be blamed for what he subsequently did, the group was open to abuse by obsessed or unscrupulous individuals.

There was some contact between May and his wife. She relented a little and agreed that he should have some access to his children. On 10 January 1996, May's parents dropped the children off at his address. One of the parents enraged May by telling him that the family, without him, had had its best Christmas in years. May took the children on a holiday, in all probability extracted his wife's address from one of them, then killed his children. On 25 January, carrying a 30-30 Winchester, he broke into his wife's home and killed her, along with his parents-in-law and himself.

The Queensland Government announced that it was introducing legislation to prevent private detectives tracking down women and children. It also said it would take steps to make it harder for people to discover where women's shelters were – another instance of the courts and legislatures grappling with the realities of broken relationships where hatred and love existed side-by-side and tended to become indistinguishable. In the meantime, the use of AVOs was soaring. In New South Wales in 1996, a total of 14,068 AVOs were granted. On any day, local court lists were full of people, overwhelmingly men, who had breached AVOs. Just as the drug menace was filling court lists and prison cells, the opening up of the police and judicial system to the area of personal violence was occupying more and more police and court time. But it could hardly be avoided.

There were other developments aimed at finetuning the system. In 1997, a woman wanted to move from Cairns in North Queensland to Bendigo, Victoria, to remarry, and to take her children with her. Her former husband, who had access, opposed it on the grounds that such a move would deny him access. The Full Bench of the Family Court decided it was in the best interests of children that they go with her to Victoria. Paul Whyte, spokesman for another group, Sydney Men's Network, disagreed with the decision, saying the deepest relationship a man could have was with his children, and that to take children away from their father was an act of 'deepest cruelty', and that the Family Court remained biased against men.

And still, despite the safeguards, the years of thought, and study, the mixture of hard-line policing and humanity, the outrages kept coming. At Dandenong, Victoria, Robert Clive Parsons, 54, felt his former de facto wife, Angela Elizabeth Parsons (she had changed her name by deed poll) was making an unjust demand for higher maintenance payments. They had broken up several years before and Parsons, a merchant seaman with considerable financial resources, had been paying maintenance from 1992 until February 1997. Ms Parsons wanted more, and said that unless she received it, he could no longer see his children. Parsons, described later by psychiatrist Dr Tim Watson-Munro as having an obsessive personality and suffering depression and anxiety, turned to the group Parents Without Partners, which, like similar support groups, while officially not sanctioning any violence, provided a sympathetic ear.

Angela Parsons took her case for increased maintenance to the Family Court at Warnambool, Victoria, and the case was listed for hearing. She was asking that Parsons put $47,000 into a trust account until the maintenance issue was resolved. Driving to the court on 10 December 1997, Parsons saw his former de facto, grabbed a knife from under his front seat, then ran towards her. He stabbed her 41 times, screaming: 'It's over now, bitch! It's over! You can blame the Family Court for this!' Eight of the stab wounds went through her heart. When police searched Parsons' car, they found a bundle of Family Court documents with the word 'Slagfile' written on it. On 24 May 1999, Justice Philip Cummins in the Victorian Supreme Court said he rejected arguments put up on behalf of Parsons that his wife had said she was taking the children away from him and that she had provoked him by shouting and laughing. He sentenced Parsons to life imprisonment.

That tragedy was echoed in the murder of Jean Lennon outside the Parramatta Family Court in 1996. This event had its origins in 1978 when a Jordanian migrant, Hos Majdalawi, met Jean Lennon, then 19, a New Zealander. They were neighbours in Marrickville in inner Sydney. The two went out together, fell in love, lived together, had two children, married in a Muslim ceremony in 1984 and had a third child. Happy for the first five years, they moved to Katoomba in the Blue Mountains, where Majdalawi ran a tiling business. Then they struck problems. They went to live in St Marys, in Sydney's west, and there was a marked deterioration in Majdalawi's attitude, which affected his marriage and business.

The couple moved to Canberra for work purposes, then to Baulkham Hills, in Sydney's north-west, but Majdalawi sought the company of at least two other women and lost money on gambling. In 1994, Jean Lennon complained to a counsellor that her husband was beating her up. She obtained an AVO against him.

In May 1995, Jean Lennon left the family home, went with her children to a family refuge in Canberra, then moved to refuges in Brisbane and the Gold Coast. The couple had a reconciliation, then moved to Perth, but Ms Lennon decided her husband had not changed and left again, to live in a town house on the Gold Coast. Majdalawi found them there, moved in, became violent – including several threats to commit suicide with a pistol – and Jean fled with the children to a refuge at Toowoomba, taking out a second AVO. She returned to the Gold Coast, where she retained custody of the children and Majdalawi had weekend access. He said he had given up violence and had handed his firearm to the police. But he swore on the Koran that if she fled again, he would kill her.

She did move out again, twice, and on 12 December 1995, moved to Sydney. In February 1996, police charged Majdalawi with breaching an AVO. Ms Lennon took out a third AVO on 20 March that year. On the same day, her mother received a phone call from Majdalawi, who said: 'You are going to be very sorry and very sad and you will be crying tomorrow.' On Tuesday 21 March, the day of the Family Court hearing of their case in Parramatta, Majdalawi arrived first, carrying in a bag $1,900 in cash, papers supporting an application for joint custody of his children, and a Russian Tokarev self-loading, semi-automatic pistol with a full magazine of eight rounds. He saw her approaching, and according to a later account, said: 'Don't make it difficult for me to get access to the kids. I only want access.' Her reply was: 'No way, no chance! You are in Australia, not Jordan!' Majdalawi then pulled out a pistol, shot her four times as she tried to run away, then, standing over her where she fell, fired another shot into her head, before walking into the court and saying to an officer: 'I just shot my wife. Call the police.'

Majdalawai went on trial for murder in May 1998. Evidence was presented that he had been raped by a relative in Jordan at the age of nine and that, when he confronted his wife and she told him to go away, those same feelings of revulsion returned. 'I feel like nobody,' he said. 'I feel very low, like dirty... the same feelings I had when I was raped... I was upset with her, I was angry because [of] what she had done and like all the memories came back to me and after that I don't know what's happening.' Majdalawai was convicted of murder and on 12 June, 1998, sentenced to 18 years.

The Family Court reviewed its security, canvassing an option that women seeking AVOs should be escorted to and from court hearings. But such measures, including the nomination of safe areas within Family Court premises, the enforcement of AVOs, counselling, therapy could all be scrutinised. But there never will be a failsafe method of preventing the totally obsessed and totally determined individual bent on revenge, short of a total abandonment of the principles of fairness, justice, civil liberties, innocence, until proven guilty and the benefit of the doubt.

As the Family Court said, after a quarter of a century of operation and many thousands of cases, the outcome of its intervention into the private worlds of troubled individuals had been as favourable as it could be, taking in all the circumstances. But no system could ever be found that could cope with the violent emotions that were aroused by so many broken relationships, where the affected individual was pushed to the extreme. The institutions of the State, in whatever form, had to be based on the premise that the State was dealing with essentially normal people. When the person at the centre of the action was totally unbalanced, and had been pushed over the edge, anything, as the next chapter demonstrates, could happen.

MAYHEM IN SOUTH AUSTRALIA

Civilisation begins with order,
grows with liberty and dies with chaos.

Will Durant

Geoffrey Bowen, 36, on secondment to the National Crime Authority (NCA) from the Western Australian Police Department, did not like surprises. Like any good police officer, he wanted to know what he was dealing with, to be in control of the situation. So when a parcel arrived for him at the NCA's Adelaide headquarters in Waymouth Street on the morning of 2 March, 1994, he was naturally curious – and apprehensive. Standing in lawyer Peter Wallis' office on the 12th floor, he casually joked: 'It might be a bomb!' He took the cardboard box out of the Express Post plastic bag, cursing as he used a pair of scissors to cut away the sticky tape binding the box. At precisely 9.15 am, he lifted the lid of the box a few millimetres...

Within one thousandth of a second Geoff Bowen was dead, blasted to death by an elaborate bomb. The plate-glass windows were blown out, debris flew onto the roofs of adjoining buildings, and pedestrians on the street below were showered with bits of furniture, paper, office litter. Wallis, 47, severely injured and blinded, called for help, not knowing whether his colleagues were alive or dead. 'I remember a loud crack like a high-powered rifle,' he said later. 'There were two explosions, the crack and then the big one. I remember being buffeted around like in extremely heavy winds. I realised it was a bomb. My thoughts were: "Oh, no, it was a bomb." There was this incredible blackness. If you shut your eyes, you don't see black the way I saw black. It was just total pitch dark because both my eyes were out.'

In the immediate aftermath, smoke billowed from the burning office – an image that became a lasting reminder of the day terrorism came to Adelaide. People rushed into the premises, a crowd gathered in the street outside. They included, for a brief period, Domenic Perre, 40, a surveillance target of the NCA, who had been tailed that day by NCA officers and had apparently chanced upon the bombing.

Wallis heard people arrive, felt a firefighter reach down to pull at his belt buckle, which was fused to his skin. 'It took them five minutes to get me out, but it felt like five hours,' he said. 'I knew I was in trouble. I was still burning when they got me out because they had a fire extinguisher to put me out. I was focused on staying alive. I had thoughts of my children and what's going to happen to them.' Wallis lost an eye and was left with terrible scarring.

At the time of the blast, one of the main activities of the Adelaide NCA office was investigating Italian organised crime. It was part of an Australia-wide operation code-named Cerberus. Bowen and Wallis were the mainstays of Cerberus in Adelaide. Perre, who lived in Salisbury North in Adelaide's north, had been of particular interest. He was one of five men charged by Cerberus detectives over a $40 million marijuana crop at Hidden Valley, Northern Territory, in August 1993. In addition, Bowen had in fact arrested Perre at his home for possession of telephone intercept equipment, and Perre was due to face court the day after the blast.

A task force of more than 40 detectives was assigned to investigate the bombing. Perre quickly became a prime suspect. Police investigated him for nine days, searching the homes of his friends and associates and a gun shop at Prospect owned by one Alan Chamberlain. They searched Chamberlain's home at Wynn

Vale, and there found books on explosives, detonators, fuses and a cache of weapons. Then they swooped on Perre's home, arrested him and charged him with the murder of Bowen and attempted murder of Wallis.

At the committal hearing in the Adelaide Magistrate's Court, apparently damning evidence against Perre was produced. Perre had had access to publications on explosives manufacture. A few weeks before the blast, he had told a man he had tested a bomb. Hours before the blast, he had left fuses, detonators and a cache of guns at a friend's house. Perre was known to have been enraged over the police search of his house which had turned up the telecommunications equipment. He was committed for trial in the Supreme Court of South Australia. But just before the trial was due to start, the South Australian Director of Public Prosecutions (DPP), Paul Rofe QC, dropped a bombshell by deciding, after a review of the evidence, not to proceed. 'On the evidence... there was not a reasonable prospect of conviction,' he said.

Investigating police went about getting more evidence in a proactive manner. In mid-1995, they devised an operation, code-named Arba, in which it was hoped Perre could be caught obtaining or possessing one of the key ingredients used in the NCA bomb – red phosphorus. Red phosphorus was an ingredient used in both explosives and amphetamine manufacture. The operation involved setting up a police-sanctioned amphetamine laboratory. Two undercover police officers were brought from Victoria to lure Perre into the venture. Perre was lured, and gave the police $60,000 to get laboratory equipment. Following that, an amphetamine laboratory was set up in the northern Adelaide suburb of Angle Vale. For months police watched every move, every step Perre made. He was followed by surveillance teams around the clock, his telephone calls tapped, his conversations with the undercover police taped. He was photographed with everyone he met. But despite considerable coaxing and urging, Perre could not – or would not – make a move to obtain the red phosphorous.

After six months, the operation was called off. Police raided the amphetamine laboratory, seizing about 500 g of amphetamines and enough chemicals to make another 40 kg with a street value of about $5 million. Perre was one of six arrested. In July 1997, he pleaded guilty to charges of producing amphetamines and was sentenced to six years' gaol. Charges against his five co-accused were dropped.

But the operation had not yielded enough evidence to lay fresh charges of murder and attempted murder. The South Australian Coroner, Wayne Chivell, began an inquest into the bombing on 6 April 1999. It started in sensational style. The Federal Government moved to block serving or former NCA officers from giving evidence on the grounds that their information might compromise existing operations. Bowen's widow, Jane, said she believed the truth would never emerge. Eventually, the Coroner rejected the Federal move.

The early stages of the inquest examined the security arrangements of the NCA office and the composition of the parcel bomb. Ironically, when a replica bomb was subjected to a metal detector – the one used to screen the parcel bomb that killed Bowen – it beeped loudly. The court heard that the explosive used in the bomb was most likely PETN, surrounded by red phosphorus. PETN is obtained from explosive fuse cord. The inquest heard that Perre had access to fuse cord and that fingerprints belonging to Perre had been found on the page of a book describing ways of extracting PETN.

Alan Chamberlain was produced as a prosecution witness. Police had seized a number of publications in his home and had had them subjected to fingerprint analysis. An expert said partial prints with several characteristics similar to Perre's prints had been found in books entitled *Sneak it Through: Smuggling Made Easy*, *Homemade C4* and *Homemade Grenade Launchers*. A partial print of Perre's left index finger and a positive print of his left ring finger had been found on the book *Sneak It Through*. A partial thumb print, a partial right middle-finger print, and a partial right index finger print, all similar to Perre's, were found on *Homemade C4*, and a partial print of Perre's left middle finger was found on *Homemade Grenade Launchers*.

The inquest heard of several possible motives for the bombing. Mostly, the evidence revolved around Perre and his associates. The director of the NCA's Adelaide office, Detective Chief Inspector John Ganley, told the inquest that Bowen might have been murdered because he had helped arrest a leader of the Italian crime gang N'Dranghita, the Western Australian criminal, Bruno Romeo Snr, who was married to Perre's cousin. Ganley said the crime group had its origins in the town of Plati, in Calabria, southern Italy. Romeo, Perre and other known underworld figures were from the same town. Romeo had been convicted in connection with two major drug crops in Western Australia after being caught on a third at Lismore, northern New South Wales. Bowen had played a key role in Romeo's capture and extradition to Perth.

The inquest heard that Perre had written a letter from Yatala Labour Prison to fellow gun enthusiast Stan Tettis. In the letter, which was intercepted by prison officers, Perre had asked Tettis to tell police that Alan Chamberlain had mailed the bomb; in this way, Perre could implicate Chamberlain, get Chamberlain's gun collection and collect a reward offered for information. Perre had written: 'He is the lowest scum and he used all of us for his profit while pretending to be our friend. Don't be afraid. Cooperate and you will be doing the right thing and I will look after you as my brother and my lawyer will help you any time.' Perre was charged with attempting to pervert the course of justice over the letter, but was acquitted.

Perre was not the only person trying hard to implicate Chamberlain. Private investigator Frank Carbone, who was charged with Perre over the amphetamines laboratory, did his best. Hired by Perre's lawyers, he told the inquest he believed police had charged the wrong man. He had tried to steer police in the right direction, but had been told he could not be trusted. He believed Chamberlain knew more than he was saying, and after interviewing about 20 witnesses, he had formed the opinion that Perre had been wrongly charged. He had gained the impression from police that his help was not wanted. More information about Operation Arba came to light.

Two undercover officers, who had gone by the names Jimmy Anderson and Jack Pahia, had been told to discover whether Perre could obtain red phosphorus. However, when asked how to get it, Perre had told the pair to look up chemical companies in Yellow Pages if they wanted it. But then, Perre had hired Frank Carbone to obtain red phosphorus, and a third undercover officer had supplied it to Carbone. Pahia said he had worked tirelessly to win Perre's trust, but Perre had become aggressive whenever the bombing was mentioned. Pahia did obtain a taped conversation with Perre in which Perre said: 'Down the track they f***ing annoyed me so much, I wish I'd gone and taken out the whole f***ing building. F*** them, the f***ing bomb, I dream about it.'

Anderson said he and Pahia had told Perre they were getting red phosphorus from Sydney. But when it arrived, it just happened that the jar had been broken and the red phosphorus was contaminated. Perre had then been asked to get the chemical at short notice. Anderson said Perre had appeared very reluctant. 'He indicated that every detective was waiting for him to do that... he said he would rather stick his dick on the chopping block,' Anderson said.

On 17 September 1999, Chivell handed down his findings, and they were worth waiting for. The last words on page 95 were more than the police anticipated. 'The circumstances of the death of Detective Sergeant Geoffrey Leigh Bowen were that he died when he opened a parcel bomb, sent to him by Domenic Perre, and the bomb exploded in his hands,' Chivell said. He gave 19 reasons why he believed Perre had killed Bowen. Some of the evidence he had heard might not be admissible in another court, but: 'In my opinion, however, the only reasonable inference to be drawn from the evidence is that Domenic Perre was responsible, in the sense that he constructed the bomb, and either posted it or arranged for someone else to post it on his behalf to Detective Sergeant Bowen. From the evidence, I am unable to find whether Perre acted alone or in concert with another person or persons.'

Jane Bowen, the South Australian Police investigators and Geoff Bowen's NCA colleagues were elated. The DPP was also studying them intently. Perre was outraged, claiming he had been unjustly labelled a killer. His lawyers lodged an appeal in the Supreme Court challenging Chivell's findings. At the time of writing that appeal was still to be heard.

The next bomb to take South Australia by surprise came seven months later. This time, it came with a sarcastic note inscribed on the Postpak delivered to 27-year-old Ronald Brian Pettit: 'From a secret admirer.'

On 13 October 1994, sitting on the verandah of a friend's home in Jacob Street, Gawler, South Australia, Pettit was interested in what the package might contain. As he lifted the lid, the bomb exploded, blowing jagged pieces of shrapnel in all directions. Pettit, taking most of the blast, was killed instantly, all but the seams of his clothes ripped from his body. The blast shot shrapnel through the Colorbond verandah roof and onto neighbours' roofs. Three people in the backyard were lucky to escape injury.

Senior Sergeant Doug Kokegei had his head buried in files on another murder case when the call came through to the Major Crime Task Force office at Adelaide Police Headquarters. His team members flinched.

The same thought ran through their minds... bombings and arsons were always the hardest to crack. Immediately after visiting the scene, Kokegei and his partner, burly no-nonsense David Modra, went to the nearby Gawler police station. It turned out Pettit had a police file, and the information it contained provided a starting point for the inquiry. 'They had records of a custody battle going on between a woman called Angela Sinclair and Pettit,' Kokegei said later. 'He had been giving her a fairly hard time. After that meeting, I had a gut feeling she had to be implicated. I wanted to be the one to advise her of his death.'

Police broke the news to Angela Sinclair, then 22, at her mother's home a short time later. 'Her response was one of surprise and after a while, tears,' Kokegei said. 'There were plenty of tears. Too many, in fact, and a lot were probably crocodile tears, considering the problems she had been having with Ron.' Kokegei struck up a conversation with Sinclair's Filipino mother, and formed a bond with her. With Modra, he spent a week inquiring into Sinclair, speaking to her family, associates and, more importantly, her enemies. She had met Pettit at the age of 16 and had lived with him in a de facto relationship before a falling-out. The two had split up acrimoniously in 1992. There was a constant round of domestic violence restraining orders and court proceedings, requiring constant police intervention, with their infant daughter, Bianca, caught in the middle.

Sinclair had not been fussy in her choice of associates. One of them was Hieu Duy Dinh, with whom she formed a relationship and to whom she became pregnant. Dinh, 32, was well known to both South Australian and federal police for dealing in heroin. He was also known to use violence to get his way. In all, he was a nasty little thug, and he did not like Australians. Police learnt from people who had known both Sinclair and Dinh that some time before the bombing, the couple had been talking about 'Ron going boom'.

The first major breakthrough came with a phone call from a most unexpected quarter – Sinclair's mother. 'Out of the blue she rang and said she wanted to meet us, but not at the house,' Kokegei said. 'We met around the corner from her house and went to the Torrensville police station and took a statement from her for several hours. She just let it out. She told us she had overheard her daughter and Dinh talking about the bombing and that her daughter had told her this and that about it, things her daughter could not have known unless she was intimately involved in it. But because she could not write or speak any English, we couldn't get her to sign her statement.' Police had obtained the services of an interpreter for the interview.

Surveillance teams were assigned to find where Sinclair and Dinh were living and what they were up to. Listening devices were planted. Friends of the couple were brought in for questioning. Dinh and Sinclair, getting wind of the fact that they were the centre of the investigation, resorted to what they knew best – violence. Witnesses were threatened and some were assaulted. Sinclair was proving herself to be someone to be reckoned with. Two acquaintances she felt had wronged her had their cars firebombed.

Teamed with the aggressive Dinh, Sinclair now acquired the confidence she had been lacking. But it did not deter the police, who put together a profile of the couple and the probable motive for the bombing. According to Kokegei, Pettit had wanted custody of the child and Sinclair was strongly resisting. Pettit had told people Sinclair was dealing in heroin, and he was going to use this against her in the Family Court.

Once the suspects had been linked to the bombing, the police hierarchy wanted arrests. That bureaucratic pressure almost resulted in Kokegei walking away from the inquiry. But the DPP, Paul Rofe, took an even-handed view of the evidence and told the hierarchy they would have to be patient.

Scientific examination of the bomb debris was starting to produce results. The scientific team, led by Sergeant Paul Sheldon, did a painstaking job, collecting hundreds of pieces of shrapnel and shredded Postpak. The shrapnel, most of it gold-coloured pieces of copper wiring not larger than 5 mm, had come from the casing of the bomb and the nine-volt battery used to power it. Initially, the team could not determine the type of explosive used and there were fears that the failure to identify the explosive would become a major stumbling block. But further chemical testing of a residue found on most surfaces close to the blast provided a clue. It was ethylhexylpthalate, from the plastic cover of the explosive cord, a commercially available item that was used in quarry operations.

The gold colour of the shrapnel indicated that the bomb casing had most likely been a can of some description, probably one that once contained food. This was confirmed during testing at an Adelaide Hills police scientific facility. A short length of explosive cord had been used and the can had had several extra lids placed inside to maximise damage from shrapnel. But how could the bomb be linked to Dinh and Sinclair?

Sheldon's team, tossing ideas around, played with the notion that the distinctive marks found on many of the edges of the shrapnel might have been made by a can-opener. The team consulted with can-opener manufacturers and discovered that the marks had been left by feeder wheels on a can-opener that is rolled around the edge of the lid as the lid is cut. Police searched the houses of Dinh and Sinclair, and families and associates of the couple. They found eight used can-openers, and bought eight new can-openers for the purposes of comparative testing.

After almost 60,000 tests, they found that only one can-opener made the individual marks found on the shrapnel, and that was one that came from the home of Dinh's father. It was inspired detective work, and the evidence was extremely strong. Combined with circumstantial evidence, this could positively link Dinh with the bomb. The couple were arrested and charged with the murder of Ronald Pettit. During further searches of Dinh's house, police found jewellery and around $12,000 in cash stuffed into a bed post. 'I screwed the top off the post and it was stuffed full of cash,' Kokegei said.

Dinh and Sinclair made no admissions. Dinh's story was that the can-opener found at his father's place had been picked up at a trash and treasure sale a fortnight after the bombing.

In the meantime, the campaign of harassment and terror against potential witnesses took another turn while Dinh was in custody awaiting trial. Police intelligence sources discovered $10,000 had been offered to kill three people connected with the case. All three were Kokegei's witnesses. Underworld sources confirmed that those three had been nominated. Only one of the addresses put out was by then correct – the other two witnesses had been shifted into safe houses.

Dinh and Sinclair, on trial in the Supreme Court of South Australia, pleaded not guilty and denied knowledge of Pettit's murder. Their case, presented by Gordon Barrett QC, was that another man, Charles Atherton, who happened to be a prosecution witness, was the culprit. Dinh said in evidence that he had had drug dealings with Atherton and that he had sold $20,000 worth of marijuana and amphetamines a week for Atherton. Dinh had stored his drugs in cans and buried them, and had given Atherton a bagful of cans from his father's house on 13 September 1993, thinking Atherton had also wanted to store his drugs that way. Angela Sinclair said Atherton had heard that Pettit had made claims to the police that she was selling heroin. This, allegedly, had been part of Pettit's plan to discredit her, and so win back custody of his daughter. Atherton had become furious with Pettit.

Dinh said that after the bombing, he had repaid a $1500 debt to Atherton because 'he didn't want to be next'. The court heard that following his evidence against Atherton, Dinh had been taken into protective custody within the prison system. Atherton, in his evidence, denied he was drug dealer, saying he was only 'a casual user', said he had not received any cans from Dinh, and that he had had no involvement in the murder.

On 22 August 1996, after a ten-hour deliberation, the jury returned a guilty verdict against Sinclair and Dinh. Both received life sentences for murder, Dinh getting a 24-year non-parole period. Sinclair received 17-years non-parole – her daughter, Bianca, of whom she had been so determined to be awarded custody, would be 21 years old when she was released, and her younger daughter, from her relationship with Dinh, would be 18.

There was a strong circumstantial case, but the can-opener was the clincher, 'the cream on the cake,' Kokegei said. Later, in retirement, he said the case had been one of the most frustrating he had worked on. 'I felt more pressure in relation to the witnesses than in any other case,' he said. 'Knowing I had built up a bond with them to get them to testify, I also knew that if anything really happened, I could not protect them. If Dinh had been acquitted in the trial, they would be dead. That's the type of man he is.'

Evidence that locked the door on Dinh had come from the bomb itself. So many bombers think that a bomb, like a fire, will simply destroy everything and leave no clues. That was certainly the case in a bombing the South Australian police had to deal with three years earlier, in 1991.

That bombing on 5 November, 1991, came to the immediate attention of one James Peterson, who happened to be walking past the ground floor flat in Nicholson Avenue, Whyalla, a steel town in South Australia's mid-north. He caught some of the blast when the bomb inside the flat went off. Temporarily stunned, and instinctively shielding himself from the flying glass, he turned to see flames billowing from what had been the window. He was soon joined by neighbours, who began fighting the fire with buckets of water and a garden hose. Then Peterson had another shock. Through the smoke and diminishing flames, he saw a woman's body on a bed – she was on her back, naked, the lower portion of her body covered with a quilt, and quite dead.

It turned out she was a Whyalla nurse, Cheryl Allen, 23, and the explosion and fire did not obliterate how she met her end. She had suffered a violent death – stabbed 35 times – and she was already dead when the explosion, triggered by a time-delay switch, ripped through her flat. The multiple chest wounds could be clearly seen, along with cuts to her forearms where she had tried to fend off the repeated knife blows. Whoever had killed her had made no effort to conceal the cause of the explosion. A near-empty 20-litre drum of high-octane racing fuel was sitting in a corner of the bedroom.

Next morning a team of Major Crime Task Force detectives, headed by Doug Kokegei, arrived to begin the investigation. Forensic pathologists took samples from the body and established that the woman had had sexual intercourse, possibly as a result of rape, some short time before she died. It did not take them long to find a prime suspect, one Steven Paul Stackhouse, 27, who had lived in a flat next door. He was not there when police came knocking. A search of his flat revealed a huge collection of ammunition and disarmed artillery shells. Police also found a book detailing how to make booby traps, bombs and time-delay switches.

'A lot of the stuff in that book related not just to army stuff, but to ingredients that could be found around the house,' Kokegei said. 'And there was one in there that related to racing fuel as an ingredient.' Police found a note from Stackhouse to his parents. It was in essence a suicide note. They also learned that he had borrowed a rifle from a friend the day before. Police started a search of the nearby scrub, with members of the force on the ground and in a helicopter. For a week, they found nothing. Then they found him, dead, with a single gunshot wound to the head, the borrowed rifle, its butt sawn off, cradled in his arm. Pathologists put his death on or about 5 November.

Kokegei and his team figured the case was all but closed. They believed the DNA test results of sperm found in Cheryl Allen would match Stackhouse and that the case would be filed as murder/suicide. But just a few weeks later came the bad news – the tests showed that the sperm in Allen's body and from Stackhouse's body did not match. 'It was a complete surprise,' Kokegei said. 'We were totally dumbfounded. While Stackhouse remained a firm suspect, we had to look elsewhere for the person who had sex with her, to eliminate him or link him with her murder.'

That is when things got tricky, and the Major Crime detectives were soon to wear out their welcome with the local police at Whyalla. Letters Allen had written to one of her girlfriends revealed that she was seeing a man she named as Constable Adams. A check revealed there was no Constable Adams working in Whyalla, but Kokegei's team figured he may still have been a police officer, but using a false name.

The task force broke the news to local police that they would all have to undergo DNA testing. They got a great reception from the Whyalla police. They just loved being treated as suspects in a case of rape/murder. While most obliged and were soon eliminated, some refused and other methods were used to clear them. DNA tests were also conducted on Stackhouse's Army Reserve mates and other possible suspects. All test results were negative.

For the next 12 months, all lines of inquiry were exhausted. Finally, Kokegei aired his suspicions that the original DNA tests were faulty and made approaches to have the samples subjected to more rigorous testing. This was refused. Seeing no alternative, Kokegei ensured that the unsolved case was presented to Coroner Chivell. At Chivell's inquest, Kokegei expressed concern about the DNA analysis. He said new, updated testing methods and equipment were now available, and requested the tests be redone. Chivell's request was forwarded to forensic scientists, who were extremely irritated.

But the new test results did show up the original ones as false. It was Stackhouse who had had sex with Cheryl Allen a short time before she was murdered. 'We just could not believe it,' Kokegei said. 'We had wasted thousands of hours of our time and the case had dragged on for years because our initial request for the tests to be redone had been refused. Not to mention the years of anguish both the Allen and Stackhouse families were put through.' A firm motive for the murder was never established. Kokegei believed Stackhouse might have developed an attraction for Allen, ending in rape and murder, a bombing to destroy evidence, and suicide.

Evidence suggested that Allen and Stackhouse had not been in the sort of relationship in which voluntary sexual intercourse might have taken place. And if it was rape, the logical connection was that the rapist had been the murderer. 'It was a frenzied attack,' Kokegei said. 'The blows were delivered with tremendous force. They cut and broke bone and it would have been over in a few minutes. I think something just made him snap, but we will never know what.'

Of course, many sex attacks are frenzied. The perpetrators, living for years with the sexual monster living within them, dropping in and out of a fantasy world, snap, just as Stackhouse did, and in many instances the life of an innocent person is ended.

In June 1993, Shirree Turner was attacked and stabbed five times through the chest, including once through the heart, on an isolated reserve in the Adelaide suburb of Marion in the early hours of the morning. She was still alive in the immediate aftermath, but the single-edged blade had done its job, and she was bleeding badly. Her attacker sped off in his car, and she made for a house, whose lights she saw about 100 metres away. She was crawling, staggering, crawling again. She made it onto the front porch, and called for help, banging, probably yelling and pleading, but in vain. The house was empty.

Detective Senior Sergeant Mick Johnson arrived at the scene on the morning of 6 June 1993. Shirree had died on the porch. He admired her courage and will to live, but knew that the wounding was so severe that she would not have survived more than a few minutes. Police searched the area and found precious little, although they did retrieve three handbags on the side of Marion Road, a short distance from the reserve, probably thrown from a vehicle leaving the scene. Instinct told the burly detective that the investigation was going to be one of 'the hard ones'. And his team from the Organised Crime Task Force detectives had to do it because the Major Crime Task Force was otherwise engaged.

It did not take long for Johnson's team to put together a picture of what might have happened. When news of the murder hit the airwaves, two of Shirree's friends contacted police, telling them she had been in the city the night before, visiting nightclubs in Hindley Street, a seedy entertainment strip. The last time they saw Shirree alive had been in the Charles Sturt Tavern on the night of 5 June, when they had asked her to hold their handbags so they could dance. The last confirmed sighting was in front of the Prince Berkeley Hotel, Hindley Street – a bouncer saw her, and she appeared visibly intoxicated, holding three handbags.

'After that sighting, it was just a vacuum,' Johnson said. 'We had no idea who she was with or where she was from there. But she obviously went with her killer, probably voluntarily, to the reserve.' There was little for forensic scientists to work with: no fibres from the scene or on Shirree's clothes, no fluids from a sexual assault to examine, no fingerprints on the handbags.

For the next two years the case was virtually at a standstill because little new evidence was uncovered – until the phone rang one afternoon in the Major Crime Task Force office. Detective Senior Constable Bill Cunningham took the call. The caller said he had information about the Turner murder and who might be involved. Although the caller was reluctant to come forward, Cunningham, an amiable Scotsman with gentle powers of persuasion, arranged a meeting. On a cold August night in 1995, Cunningham and Johnson met the caller in the grounds of a southern suburbs school. 'He told us about a conversation he had overheard,' Johnson said later. 'He gave us the names of those involved in this conversation and that basically pointed us in the right direction.'

The thrust of the information was that a man named Frank Mercuri had returned home to his flat in the suburb of Park Holme, near the murder scene, on the morning Shirree was killed, in an extremely agitated state. He also gave other information to suggest that Mercuri might have committed the murder. It was certainly worth following up, and a new investigative team was formed. The detectives soon identified a group they needed to interview, all friends and associates of Mercuri.

Johnson and his team planned a synchronised operation that would see all the men in the group interviewed at the same time. When that was accomplished, it emerged that Mercuri had allegedly told one of his friends, Scott Schinella, that he had been in a reserve with a girl and another man had come up and attacked him. Mercuri had allegedly said he responded by stabbing the attacker, and when the girl screamed, stabbing her. Another man, Julian Berti, present when Mercuri made his alleged confession to Schinella, gave confirmatory information. A third man, Chris Thallas, told police that Mercuri had said the day after the attack on Shirree: 'I've killed a bird.'

Mercuri himself was nowhere to be found in Adelaide. An all-points bulletin was put out, and Mercuri turned up – in Victoria's Pentridge Gaol. The team were astonished by what they found out then. After the death of Shirree, Mercuri had gone to Melbourne. One night in 1994, a day after serving a prison sentence on other offences, he had invited a woman back to his motel room, where he had produced a knife and tried to rape her, stabbing her when she resisted. She had escaped and, not mortally wounded, had been able to survive to give evidence against him. Cunningham and another detective visited Mercuri in gaol on 16 September, 1994, and charged him with the murder of Shirree.

It turned out Mercuri had spent most of his adult life on the wrong side of the law. By the age of 27 he had been convicted nearly 50 times, mainly for offences of robbery and dishonesty. But evidence of prior convictions was inadmissible, and the team had to rely on the evidence of Mercuri's associates.

Schinella and Thallas were not convincing, and Mercuri's gun lawyer, astute QC Lindy Powell, had a field day at the trial tearing their statements apart, accusing them of concocting their stories about Mercuri. Berti threw the final dagger into the Crown case when he told the court his view of the events in Schinella's flat was quite different. He said Mercuri had arrived home looking agitated, but had not said anything about having stabbed a girl.

When Mercuri took the stand, he said he could not remember what he was doing on the night of Shirree's murder. He had been given a knife a short time before Shirree had been attacked but it was double-edged, whereas the murder weapon was single-edged. The trial took less than half the time allotted and the jury took just one hour to return with its verdict: Not guilty.

Johnson and his team were shattered. 'The only explanation was the witnesses let us down,' he said. 'I don't know to this day why they turned in court. I think they just didn't want to know about it and that was that. The jury could see they were having problems and that was the end of it.'

Shirree's father, Ken Turner, was not prepared to let the matter rest. In an Australian first that mirrored the O.J. Simpson case in the United States, Turner started suing Mercuri for damages in relation to his daughter's death. He alleged Mercuri was responsible for Shirree's death and the suffering he had endured as a result. He was working on the principle that in civil proceedings, a claim can be proved on the balance of probabilities, a lower standard than in criminal proceedings, where proof is required beyond reasonable doubt. As well, in a civil case, Mercuri's criminal record could be used.

But Ken Turner's health gave out. On 11 October 1999, the day the civil proceedings were due to start, Turner's lawyer told the District Court his client had been advised not to go ahead because the trial would adversely affect his health. His psychiatrist warned that it would worsen his post-traumatic stress disorder and other related health problems.

Turner said later that he had taken notice of his doctor's advice, but he would lobby the South Australian Government for changes to legislation to allow similar fact evidence to be admissible in criminal trials. 'I can't seen how anybody can make the right decision without knowing all the facts,' Turner said. 'You can't delete the character of a criminal when he's accused of such a horrendous crime as murder.' Interestingly, Mercuri's trial lawyer,

Lindy Powell QC, in a column written for the *Advertiser*, said she believed the relevance of previous convictions was 'far outweighed' by their prejudicial effect.

We might round off this section on South Australian crime with a gangland/bikie-type murder, and take the clock back to shortly after midday on 15 August 1997, and to Les' Auto Repairs, at Lonsdale, a working-class suburb 15 kilometres south of Adelaide.

On this occasion, Gerry Preston, 36, might have been just another customer, until he pulled a stocking mask over his head, adjusted his black-rimmed glasses and pulled a 9 mm Luger pistol from his jacket. With a purposeful spring in his step, he walked into the office where two men, Les Knowles, 37, and Tim Richards, 28, were sitting. He said to Knowles: 'Are you Les?' Knowles replied: 'I'm not Les… ', but barely had time to get it out before Preston took a step back and asked again: 'Are you Les?'

Then Preston fired, hitting Knowles in the temple, and swinging around, asked Richards the same question. Richards denied he was Les, but Preston fired anyway, hitting Richards just below the left eye. Turning to leave, he spotted a mechanic, Kym Traeger, 43, and fired. Traeger, hit on the wrist but only grazed, dived behind a car seat. Preston, having killed Knowles and Richards, and apparently thinking he had done the same to Traeger, walked to a yellow Econovan, driven by his 33-year-old associate, Kevin Gillard.

Veteran homicide investigator Senior Sergeant Gerry Feltus was at home when the call came through. He was working the afternoon shift that day, but went in early. He took one look at the murder scene and formed the viewpoint that this had been a professional hit: two head shots and two bodies. 'It was very obvious it had been a well-planned assassination,' he said later. 'They were not concerned about witnesses and they had planned their escape carefully.'

Feltus and his team were still at the scene when information came through that a yellow Econovan had been found burning behind a block of shops on Beach Road at Christies Beach, about four kilometres away. Problem was, the van had different number plates than witnesses had reported. Was the burning vehicle a ruse to give the assassins more time for their getaway, or had the plates been switched?

The latter scenario was more likely. The initial days of the inquiry revolved around building a picture of the victims and appealing to the public for any information on the yellow Econovan. A yellow Econovan had been stolen from the city a few days earlier and was at that point their only real potential lead.

Les Knowles was well known to police. In Feltus' words, 'he was not a nice person', with form for amphetamine dealing, armed robbery and an attempt to run over two officers while they were trying to arrest him. Among his more serious crimes were the robberies of a car yard and a State Bank branch in the 1980s.

In 1987, Knowles had been sentenced to 14 years' gaol and, just four months before his murder, he had appeared in court charged with assaulting police and driving dangerously. He had probably been involved in other crimes that had occurred just before his death. His drug activities in the southern suburbs were well known. He had been something of a standover man, respected in the local pub because of his tendency to violence. Over a criminal career of more than two decades, he had made plenty of enemies.

Police searching the workshop found $70,000 in a cash drawer, still bundled in the distinctive straps and manner used by the counting houses of armoured car companies. There had been two armoured car-related jobs in the previous fortnight and several others interstate. Although it was never confirmed, police suspected the cash was from one of them because of the way it was bundled. Knowles had either been involved or the cash had been given to him as payment for drugs.

Tim Richards was not in Knowles' league. Police formed the view that Knowles had been the target and that Richards had been, as the saying goes, in the wrong place at the wrong time, as was Traeger. 'We believed pretty well straight away that, because of his lifestyle, Knowles was assassinated for either welching on a drug deal or stepping on someone's toes in relation to territory for distribution,' Feltus said. 'The only alternative we did consider was that because he was a standover man and not very nice when he got on the booze, maybe he had upset an individual who wanted to pay him back.'

As with many complex murder investigations, police relied on public assistance, and plenty of information came in, including calls from people dobbing in somebody they did not like. Police received snippets of information on possible sightings of the Econovan between 12 and 15 August. As so often happens, there are gems in the mass of information, if police have the patience and acuity to detect them.

One caller nominated a man named Gerry Miller as the killer and another provided details of the Econovan being parked at a unit in Washington Street, Hilton, an inner-city suburb. Initially, police did not make a connection between the two items of information. But inquiries with the unit's owner found it was rented by a man named Ron Preston. Among contact numbers left with the unit owner, for people who could provide references, was the name Gerry Miller.

Their curiosity aroused, police checking the background of 'Gerry Miller' in South Australia and Victoria soon discovered Miller was in fact Gerry Preston. They looked at Preston's police record and found he was a heavyweight. He had been involved in crime of various types for many years, including burglary, armed robbery and receiving. At one stage, he had been making $3500 a week from selling marijuana. Although he claimed to have been on the 'periphery', Preston had been part of a stolen goods racket involving cars and computers throughout the 1980s, and had been caught trying to rob a computer store. He had been convicted in 1980 of a series of robberies, and had served a six-year gaol term in Pentridge Gaol.

It was obvious that there should be a lot more inquiries about Preston. 'Because of the circumstances, we thought it would be a waste of time talking to them [the Prestons] straight away,' Feltus said. 'We didn't want them to realise they had come under scrutiny, so we went about gathering evidence in other ways.' Police obtained listening device warrants and placed the devices in Ron

Preston's unit at Hilton and Gerry Preston's at Christies Downs. They also tapped telephones. Both brothers were placed under surveillance. An undercover police officer befriended Ron Preston.

At one stage during the inquiry, Gerry Preston travelled to Melbourne. Among the people he met was a member of the Hells Angels bikie gang, Terry Tognolini, a long-time associate who had been the best man at his wedding. Preston also visited his former wife, Vicki, the mother of his young son who had changed her name to Jacobs. Police tapped telephones in Melbourne as well.

With the electronic surveillance in place, it was time to tip their hand. Ron Preston was questioned over the Econovan seen at his unit, and about his movements. He said that at the time of the shootings, he had been visiting his dentist, something which police confirmed. But Feltus felt it was all a little too neat. 'The fact he had made a dentist appointment for the exact time of the hit, and a conversation we intercepted between him and his flatmate indicated to us that we were on the right track,' Feltus said. 'If he wasn't involved, he certainly had knowledge of it. But we were still very short of evidence against Gerry Preston.'

After weeks of checking and rechecking Preston's associates, his previous crimes and even his bank accounts – which revealed a recent $10,000 deposit – police were almost certain Gerry Preston was the principal offender. They had got onto Kevin Gillard, a criminal associate of Preston, and had formed a suspicion that he had been the getaway driver. 'We knew we had to come up with some ploy to get some activity out of them,' Feltus said. 'They were very guarded on the telephone.'

It was necessary, as they say in the movies, to 'rustle the grass to frighten the snakes'. A story was fed to the *Advertiser* to run on a Saturday morning and be followed up by the television news bulletins that night. The story was essentially that the Econovan had been positively linked to the hit. 'Our undercover operative was to show the story to Ron Preston that morning and get him talking about it, but it didn't work out that way,' Feltus said. 'Ron had been drinking heavily the night before and really didn't want to know about it.'

But the television news item was still to run, and it paid dividends. 'After the first news service, things started happening. Gerald Preston made contact with his father, also called Gerald, and spoke in a coded manner, telling his father to expect a visit from us because things were hotting up. He also told him to dispose of a weapon.' Preston urged his father to watch the next television news if he wanted to know any more.

As far as Feltus was concerned, the reaction of Gerry Preston that night was the clincher; there was now enough evidence to make arrests. A meeting was hastily called and plans for a series of raids on early Sunday morning were made. Preston's father's house at Moonta, about two hours' drive from Adelaide, was raided first. A search found a block of still-damp cement in the boot of his car. A 9 mm Luger pistol had been set in it. Police also found an ignition switch for an Econovan.

Gerry Preston was arrested at his home and said nothing, maintaining his silence during interviews when the allegations were put to him. But he was charged with two counts of murder and one of attempted murder. Ron Preston, arrested the same day, decided to roll over, and was granted immunity from prosecution in return for giving evidence against his brother. Gerry Preston's father was charged with attempting to dispose of the pistol, but the charge was later dropped. Gillard fled but used his credit card, which showed him moving through Victoria and Tasmania. Arrested in Queensland, he was charged with two counts of murder and one of attempted murder.

The trial started in the Supreme Court of South Australia in June 1998, but there was evidence of some attempts, real or anticipated, to distort it. Vicki Jacobs expressed fears for her safety and that of her son. Tognolini was arrested at the home of Preston's father after travelling from Melbourne. He was making overtures to Preston senior not to give evidence against his son. Police arrested him for that, and he was given bail on the condition that he not return to South Australia.

The trial proceeded, the Crown arguing that Knowles and Richards had been killed after a contract was taken out by a Hells

Angels member in Melbourne. The bikie had agreed to pay Preston $10,000 for the hit. After sitting for 70 days of evidence, the jury, deliberating for eight days, returned guilty verdicts against Preston and Gillard on all charges. Preston was sentenced to life in prison with a 32-year non-parole period, and Gillard to life with a 25-year non-parole period. Both appealed their convictions.

'We were always aware that the trial was going to be tough, but its length surprised everyone,' Feltus said. 'There was always the possibility of separate trials and there was the possibility of witness intimidation, which occurred in a roundabout way.' Although no exact reason for the hit was outlined, Feltus has his own theories. 'I think it basically got back to one or two things,' he said. 'He, Knowles, either trod on the toes of someone with his drug dealings or he had moved into an area or category of time which controls a particular drug or a particular area and he was assassinated for that. The people he had moved in on sent out feelers to see if they could get the job done and ended up obtaining the services of Preston and Gillard.'

Those who did the hiring had not been identified at the time of writing. Preston, in gaol, could probably have given police a lot of help, but in all probability knew that if he did disclose such information, he would be killed. Retribution was certainly exacted elsewhere. In the early hours of Saturday 12 June, 1999, Vicki Jacobs, asleep in her home in Bendigo, was shot twice in the head and twice in the back by a killer who had climbed in through a window and crept past her sleeping niece. A week later, Feltus and another detective interviewed Preston about the murder in Adelaide's Yatala Gaol. He told them nothing.

part two

THE MULTIPLE KILLINGS

massacres

disappearing women

the monster of Belanglo

MASSACRES

What! All my pretty chickens and their dam,
at one fell swoop?

William Shakespeare
Macbeth

Wade Frankum, a shaven-headed, failed public schoolboy, business manager and lover, and in his own mind a failed son, drank four cups of coffee as he sat for an hour in the Coffee Pot, Strathfield Plaza, Sydney, on the afternoon of Saturday 26 August 1991. He did not display emotion, but his stares were disconcerting to the few who noticed him. At 3.30 pm, he finished his fourth coffee, a cappuccino.

Nearby, 15-year-old Roberta (Bo) Armstrong was sitting talking excitedly with a friend. A ballet student at the nearby McDonald Performing Arts High School, she was to attend her Year 10 formal and had bought a dress for it. Due to go dancing that night, she was talking about boys and clothes. Nearby, Carole Dickinson, 47, of Greenacre, and her daughter Belinda, 21, were having coffee with Rachelle Milburn, 17, a student and volunteer social worker, who had arrived from Newcastle and was to be the bridesmaid at Belinda's wedding. At another table, Patricia Rowe, 37, and her mother Joyce Nixon, 61, from Sussex Inlet, a resort on the New South Wales south coast where the family had long been in business, were sitting with Mrs Rowe's sons, Kevin, 14, and Nathan, 9. They had all visited Joyce Nixon's husband, Bob, who was in hospital, as he had just had a cancerous growth removed.

In the kitchen, the proprietor, George Mavris, was talking to friends. Aged 51, he had worked hard since his arrival from Greece 34 years before. Now the owner of his own business, he had friends around on Saturday afternoons to talk and play the card game viftiko. He had provided a good home for his family and had made enough money to send his sons to Sydney's Newington College.

It was a scene that could be replicated anywhere – normal, happy people, caught at a moment of time, busy with the details of their lives. Except that Wade Frankum was not one of them.

Frankum's life had crashed. His outlook had deteriorated, and his appearance and behaviour with it. After a catastrophic meltdown, fuelled by bitter personal experiences as he was growing up and the suicide of his mother, he was ready to throw in the towel. But he was going to take people with him. Who they were, he did not really care.

Those normal, well-adjusted individuals were people he hated. They had what he did not have. In his mind they were the people who, when forced to notice him, were likely to react with indifference, or even scorn. It had happened before. He had been a pupil at Newington College, where the fit and manly flourished, and those who could not keep up – as at any school – endured torment. Because of his pudgy appearance, he was called 'Pig'. He became a chronic truant and was expelled.

Frankum was always a candidate for psychiatric breakdown. With borderline personality stability, he did not need much to push him over the line.

After his expulsion, he had completed his schooling at Homebush High School and had entered working life with the T.J. Maxx chain of clothing stores. He rose to the position of stock controller, performing his job competently and earning respect from the staff. He was there nearly five years, but lost the job over a staff dispute. In 1988, his father died after a long illness. His mother, reacting badly, became vague and irrational and was hardly any help to Frankum. Nor was the decision of his girlfriend to break off their engagement shortly before the wedding date. In 1989, Frankum stopped jogging and swimming, gave up social life, let his appearance deteriorate and fell to pieces in his behaviour.

In May 1990, his mother, suffering depression, gassed herself in her Ford Laser sedan at the family unit in Baronga Street, Strathfield. Frankum, with his sister, Gaynor, inherited the unit and moved into it. Distraught over his mother's death, he plastered her pictures over his bedroom wall and blamed himself for not having been more attentive to her. He gave up his sales job and worked casually as a taxi driver, started wearing tracksuits and army shirts and shorts, and spent a lot of his $30,000 share of the inheritance on prostitutes. He acquired a stock of magazines depicting violence and a copy of *American Psycho*, a novel about a serial killer. He also obtained a shooter's licence.

Recognising at least some of his problems, Frankum turned to a psychologist for what were to be five consultations. Psychologists, bound by professional protocol, committed to maintaining a professional detachment, discouraged from taking an intrusive role in patients' lives or telling them what to do, are restricted. The psychologist did note the hatred Frankum bore his mother, and at the same time his attachment to her and apparent inability to form relationships with women. Seeing the psychologist might have been a desperate plea by Frankum for help. It might have been, in his mind, the last chance he was giving society. In January 1991, out of funds, Frankum withdrew from treatment.

On 16 January, he bought a Chinese-made SKS semi-automatic rifle, telling police he wanted to go pig-shooting. He bought one hundred rounds of ammunition, three magazines with the capacity of 30-rounds each, and a 30 cm Bowie knife. In April that year, police questioned him because there had been a number of crimes committed in which a rifle similar to his had been used. Frankum was cleared, but, on later coroner's court evidence, might already have been planning a massacre. He might also have been hoping for some sort of shoot-out with police, which would fulfil a violent fantasy and be the ultimate thrill, ending in his own death. In July, he took his knife to a Mister Minit store to make it razor-sharp. Innocent, well-adjusted people were going to be caught up in all this and they would pay the penalty for all the taunts, sneers and insults the world had heaped upon him.

It appeared later that Frankum initially planned the massacre for North Strathfield station, choosing a place and people he had daily contact with. He knew the stationmaster, Clive Young. Strathfield Plaza, a place with many people, also suggested itself. He might have been thinking of setting up a sniper's nest in the Department of Social Security offices there. At North Strathfield station he lingered. He said to Young: 'You had better go home, Clive.' He did not catch the next train. Then, at 1.48 pm, he got on one for Strathfield, carrying a black bag in which he had his knife, a tubular Postpak containing his rifle, and three loaded magazines. Alighting at Strathfield, he went to the shopping plaza.

When he started killing, it was swift and brutal. Smiling and laughing, he plunged his Bowie into Bo Armstrong, who screamed and slumped. Taking up his rifle, he trained it on Nathan Rowe. Patricia Rowe hurled herself in front of Nathan and Joyce Nixon overturned the table to shield Kevin. Frankum shot both women dead. Carole Dickinson hurled herself over Belinda and was shot dead. So was Rachel Milburn. George Mavris emerged from his kitchen and was met with a bullet.

Frankum walked into the shopping centre and started firing indiscriminately. People were running wildly or taking shelter, urged on by Greg Read of Homebush, one of seven who was wounded that day but not killed. He ran through the shopping centre warning people. Frankum killed Robertson Kan Hock Vool, 51, of Croydon. But he was still after more. This writer, reporting on the massacre the day after, interviewed a shopper who had dodged and danced in a macabre duel with Frankum, who fired several times trying to pin him.

Frankum, apparently unable to get into the Society Security offices, walked out of the shopping centre, bailed up a motorist, who thought she was about to live her last few minutes, and told her to drive him to Enfield. With sirens of approaching emergency

The twisted remains of the garbage truck in George Street, Sydney,
after the Hilton Hotel bomb explosion on Monday 13 February 1978.

Emergency services at the scene of the Hilton Hotel bombing.

Evan Pederick leaving gaol after serving eight years for his part in the Hilton Hotel bombing.

Aarne Tees was a senior detective assigned to investigate the Hilton Hotel bombing.

Tim Anderson, the Ananda Marga public relations officer, after his acquittal.

Dean Waters, a former heavy-weight boxing champion, with his coach and father, Cec.

Below: Dean and Cec Waters arrive at court on 29 March 1989, to face murder charges.

Prime Minister Bob Hawke (centre), NSW Premier Neville Wran (right) and Peter Barron (left) before a press conference at the Regent Hotel after the bombing of Judge Ray Watson's Home in 1984.

Hos Majdalawi being led from court after being found guilty of shooting his wife dead in front of Parramatta Family Court.

Bomb disposal experts scale the exterior of the building where a parcel bomb exploded in the offices of the National Crime Authority, killing NCA officer Geoffrey Bowen.

Domenic Perre, alleged South Australian drug dealer and NCA bombing suspect, leaving court on 16 December 1994.

Peter Wallis, who survived the NCA bombing, suffered severe burning and lost an eye.

An artist's impression of Hieu Duy Dinh and Angela Linda Sinclair. Both were found guilty of murdering Ronald Pettit.

Angela Sinclair who was locked in a custody battle with Ronald Pettit at the time of Pettit's murder.

Frank Mercuri after the civil lawsuit for wrongful death charges were dropped by Shirree Turner's father, Ken.

Gerald David Preston who was found guilty of the murders of Les Knowles and Tim Richards.

Julian Knight is led away by police after the Hoddle Street massacre, in which he killed six people.

Frank Vitkovic is caught on security camera during the Queen Street massacre, in which he killed nine people.

Martin Bryant, three days before the Port Arthur massacre.

Below: The smouldering remains of the Seascape Guesthouse, where Martin Bryant began and ended the massacre at Port Arthur.

Lindsay Beckett shows police the place where he and Camilleri picked up Bega schoolgirls, Lauren Barry and Nichole Collins.

Leslie Camilleri is escorted from the court after being found guilty of the murders of Lauren Barry and Nichole Collins.

(Left to right) Garret Barry, Graeme Collins, Delma Collins and Cheryl Barry, the parents of Bega schoolgirls Lauren and Nichole, after the trial which found Camilleri and Beckett guilty of murdering their daughters.

Michael Murphy (covering face) and detectives in the paddock where Anita Cobby's body was found.

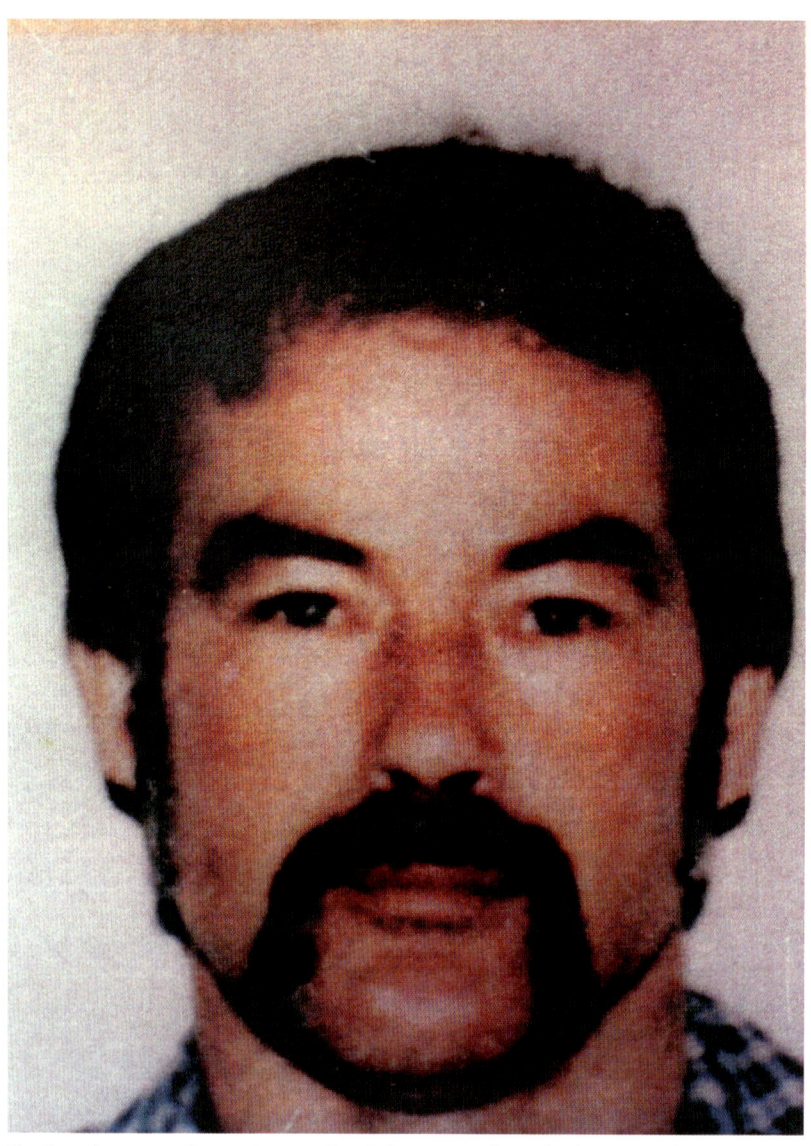

Backpacker murders witness, Paul Onions, identified Ivan Milat (above) as his attacker from this mugshot.

Above: Challinder Hughes, girlfriend of Ivan Milat, with her lawyer, Leigh Johnson, arrives at the court for the Backpacker murders trial.

Ivan Milat's former prison cell at Maitland Gaol.

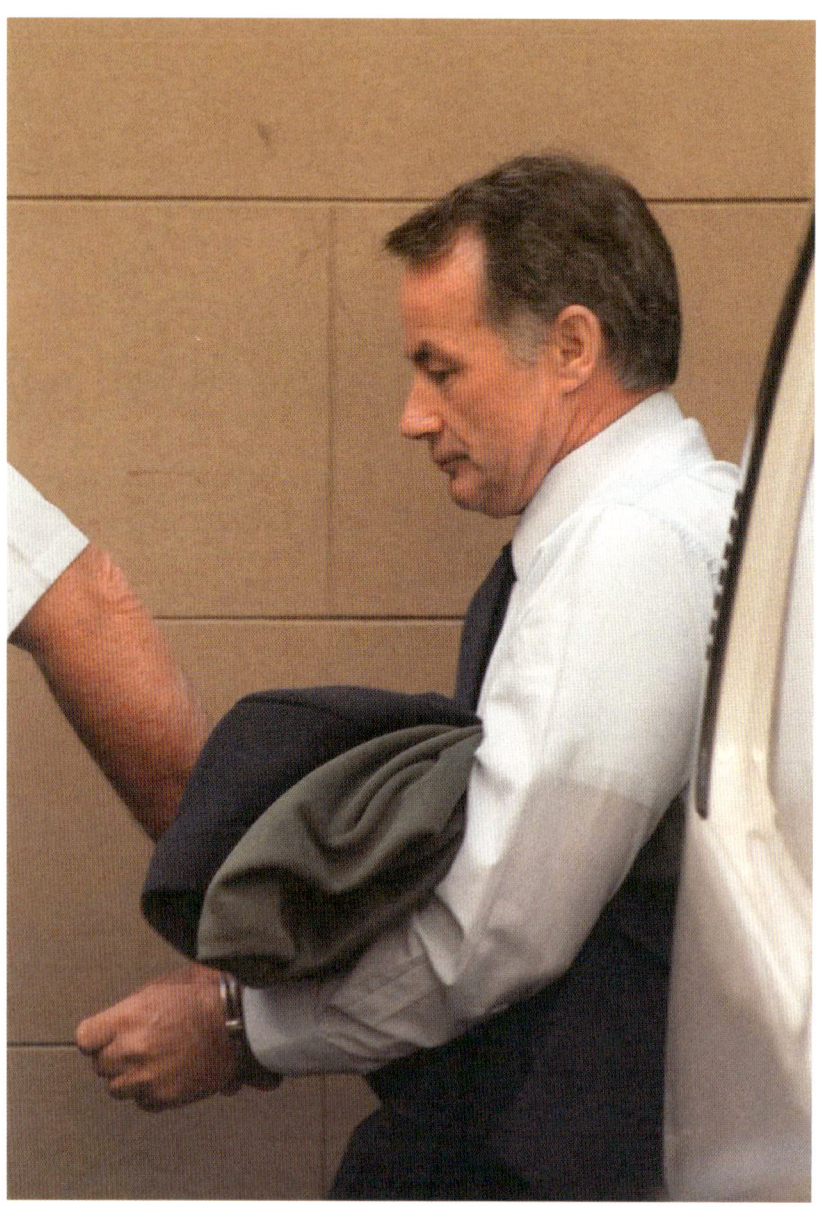

Ivan Milat is led into court by police to face trial for the murders of
seven backpackers, whose bodies were found in the Belanglo State Forest.

vehicles growing louder, Frankum apologised, got out and shot himself through the head.

The M'Naghten Rules relating to crime and mental illness – that an individual did not know what he was doing or did not know the difference between right and wrong – are the established legal tests for mental illness, but the law also recognises degrees of madness, as in 'diminished responsibility'. Had Frankum lived, he could have pleaded not guilty to murder charges on that basis, but the calculated actions, and evidence of planning, would probably have gone against him.

There is usually a degree of mental illness in people who perpetrate massacres. Otherwise, it can be argued, they would not do it. The common feature in nearly all massacres has been access to firearms, though there are other means available. On Christmas Eve, 1975, a hapless homosexual misfit, Reginald John Little, disappointed his boyfriend had not turned up, feeling the particular bitterness that Christmas often brings, particularly to misfits, set fire to the Savoy Hotel in the heart of Kings Cross, killing 15 people. I interviewed Little several days later while he was leading a rally calling for stricter fire regulations. Little did seem totally preoccupied when I spoke to him. He was given maximum media exposure, which brought him to the attention of Newcastle police, who knew he had an extensive record for arson. They rang Darlinghurst detectives, saying: 'You've got him!'

On 18 August 1983, Douglas John Edward Crabbe, 36, truck driver, ejected from the bar of the Inland Motel at Ayers Rock, had a violent impulse to get back at the people there, and with his self-restraint weakened by the effects of alcohol, he drove his truck at speed into the bar, killing five people. In Alice Springs Magistrate's Court on 19 November 1983, his counsel, Kevin Borick, said: 'The accused has instructed me that he bitterly regrets the tragic consequences of the events that led to him being here today.'

But firearms are the main issue in mass killings. Every firearms outrage has been followed by calls for severe limitations on ownership; there were constant battles because of the powerful gun lobby, and usually some sort of compromise. The Prime Minister of the day, Bob Hawke, had called a national 'gun summit' in 1987, including ministers from States and Territories. But there was always opposition to gun law reform. The then New South Wales Premier, Barrie Unsworth, stormed out of the meeting in exasperation, saying: 'It will take a massacre in Tasmania before we get gun law reform in Australia.' That State, and Queensland, he was later to declare, were 'black States', intransigent on the issue of firearms law reform. On the ropes politically, and seeking an issue, he decided on firearms control for the New South Wales State election of that year.

Unsworth lost the election decisively, and part of that loss was attributed to a groundswell opposition, particularly in rural areas, to the threat to take away firearms and, so the argument went, the inalienable right of an individual to protect himself and his family. After the election, the Sporting Shooters Association of Australia wrote to this reporter, who had been covering the issue, and said that the election result was 'a lesson', and nobody should ever dare bring up the prospect of banning firearms again.

Massacres have occurred in Australia from the time of colonisation, the earliest victims being Aborigines. Wherever there was competition for land – and that was inevitable when sheep and cattle were introduced – violence broke out. It happened in Tasmania, and in fact in every State, fuelled by racism, boorishness, lack of understanding. On one estimate, 100,000 Aborigines died in massacres, but because New South Wales Governor Gipps insisted on hanging seven perpetrators of the 1838 Myall Creek massacre, word went out to be discreet.

The so-called 1984 'Father's Day Massacre' at the Viking Tavern, Milperra, in south-western Sydney, involved members of the Bandido and Commanchero motorcycle clubs and resulted in the deaths of six bikers. A seventh victim, a 14-year-old girl, was caught in the crossfire. But that might be classified differently – as a battle, in which both sides had armed themselves. The mainstream 'massacre', as understood in today's Australia, involves one person armed and the victims defenceless. This sort of massacre is normally perpetrated by someone who has given up, overwhelmed by the pressures of life. The pressures might have arisen within himself (or herself), or in the external world. It could be, and normally is, a combination of both, a vicious circle, where the disturbance within the individual makes him less capable of dealing with the problems of life, and then the problems of life increase the disturbance and so on.

When the outcome is violence, it can be directed against himself, and there will be a suicide. A man killing his entire family often does it as an extension of suicide. In July 1985, psychiatrist Harold Leyton was oppressed with mounting financial difficulties and facing a sexual harassment case brought by a former patient. He had warned another psychiatrist nine months before that he felt like killing himself and his family. The psychiatrist had taken it seriously enough to warn Leyton's wife, Gail. Harold Leyton, obliged to move from his $650,000 house in Pymble to a far humbler home in Chatswood, shot Gail and their sons aged ten and twelve in their beds, tried to burn the house down and then committed suicide by slashing his wrists.

In 1992, another eruption of twisted passion was building up on the Central Coast of New South Wales. Malcolm George Baker, a 45-year-old unemployed mechanic and panel beater, had split with his girlfriend of seven years, Kerry Anne Gannan, at Terrigal. Kerry had wanted to end the relationship. Baker was bitterly resentful and thought his son, David Malcolm, who had a wife and child at Bateau Bay, was having an affair with Kerry. Kerry Gannan had taken out a restraining order against Baker, and he also resented that, as well as the rest of her family, for interfering. That included Kerry's father, Tom Gannan, 43, and Kerry's pregnant 18-year-old sister, Lisa.

Baker had voiced some warnings about the way he felt. He told a new girlfriend: 'I'm gunna crack and when I do, I don't care if I take a pregnant woman with me.' On 22 October, Baker told his 21-year-old daughter that he would kill himself. She had told him it was not worth it, and he had replied: 'I am going to shoot them… when the time's right, I will kill them.' Shortly after 9 pm on 27 October, armed with a rifle and in breach of the restraining order, Baker went to Kerry's home to 'rectify' the relationship. He later told police: 'I found out about her having an affair with my son and getting dope off him for three years. I was not going to do anything, just threaten them.' On his account, he stood outside the bedroom and heard Kerry and her new boyfriend, Christopher Gall, talking about sex. He shot the lock off the door. Kerry Gannan screamed: 'It's Mac! It's Mac!'

Baker shot Gall in the face, and Kerry. Losing all restraint, he went through the house shooting anyone else who was there, including Lisa Gannan. Tom Gannan managed to get out of the house, but Baker cut him down. With Kerry, Tom and Lisa dead, Baker drove to Bateau Bay, shot his son dead, then went to Wyong and shot Ross Warren Smith, 35, whom he told police had owed him money, and Smith's de facto wife, Lesley Joyce Read, 25. Later that night, with only Gall surviving, Baker gave himself up to police. On 6 August 1983, he was gaoled for life.

Baker had a passionate hostility towards a group of people for specific reasons. When he had killed them, he was done. In other cases, the killer might take action against the one or two people for whom he has nursed hostility, and then with restraints gone, go for anybody else. The people then chosen might have done something to annoy the killer, but whatever their fault, they hardly deserve the death sentence they'd received.

Other attacks are totally tokenistic. Paul Wade Streeton on 10 October, 1996, engaged in an act of pure tokenism. He decided to make a six-year-old Aboriginal boy, Tjandamurra O'Shane, playing in the schoolyard at Cairns North Public School, pay for what he felt society, or at least its school system, had done to him. Streeton poured petrol onto the child and set him on fire. Appearing in Cairns Magistrate's Court, Streeton said he had grievances against the education system which had failed to recognise his intelligence, and his parents who failed to support his claim for greater recognition. 'I just wanted people to be aware of what I am angry about,' he said. 'I could see no other solution to my predicament. I have nothing against the child, I just wanted to hurt those people who make me feel unsafe or threatened.'

Tjandamurra recovered as best he could from his burns; Streeton, whose explanation was rejected by the court, got life.

The modern era of high-profile massacres in Australia was ushered in four years to the day before Frankum's rampage. A disaffected former Duntroon officer cadet, Julian Knight, cut loose with two powerful rifles and a shotgun in Clifton Hill, Melbourne. Knight was 19 years old when the pressures of life became too much for him. Like Frankum, he had had severe disruptions in his family life. Born 6 March 1968, and adopted by Ralph Knight, a professional soldier, and wife Pamela, Knight had been drawn by his father's occupation and by normal schoolboy instincts to firearms and militarism, receiving an air rifle for his twelfth birthday. Following his father's career path, he joined the school cadets at the age of 14. When he was 15, his adoptive parents divorced. Julian, who felt he had been rejected by his adoptive father, remained with Pamela Knight and her son and daughter at their home in Ramsden Street, Clifton Hill. Ralph Knight, a major in the Army Education Corps, was posted to Townsville.

Though highly intelligent, Julian Knight failed to reach his potential. He enrolled in an arts course at La Trobe University in 1986 but left after six weeks and for most of that year was unemployed. For his 18th birthday present in March that year, he received a Ruger .22 calibre semi-automatic rifle. The following month, he applied for a shooter's licence, answering the questionnaire correctly. He also discovered that he had been adopted, and tried unsuccessfully to make contact with his natural mother, whom he believed lived in South Africa. His girlfriend of 17 months, Renee Cross, saw weaknesses in him. She had never seen a man cry as much as he had, she said later. She suggested he seek psychiatric help. Instead, Knight acquired more firearms: a .38 calibre M14 and a pump-action shotgun.

Knight joined the Army Reserve, and then in January 1987 was accepted as an officer cadet at Duntroon. Life in officer school is tough. It is designed to be so, since army officers have to be trained to tolerate great stress. The so-called 'bastardisation' is designed to weed out the temperamentally unfit. Knight lasted six months before becoming involved in a Canberra nightclub brawl and stabbing an army sergeant with a pocket knife. He was charged with malicious wounding and was due to appear in the Canberra Magistrate's Court. In July 1987, he was asked to resign from Duntroon and did so.

Knight returned to Melbourne, tried to re-establish his relationship with Renee without success, then fixed his attention on another woman, aged 29, whom he saw at the Royal Hotel, Clifton Hill. He tried to get to know her, meeting her outside the hotel and offering to take her home. She was unresponsive. On Friday night 7 August 1987, Renee had a party at her home and did not invite him. Knight was upset by this. At midday on Sunday 9 August, he went to his grandmother's home, where the family had gathered to celebrate his mother's birthday. He left there and went to a friend's home. When he went to depart at 5 pm, he found his gearbox had packed up. It might, his counsel said later in court, have been the 'final trigger' that tipped him over the edge.

Knight returned to the family home, then decided to go to the Royal Hotel, arriving at about 7 pm. He saw the woman who had attracted his attention, but made no move towards her. He stayed more than an hour, bought a packet of John Player cigarettes and drank at least three schooners of Carlton Draught. A group of about 20, including the woman he had had his eye on, decided to leave for the nearby Normanby Hotel, where an Irish folk group was playing. Knight did not try to join them. Maybe trying to join them, after all the rejections and rebuffs, would have meant he was still trying to make it in the real world. Being asked to leave Duntroon, though hardly unexpected, had been a bitter blow. The rejections by the two women were magnified in his mind.

Knight left the Royal at 8.15 pm. Returning home, he strapped on an ammunition belt, took the rifles and shotgun, and at about 9.15 pm left the house to make his way towards Clifton Hill station. At 9.45 pm, he took a kneeling position near the station and raised one of his weapons to his shoulder. In the 15-minute mayhem that followed, he fired shotgun blasts and discharged more than 120 bullets, killing six people and wounding 18.

In the ensuing media coverage of the event, there was particular attention – even a fascination – with the fact that the people there at that point in time could have been anyone. And indeed that was true. A moment's hesitation by one of the people who was to become a victim, a decision to have another cup of coffee, anything, could have saved them – or killed them.

Kevin and Tracy Skinner had attended a birthday party for Kevin's brother and were returning home with their 18-month-old baby, Adam, whom she was nursing. She had her face blown to pieces and Adam was wounded. Venna Markouska, 25, a migrant from Yugoslavia, was driving her father's car. She heard a loud bang, thought the motor had packed up, got out and was hit in the neck. Dusan Flajnik had migrated from Yugoslavia 28 years before, worked on the Snowy Mountains Scheme and for 25 years for Carlton and United Breweries. Due to start his 10.30 pm shift, he was driving to Abbotsford brewery for his usual early start. He was hit by a single bullet. Bob Mitchell had been visiting friends and saw what he thought was a car accident. He saw the bodies of Vesna Markovska, 24, who had been shot, and her boyfriend, Zoran Trajceski, 22, who was shot as he tried to pick her up. As Mitchell tried to help, Knight cut him down. Zoran, hit twice, ran 500 metres to Vesna's home to get help.

John Peter Muscat, sitting in a lounge, heard what he thought was a car accident. Ignoring the pleas of a woman friend who realised what was happening and was tugging at his jumper, trying to make him stay, he ran out and was hit by two shotgun pellets in the forehead and one behind the ear. Gina Papaioannou, 21, got out of her car to help a victim, and was hit several times. She died 11 days later. Making his way towards the railway station, Knight abandoned the shotgun and Ruger but kept the M14. He saw Kenneth Shane Stanton approach on his 250cc Kawasaki road bike to start his 10 pm shift at Australia Post. Stanton was riding because he and his wife Debbie feared their Camira sedan might be stolen if parked in that area. Knight put a bullet through his head.

Knight, cornered by two police officers, surrendered. He told police: 'I wanted to see what it would be like to kill someone, because I knew as soon as I did, the police would come along and then the SOG (Special Operations Group) would come along and finish me off.' Ultimately charged with seven counts of murder, 39 of attempted murder, 12 of intentionally causing serious injury and 10 of intentionally causing injury, Knight pleaded guilty, and on 10 November, 1988, was given seven life sentences and a total of 460 years on 46 counts of attempted murder. His minimum term was 27 years.

From gaol, Knight appealed for greater controls on firearms, a reaction that seemed like Little's in the arson case – looking for contributing causes to the disaster beyond himself. He sent a seven-page submission to the Victorian Parliamentary Committee investigating causes of criminal violence. In July 1994, Knight wrote to this writer from Pentridge Gaol, introducing himself in a paragraph in which he described his role in the massacre, but appearing to be dismissive of it. He invited me to edit a proposed Encyclopaedia of Australian Crime. I declined on the grounds that it was too big a task, and being incarcerated he would face an uphill battle. I suggested he take up a more uplifting subject, and expressed the view that a man with his record might have problems being accepted by publishers or book buyers.

On 28 December 1994, he replied: 'In relation to myself and alternative writing projects; I must admit that I was astounded by many of your comments, especially in light of your 23 years as a journalist. I readily accept that I am *persona non grata* as far as society is concerned. In fact, I would say that I am generally despised by the vast majority of the population at large. As I often facetiously say: "You can't run around shooting people and then expect to win popularity contests." I expect that this general principle applies also to journalists and prospective publishers. I simply cannot, however, accept that the vast majority of journalists and publishers would be dismissive of any writing proposal I put to them – especially an autobiography.' He likened his story to the accounts of the life of Victorian criminal Mark 'Chopper' Read.

There was in his writing no expression of remorse, and Knight continued to suggest that having committed a massacre made him someone important. He was not. Perhaps, in taking up his weapons on that fateful night, he was fulfilling a deep-felt need; for the first time, as he gunned people down, he was being taken seriously.

Seven years afterwards, Knight had a right to try to make something of himself, to try to salvage something from the wreckage of his life. But the surliness and bitterness also still came through. He expressed dismay at researchers who had written to him or interviewed him, then used what he had told them privately to write articles on him. I suppose I am doing that now. Knight retained his greatest vitriol for crime writers, the group he appeared anxious to join: 'An associated fact is that the vast majority of crime reporters, being the despicable, dishonest and blood-sucking, gutless desk-bound maggots that most of them are, would do a book deal with Charles Manson if there was heaps of royalties to be gained from it. Given that I am fully aware of the true nature of "crime reporting" in this country, I would do a deal with [he named two Melbourne crime reporters] but I wouldn't piss on them if they were on fire; although I might if they were holding my royalty cheque...'

The Clifton Hill Massacre might have provoked other outrages. In England ten days afterwards, one Michael Ryan went on the rampage at Hungerford with a rifle and revolver, killing 16 people before committing suicide. In December 1987, in Knight's home town, Frank Vitkovic, a 22-year-old university dropout with a brilliant academic record, a good sporting past and a wonky knee, went on a rampage, killing eight people and wounding five in what became known as the Queen Street Massacre.

In the inevitable inquiry into Vitkovic's background, it was evident that he was mentally ill. There was nothing in his background that seemed likely to have provoked his disturbance. Born on 7 September 1965, Frank Vitkovic went to a Marist Brothers College. He excelled at his studies but ran into one spot of trouble with the law at the age of 17, when he was caught lifting a woman's dress. He was referred by police to a psychiatrist. He did brilliantly in the Higher School Certificate of 1983, especially in accounting, and won the local tennis club championship. In 1984, he enrolled in a four-year law course at Melbourne University. A knee injury suffered while playing tennis caused him to limp and ultimately forced him to give up the sport, which depressed him.

Vitkovic completed his first two years of law and underwent a series of knee operations in 1986. In his second term, he deferred his law studies and helped his father, who was a housepainter by trade but handicapped by a back injury. Vitkovic resumed his studies, but in December that year, the sub-dean became disturbed by the contents of an idiosyncratic essay Vitkovic had written on justice and referred him to a psychologist, Malcolm Morgan. Morgan recognised anger and bitterness in Vitkovic. 'Frank was a person who, if not psychotic, was in the hinterland between functioning normally and not... he was severely disturbed and on his way to becoming psychotic,' he said later. 'He was disturbed by violent fantasies which focused on himself and others. He was painfully aware of the problems he had in his life.' But Morgan felt restrained by professional considerations relating to the breaking of patient confidence and did not report him, although it is not clear what on earth he would have been able to report that would have justified any sort of official action.

In January 1987, Vitkovik was suspended from the university for 'unsatisfactory progress'. He was due to see Morgan for another session in March that year but did not keep the appointment. Perhaps the suspension was the trigger – a young man with so much potential on the scrapheap. He was in desperate need of psychiatric treatment, but would have needed to seek it himself and persist with it. The only other person to encounter Vitkovic in this vein was Eleanor Simpson, a volunteer with the Church of Scientology, a faith which believes it has a better approach to mental health than conventional practitioners in that area. She gave him a personality test, and, alarmed with the results, offered him a church pamphlet and a course which he did not take up. The Church of Scientology has a record of contributing positively to mental health, particularly in helping to unravel the Chelmsford Hospital scandal in New South Wales, but any involvement by anyone in the area of mental health carries risks.

In mid-September 1987, Vitkovic obtained his shooter's licence, though he answered one question, whether firearms should be unloaded before being taken into a house or shop, in the negative rather than affirmative. At that time, on 16 September, he started a diary, writing: 'I am in hell and there seems no way out, I feel the end is near for me. I don't know why I say that but I feel it is true. I cannot control myself... this time things have destroyed me, my ego has gone completely. Many times I feel like exploding. I wish all would end. I am isolated totally – I never go out socially any more. After I was dead, my torture would be over, it's mainly mental torture I feel.'

He wrote about 'rejection, loneliness and ill-treatment', and 'a fascination with guns' as being the ingredients of a massacre. Perhaps he was thinking about Julian Knight's massacre. He referred in his diary to 'Rambo', an all-action macho man regarded with amusement by normal people, but whose effect on an unbalanced mind might be quite different. In October 1987, Vitkovic went to a doctor suffering tension headaches and received tranquillisers. He bought an M1 carbine, telling police he wanted to 'go hunting', and shortened the stock and barrel until its combined length was 75 cm.

His school friend, Con Margelis, rang him in October, and Knight told him to leave him alone. In fact, Vitkovic's hostilities were starting to centre on Margelis, who was blameless. He wrote that Margelis had only wanted him to be a partner to play snooker in front of his friends. 'He treated me like dirt,' Vitkovic said. 'Something should be done about others like him. I long for the end now. I know the end is near. I have so much hostility built up inside me – everyone else treats me like dirt... I have never felt so lonely or inadequate in my life. I cannot live in this world – there is no place for me.'

In November 1987, Vitkovic reapplied for entry to Melbourne University and this time switched to arts. But by now he was virtually beyond redemption. A forensic psychiatrist, Dr Allan Bartholemew, said that by that time, Vitkovic would have been suitable for certification under the *Mental Health Act* as a paranoid schizophrenic, which meant Vitkovic could have been detained for his own good and the good of society. On 8 December, Vitkovic penned a suicide note. It said: 'Today is going to be the day. The time has come to die. There is no way out... anger in my head has gone too much for me. I have got to get rid of my violent impulses.' Carrying his rifle, ammunition and a change of clothing in a bag, he went to Melbourne University, where he spoke to a receptionist he knew, Mary Cooke, and told her he had failed his exams and that he had, 'a job at the post office today'. He then went to the Australia Post building in Queen Street, Melbourne, specifically, it appears, to kill Con Margelis.

Margelis, a credit officer at the Telecom Credit Union on the fifth floor, heard that someone wanted to see him at the counter. When he went there, Vitkovic smiled and pointed the M1 at him. Margelis bolted, and sought refuge in the women's toilet. Abandoning any pursuit of him, Vitkovic started killing indiscriminately. Judith Anne Morris, 19, was hit in the chest. The next to die were Julie Faye McBean, 20, and Warren David Spencer, 29, who was at the photocopier. Vitkovic went to the 12th floor, where he killed Annunziate Avigone, 18. Police were on their way. Vitkovic took a long-distance shot at a motorcycle officer.

Going to the 11th floor, he shot Michael Francis McGuire, 38, father of three, in the data processing room, then opened fire on the finance and accounting department, hitting Marianne Jacoba van Ewyk, 38, and Catherine Mary Dowling, 28, as they crouched beside a desk, and Rodney Gerrard Brown, 32, at his desk. An assistant manager, Tony Gioia, rushed at Vitkovic, grabbing him around the chest. Another employee, though wounded, helped Gioia. A third grabbed the rifle and hid it in a refrigerator. Vitkovic fought to get free, broke the grip of the two trying to restrain him, rushed to the window and hurled himself 60 metres to his death.

Marianne van Ewyk, 36, a migrant from Holland who had worked for Australia Post from her teens, died beneath a calendar which she had used to calculate the holidays she would spend with her son, Peter. The birthday cake had been made and the candles placed for the fifth birthday of Tony McGuire's daughter. He was to have blown the candles out. Again there were the recriminations, the soul-searching, the debate about firearms control. Security systems at the building were looked at and found to be adequate for everybody but a determined madman.

On 28 April 1996, Tasmania had the massacre Barrie Unsworth had feared. A mentally retarded, psychiatrically twisted 28-year-old, Martin Bryant, sought out two people he knew, David and Sally Martin, who had run the Seascape guest house at Port Arthur for many years and whose son, Darryn, had played with him as a boy. Bryant had a mortal hatred of them, apparently over a property dispute. Bryant went in with his SKS rifle, the same type of weapon that Frankum had used, banned in New South Wales after the Strathfield massacre but still available in Tasmania. He also had an AR-15 0.233 calibre semi-automatic. He shot David and Sally Martin dead.

In the aftermath of the massacre, the public had a natural curiosity as to what sort of a person Martin Bryant was, and how that related to what he did. So let us look at what was discovered.

Some enterprising reporters gained unauthorised access to Bryant's house at 30 Clare Street, in the northern Hobart suburb of New Town and got family snaps, which were published nationally, along with various accounts of his life. Martin Bryant was born in 1966, son of Maurice and Carleen Bryant. Maurice worked as a wharf labourer and on the domestic scene was said to be a bully. But in at least some aspects it was a normal enough family life. The family snaps showed Carleen full of the new mother glow, cuddling infant Martin. The family had a seaside cottage on the Tasman Peninsula, north-west of Hobart, and Bryant knew Port Arthur well. Blond-haired, he was an angelic-looking child, but dull. At New Town High his grades were poor and his deficiencies were quickly recognised by his schoolmates, who called him 'dope', 'mad' and 'funny in the head', driving him into isolation.

Martin Bryant, who earned money from an early age selling vegetables from door to door in Hobart, was 12 years old when he turned up at the Clare Point home of Helen Mary Elisabeth Harvey. She was a dotty, elderly woman, heiress to the Tattersalls fortune, who had opted to look after her invalid mother, and had fallen out with the rest of her family. She felt affection for the boy. Bryant did odd jobs for her in the garden, and became close, seeking refuge from the unhappiness of his home. In the late 1980s, the family blew apart. Maurice beat Martin, Martin's sister Lindy took refuge in Melbourne, and Maurice and Carleen separated.

In 1991, Miss Harvey bought a farm, at Taurusville, near Copping, 30 kilometres from Port Arthur, and both she and Martin moved there. According to neighbours, they spent two happy but 'weird' years there, directionless, gardening and living in close company with animals. Maurice Bryant visited the farm and became a friend of Miss Harvey as well, on one occasion taking her to a country dance. Carleen came to stay there, living there for 12 months, though privately expressing hatred of Miss Harvey. There was a hint of menace in Martin Bryant's behaviour from time to time. A neighbour, Sue Featherstone, said later that on two occasions she visited the farm and Bryant had threatened to kill her.

Miss Harvey came to have more and more affection for Martin, who sometimes pushed her wheelchair as she went shopping. In early 1992, she made out her will, leaving everything to him, and naming Maurice Bryant as executor. Martin's private attitude to Miss Harvey did not match his show of benevolence. He said on occasions that he might kill her to get her money. What he stood to gain was the house in New Town, in 1993 valued at $180,000. He also stood to gain the farm, valued at $130,000, holdings in small commercial properties in Hobart, furniture valued at $103,000, and three cars valued at just over $17,000.

Bryant was starting to behave oddly. He was becoming more interested in firearms. Neighbours heard him firing at night. He also developed a practice of grabbing the steering wheel while Miss Harvey was driving. In 1992, he forced her car into a ditch. She complained about it to Barry Featherstone, brother-in-law of Sue, who helped get the car out of the ditch. She would drive slowly, but not slowly enough it appeared, because on 20 October, 1992, her car veered into the path of an oncoming vehicle, at about the same spot she had gone into the ditch two weeks before. She was killed.

Martin sustained severe neck injuries. There was later suspicion that Bryant had deliberately killed her, but that was never proven. An action was taken in the Supreme Court of Tasmania to ensure strict supervisory trustee arrangements over the inheritance, because of Bryant's 'unsound mind'.

While Martin Bryant was recovering from his injuries, his father moved onto the farm and appeared interested in buying it. Money found on the farm later might have been from the sale of the family's holiday cottage, to go towards purchase of the farm. Martin apparently resented his father moving in. And Maurice Bryant was not to be around for much longer. He died in a manner which again aroused suspicion. On 16 August 1993, police divers recovered his body from a farm dam. He had diving weights strapped around his chest.

Barry Featherstone told police that Maurice Bryant had been shot twice. The police, unable to find wounds but finding that a great number of Serapax sleeping tablets had recently been consumed, formed the view that it had been suicide, and coroner Edward Vickers agreed. Martin was left the proceeds of some of his father's insurance policies. Neighbours were later to say that Bryant had said of his father that he would 'do him in'. Bryant also, apparently, visited a former schoolteacher to blame her for his failure to get ahead in life. While there, he reportedly said: 'Anyway, my father's in the dam.' But it went no further and the suicide verdict remained.

Bryant was now wealthy, but he did not have the intelligence or inclination to make constructive use of the money. His behaviour was odd and erratic. In 1993, a bus driver told him he could find another means of transport after receiving complaints that Bryant had been lifting girls' dresses. In 1994, Bryant sold the farm for about $130,000. About 1995, he changed his appearance to look like a 'surfie' with long hair. He once placed $2000 on a young woman's desk and asked her to go to lunch. He put $10,000 onto a travel agent's desk and said: 'Send me somewhere.' He twice took out Yvonne Briggs, who was old enough to be his mother. They danced and visited a casino, and he kissed her on the cheek.

Nobody to this day knows why, on Sunday, 28 April 1996, he decided to commit a mass killing. Despite the wealth he had acquired, he had not been particularly favoured by life. His family had been unhappy. As with Wade Frankum, there had been a violent death in his family. But millions of people have had such experiences. Not as articulate as Julian Knight or Frank Vitkovic, he did not commit his thoughts to writing, before the massacre or afterwards. On the Sunday morning, Bryant rose from his bed in New Town, dressed, took his rifles – for which he had no licence – got into his battered yellow Volvo, with surfboard on top, and drove to Port Arthur, stopping at a Shell service station on the way to have a cup of coffee. He went to the Seascape guest house, murdered the Martin couple, and then drove on towards the crowded Broad Arrow Cafe.

Shortly after 1 pm, Bryant arrived at the cafe, where about 60 people had gathered, and wrestled with the bulky cricket bag, containing his rifles as a diner held the door open for him. Ordering hot food, Bryant sat down, had a meal, and stayed. At 2.15 pm, he stood up, saying, 'There are a lot of WASPS [White Anglo-Saxon Protestants] about today, not too many Japs', before pulling a rifle from his bag...

When he opened fire, the diners, crammed into a confined space, had little chance of escaping. Bryant fired at 40 of them, aiming at heads and necks, killing 20 and wounding 12 others. The people who fell that day were the same normal, happy people found at other, similar massacres: unsuspecting, unprepared, reacting in various ways – in panic, in fear, courageously – but powerless. Kate Elizabeth Scott, 21, who had celebrated a friend's wedding in Hobart and was due to fly off to take up a job at a goldmine in Western Australia, was the first to die. Her boyfriend, Mick Sargent, was creased on the forehead by a bullet. Tony Kisten, a panel beater from Summer Hill in Sydney, a deeply religious man, tried to reason with Bryant, but was shot and died in the arms of his wife. Jason Winter, a New Zealander, hurled himself across his wife and child to protect them and paid with his life. Sue Ling Chong and William Ng Mokyah, on a business trip from Kuala

Lumpur, Anthony Nightingale, a man eating alone who tried to get to the souvenir shop next door, and a Victorian couple, Mervyn and Mary Hughes, trying to flee to the kitchen, were all cut down. So were friends Andrew Mills and David Capper. A local man, Peter Crosswell, threw himself on top of two women and lay there, playing dead, not moving even though shot in the buttocks, and saved both himself and them.

Gwenda Neander, 67, holidaying with her husband Ronald Neander, 65, who had retired after years of service to the funeral industry, was cut down in the souvenir shop. Jim Pollard, 72, a retired university administrator who had completed a law degree and dreamed of setting up a legal advisory service for the elderly, was standing in the car park with friends Robert and Helene Salzmann when Bryant mowed them down.

Nanette Mikac had gone to Port Arthur, where she had a job, to have a picnic on her day off with children Allanah, six, and Madeline, three, while her husband played golf. Realising something serious was happening she made a dash for safety, carrying Madeline, with Allanah running beside her. Bryant pulled up nearby. It is said that Nanette, thinking he was someone who could take them to safety, turned towards him. Then she saw the gun, turned and started running away. Bryant opened fire, the one bullet travelling through her body and into Madeline. Allanah made it to a tree and took cover, but he followed her there and dispatched her at point-blank range.

Further on, Bryant killed three occupants of a BMW, pitched the bodies onto the road and took their car. At a Kwik'n'Thrifty convenience store, he encountered Sydney lawyers, Zoe Hall and Glen Pears, on a day trip to Port Arthur. He shot Zoe and forced Pears into the boot of his car. Driving off, he shot at the Fox'n'Hounds Hotel and at two occupants of a four-wheel drive vehicle, whom he wounded. At 2.30 pm, Bryant took Pears into the Seascape guest house, set fire to the BMW and kept police at bay by threatening to kill him.

Night came and the standoff continued. An ABC reporter, Alison Smith, rang from Hobart seeking information from, she thought, the proprietors on what was happening. Bryant (almost certainly) answered, saying: 'I am having a lot of fun and right now I need to take a shower and if you try to call me again I am going to shoot the hostage.' Bryant negotiated with police by telephone, demanding a helicopter. The negotiations broke off, and he resumed firing. At 8 am the following day, smoke was seen coming from the guest house and at 8.40 am Bryant emerged, his clothes on fire. Pears was found dead.

Bryant was arrested, taken to hospital, and on 5 July 1996, charged with 35 counts of murder and charges of harm, including murder, against 70 people. After entreaties from his mother, he pleaded guilty to murder and on 22 November 1996, Tasmanian Chief Justice William Cox, saying Bryant would spend the rest of his life in gaol, sentenced him to 35 life terms for murder and 37 terms, each of 21 years, for related offences.

Prime Minister John Howard called the States together to bring in some really firm legislation. He got a favourable response, though Tasmania made some more muted regulations to restrict sale and possession of firearms. Bryant disappeared into the Tasmanian prison system. There were intermittent reports of him attempting suicide. He was a mass murderer living in suspended animation, spending the rest of his life paying for a single day, when he could have locked up his weapons, gone for a long walk and reflected. With Frankum and Vitkovic, there had been some hope; both had been struggling with their descent into madness and had tried to get help. Knight appeared to have a psychopathic detachment and delusions of grandeur. With Bryant, there was nothing – a dull, twisted brain and, as the judge said in sentencing, little hope he would ever be different.

There have always been people like them, but before the advent of high-powered rifles, the assaults on individuals or society in general would have been with knives, swords, or whatever, with fewer victims and with potential victims having a better chance of fighting back or getting away. The modern firearm had, like machineguns, bombs and shells in warfare, escalated the potential destructiveness of madness and its associated mental conditions.

DISAPPEARING WOMEN

When sorrows come,
they come not in single spies, but in battalions.

William Shakespeare
Hamlet

It was an idyllic part of Australia, the far-south coast of New South Wales, unreachable by rail, a holiday spot, a place where alternative lifestylers liked to go to build mud-brick houses in the hills, and where others braced themselves each year for the retirees – or victims – of the annual Sydney–Hobart Ocean Yacht Race. It was a place veterinarian turned worm-farmer Graeme Collins had found inviting when he moved there with his wife, Delma, and family from Goulburn in 1993. They settled at Kalaru, a settlement of about 800 people halfway between Bega and Tathra. In the same year, Garrett Barry accepted a job as planner with Bega Valley Council and moved with his family from Orange. The Collins and the Barrys became friends.

On Friday 4 October 1997, the start of a long weekend, Lauren Barry, 14, and Nichole Collins, 16, joined a group of friends at a camp outside Kalaru. The two were vigorous, outdoor girls. Nichole, with her own horse, and working part-time at a Bega supermarket, had hopes of becoming an interior decorator or a chiropractor. Lauren, a gifted athlete, wanted to work with small animals or children. The camp had been organised because Lauren was to have celebrated her 15th birthday the following Friday, but was going off to Sydney for a week with her brother, Nathan.

Teenage friends were there. Nichole's parents helped pitch the tents. On the Saturday, Lauren went to her mother's place to give her a birthday card and dine with the family before returning to the camp. Nichole's parents visited the site. That evening, Nichole had two glasses of bourbon and Coke. At 9.30 pm, she and Lauren decided they would visit Nichole's former boyfriend, David Irving, 21, who lived at Jellat Jellat, seven kilometres away. They decided to walk, and left in the clothes they wore with a torch and a nearly empty bottle of drink, probably containing bourbon. Motorists saw them on the Snowy Mountains Highway. Then they disappeared.

Nothing was heard from them on the Sunday. On the Monday, 7 October, Nathan turned up to take her to Sydney. She was not there. Nor was Lauren. On the Monday afternoon, a local resident found a blue flannelette shirt at Old Walagoot Road, Bega, near the local tip. It was Lauren's, and it was later found to have been semen-stained. With no trace of the girls anywhere, the alarm was raised. There was no earthly reason why the girls should have taken off without telling.

On the Thursday, a police task force, code-named Daloa, was formed. The desperate, frantic Collins parents, living a parent's ultimate nightmare, visited a clairvoyant. Garrett Barry insisted on doing his day's work, but afterwards went out, through the bush, across mountainsides, anywhere and everywhere, searching and searching and fighting the fear and the despair. The next day, up to 300 people were out searching, going through bushland, waterways, beaches. They included police, State Emergency Service volunteers, rescue organisations, family members, police helicopters and police dogs. They found nothing.

Days grew into weeks. Three weeks after the disappearance, information came to police that a cream and yellow sedan had been sighted at Tathra at the time of the girls' disappearance, that screaming had been heard coming from it, and that the car had been seen heading for Tathra Beach. But nothing came of this.

As Nichole's 17th birthday arrived on Tuesday 14 November, fear gripped the communities.

In fact, the worst had happened. Both girls were dead. Their bodies lay, undiscovered, in bushland on the other side of the border, in rugged East Gippsland mountain country in the Cann River district. They had been abducted, repeatedly raped, and murdered, by two men who had long before come to the notice of the police but, through the vagaries of the justice system, had been allowed their freedom.

All this was to come out. The bodies were to be discovered, the girls tearfully buried, the perpetrators gaoled. And the saga of the disappearing women, a problem that had plagued Australia from the time of colonisation – leaving thousands of women dead, in laneways, rooms, bushland, waterways, on riverbanks, anywhere – continued. The brutality of man to woman, the sexual urge that has taken Mankind from the naked loneliness of Adam and Eve, and the life-creating force, so often transforming into the very negation of itself, just go on.

Alfred Leslie (Les) Camilleri, born in Liverpool, New South Wales, in May 1969, was a small-time burglar and car thief whose criminal record stretched back to Sydney's Minda Children's Court, where at the age of 12 he was charged with breaking, entering and stealing. His record in New South Wales, Queensland and the Australian Capital Territory included convictions for theft, carrying a weapon, possession of goods suspected of having been stolen, absconding from bail and illegal use of a motor vehicle. In Queensland in 1989, the charges he faced included 215 counts of unlawful use of a car and 92 of stealing.

Lindsay Hoani Beckett, born in New Zealand 1974, never knew his natural father. According to other members of his family, Beckett's early years were troubled, the troubles compounded by an extremely difficult family environment. Beckett himself began drinking at the age of 13, started smoking cannabis at the age of 14, left school at 15, and at the age of 16 made his way to Australia, where he drifted through New South Wales, picking up convictions for petty theft. In 1992, he moved in with a pregnant teenager, Lauralee Tatt, in Griffith in the Riverina. In the next three years, Beckett and she had three more children. But it was a violent relationship.

On 4 October 1995, Camilleri was in New South Wales charged with ten sexual offences, including six of having sexual intercourse with a girl under the age of 16, and one of indecent assault. The alleged victim was 11 years old. The same year, Beckett, having left Ms Tatt, made his way to Yass, where he met up with Camilleri. In 1997, Camilleri and Beckett developed a taste for amphetamines, coming again to the attention of the law. Beckett was convicted of drink-driving and had his licence suspended. In May, he was fined $100 for offensive conduct and then charged over possession of material, suspected of being drugs, found in his car. In June, he was sentenced to eight days' gaol for failing to appear when summonsed and committed to trial on two charges of sexual assault. Given bail, he took to the roads while unlicensed, for which he was charged.

Not to be outdone by Beckett, Camilleri was charged with being in possession of a stolen Harley-Davidson. On 25 August 1997, magistrate May Jerram convicted him of receiving a stolen axe, electrical equipment and electrical cord and sentenced him to four months' periodic detention. Camilleri gained consent for his detention to be switched from weekends to midweek so that he could play weekend cricket. In fact, he was not playing weekend cricket. And he often did not turn up to midweek detention. Even though he appeared in court eight times on various charges, his breach of the periodic detention order was not mentioned.

On 8 September 1997, Camilleri went on trial before Judge Fred Kirkham in the Queanbeyan District Court. A child gave evidence that over a period of 12 months he had molested her and had penetrated her a number of times. On the second day of the trial, the New South Wales Police Minister, Paul Whelan, launching Operation Paradox, an annual New South Wales Police campaign against child abuse, said that child molesters on average interfered with 37 children before they were caught. Camilleri's defence picked that up and argued that the trial should be aborted.

Kirkham, initially rejecting the submission, eventually agreed that the remarks, if picked up by one or more jurors, could have a prejudicial effect. In fact, he said the remarks were 'extraordinarily prejudicial', and aborted the trial. Camilleri went free on bail.

Much has been said about Kirkham's decision. But in the ordinary course of events, judges have always been watchful for prejudicial events. A decision to allow the trial to proceed in the light of what Whelan had said would have been heavily criticised. Had Camilleri appeared at a later time for retrial, there would have been no adverse comment about Kirkham's decision. Trouble was, Kirkham was applying the laws of a civilised society to an animal.

Camilleri reunited with Beckett and they drove to Canberra together, where on 13 September, at Garema Place, a junkie hangout, Beckett approached a young woman, asking her to help him and his mate inject amphetamines. She agreed, but Camilleri and Beckett then seized her and drove her out of town, to rape her repeatedly at knifepoint over several hours, taking turns to shoot up on amphetamines. The two discussed how they were going to kill her, and in the early morning hours, pulled into a rest stop outside Bowral in the Southern Highlands of New South Wales. The girl dashed for freedom, fled through the bush and escaped. Camilleri and Beckett decided to claim the intercourse had been consensual; the girl did not want to press charges.

On 4 October, the two decided to make their way to Bega to visit Camilleri's de facto wife. They were driving down the Snowy Mountains Highway when they saw Lauren and Michelle. They stopped. On their later account, they chatted for a while before asking whether the girls wanted to go to the beach. In all probability, they just grabbed them. In the car, Camilleri pulled his knife and Beckett drove to Old Wallagoot Road. Beckett raped Lauren, who lost her blue flannelette shirt, and Camilleri raped Nichole. Over the next nine hours, the pair drove 190 kilometres with the girls, from Merimbula to Genoa, taking turns to have intercourse with the girls wherever it took their fancy – beside the road, in the bush, in Ben Boyd National Park, in the back seat – and later got around to discussing how they were going to kill them.

Ten kilometres across the Victorian border, in East Gippsland, and 150 kilometres from where they had picked the girls up, Camilleri instructed Beckett to find an isolated spot. They turned up a dirt road into the rainforest, got out of the vehicle and led the girls 250 metres down to Fiddlers Green Creek. They tied them up. According to Beckett's later account to the police, the girls asked whether they were going to be killed. Camilleri told them they would not be, that they would just be left there. He told Beckett to tie Nichole to a tree. Nichole was gagged with a piece of denim torn from Lauren's trousers. Then he told Beckett to kill them while he waited in the car. Beckett, in his later court evidence, said he objected, on the grounds that Camilleri had told him to do both killings and would not do one himself.

At about 6 am on the Sunday morning, Beckett took Lauren to the creek and held her head under water. He thought he had drowned her, but to make sure of it, cut her throat. Then he went to Nichole, slashed her throat and plunged the knife into her chest. 'I was trying to find her heart,' he said later. 'I was trying to kill her.' He untied her, threw her to the ground, and kicked her in the head three or four times before joining Camilleri in the car. The two went to Canberra, where they tossed the knife off Commonwealth Bridge into Lake Burley Griffin. They poured petrol on Beckett's bloodstained clothing and ropes at a Canberra lookout and burnt them. The next day, they spent several hours at a Canberra car wash cleaning the car thoroughly, inside and out. Then they went back to their normal activities.

Camilleri was arrested at Yass on 13 October and charged with having goods in custody suspected of having been stolen and possessing a housebreaking instrument, namely a sliding hammer. On 31 October, he had his bail revoked in the Yass Local Court, and was sent to the maximum security Goulburn Gaol. He appealed against the decision and was sent to the Silverwater Remand Centre in Sydney. Beckett ended up in gaol in the Belconnen Remand Centre in the Australian Capital Territory. Both were questioned about the disappearances of Lauren and Nichole. Camilleri admitted nothing, but Beckett cracked and confessed to the two murders, implicating Camilleri. He appeared briefly in the Australian Capital Territory's Magistrate's Court, where his extradition to Victoria was granted. On 12 November, he took police to where the bodies lay, 15 metres apart at a bend in the creek. He indicated where the knife had been discarded and on 13 November police divers recovered the knife. Beckett appeared in the Melbourne Magistrate's Court on 17 November 1997, charged with the two murders. An extradition order was obtained for Camilleri.

On 19 November, more than 4000 people, almost the entire population of Bega, turned up for a memorial service for the two girls in the town's central park. Bega Valley's then mayor, Tim Collins, said: 'Our safe haven has been violated in the worst possible way.' Graeme Collins said that if the loss of the girls was to have any lasting impact, it was to underline 'a right, and indeed an obligation, to demand that our children are kept safe from hideous criminals'.

Camilleri, formally freed on bail in New South Wales on 26 November, was rearrested even before he left the courthouse dock. In Beckett's pre-sentence hearing in Melbourne, his counsel, Patrick Tehan QC, said that though the horror of Beckett's actions could not be denied, Beckett had been under the influence of both amphetamines and the personality of Camilleri and recognition had to be given to the fact that Beckett had cooperated with police and Crown law authorities. Justice Frank Vincent said: 'I don't think I have ever heard a more terrible or moving description concerning the death of a person... The lives of Lauren Barry and Nichole Collins clearly possessed no significance to you... You represent the dark in which our women and children fearfully walk.' Vincent sentenced Beckett, then aged 24, to imprisonment for life, with a non-parole period of 35 years.

Camilleri pleaded not guilty. But police had Beckett's cooperation and also scientific evidence linking his semen to Lauren's shirt. Beckett said that Camilleri had threatened to kill him if he did not carry out his orders to kill the girls. A 19-year-old woman gave evidence that Camilleri and Beckett had picked her up in Victoria and raped her at knifepoint. They had driven along a highway near the Melbourne suburb of Campbellfield and then driven to an area where they said they had 'finished off' a stripper. She had bolted and escaped. Camilleri's counsel, Stratton Langslow, submitted that in regard to the murders of Lauren and Nichole, his client was 'less culpable' than Beckett, and that he should be treated as though he had 'acquiesced in a common purpose'. Vincent said Camilleri was a weak man who wanted to do the nasty things but relied on Beckett's greater resolve. He was satisfied that Camilleri had given the orders for the girls to be killed. On 27 April 1999, he sentenced Camilleri to life imprisonment and declined to specify a non-parole period.

Nobody was shedding tears for Camilleri and Beckett. But sadly, they were only the latest two in a saga of brutality that has stretched down the centuries, taking in Jack the Ripper (killer of five women in East London, 1890s), Peter Sutcliffe aka the Yorkshire Ripper (killer of 13), Ted Bundy of the United States (up to 36 victims), and Eric Cooke in Perth, who killed at least five women and a man. The men who have perpetrated these horrors have been predators, purely and simply, monsters on the rampage. The technique has been to get the victim – a young woman, a child perhaps – at a disadvantage. People could be attacked in their own bedrooms, in shopping centres, at bus stops… John Wayne Glover, the 'Granny Killer', found his victims on suburban streets and, in one case, a retirement home.

Lists of victims often include their photographs. In most cases the individual staring out from the picture is young, vivacious, attractive, still at the threshold of life. When the murderers are caught, tales of depravity often emerge. So many are individuals whose antisocial attitudes and perverse habits have festered away for years, perhaps coming to police notice, perhaps not, often fuelling a time-bomb. When the restraints of civilised society snap, there seems no limit to what some individuals can do. This writer was in England in 1979 when a man was caught for having murdered a young girl. He had murdered her, taken photographs of her naked, dead body, buried her, then, unable to resist his cravings, dug the body up and photographed it again. Let us look at a similar, local case.

Kevin Gary Crump and Allan Baker had wretched histories by the time, in 1972, they met in gaol. Crump had been convicted of a vicious sexual assault on a fellow prisoner and Baker had, in 1969, been sentenced to more than five years' gaol for shooting with intent to cause grievous bodily harm, shooting with intent to avoid lawful apprehension, carrying an unlicensed pistol, breaking, entering and stealing, and escaping from lawful custody.

Released in 1972, Baker went bush and found work at Banarway Station, 25 kilometres north of Collarenebri in western New South Wales. He was there three weeks, got on well enough with the grazier, Brian Morse, and got to know his attractive wife, mother of three, Virginia Gai Morse. He left when work ran out, and according to Brian Morse later, there was no ill feeling. A year later, teaming up with Crump, who had been released, Baker decided on crime. The two set up a base camp 80 kilometres north of Goondiwindi, which is on the Queensland–New South Wales border, and decided to make predatory raids on New South Wales, in the belief that the border, the limit of New South Wales Police jurisdiction, would be a barrier to pursuit.

In early November 1973, they made such a raid, chancing upon a cotton picker, Ian James Lamb, asleep in his car north of Narrabri. Baker shot Lamb dead and together with Crump, looted his car and body and siphoned his petrol. On the morning of 7 November they arrived outside the Banarway homestead, watched from early morning until Brian Morse drove off, then confronted Virginia Morse with a rifle. She recognised Baker and said: 'Oh Allan, you scared me!' But it was not a joke. The two bound and gagged her, drove a short distance to their own car with her, transferred her into that, and then drove 190 km to their camp.

Crump and Baker had Virginia totally at their mercy. According to Crump's later statement, she was crying, saying: 'I love my children. Please let me go home.' She also said: 'What time is it? Brian will start to get worried about me.' Crump told her to shut up. They staked Virginia to the ground, raped her, tied her to a tree, and decided to kill her. Baker demanded that Crump kill her so they would be in it together, with a murder apiece. Crump said in his statement: 'She was not crying because I think she was beyond that.' He shot her. The two performed unspeakable acts on her body, burned her clothing, then rolled the body naked into the Weir River and weighed it down.

At Banarway, the abandoned car was discovered and the alarm raised. There was a widespread search involving 120 people with RAAF helicopter assistance. Fears were raised because a young woman had been raped and stabbed on the Gold Coast the previous Monday, near the scene of the murders of Gabrielle Ingrid Jahnke, 19, and Michelle Anne Riley, 16.

Gabrielle and Michelle had been hitchhiking together on 6 October that year. They were believed to have started hitchhiking near Brisbane's Victoria Bridge and to have made their way towards the Gold Coast. On 13 October, Gabrielle's body, with a fractured skull, had been found beside the Pacific Highway south of Brisbane. On 23 October, the decomposed remains of Michelle had been found near Logan, 48 kilometres south of Brisbane. Had the murderer or murderers come south-west? Lamb's body had been found, but police were not linking it to what appeared to be a series of sex-murders.

Fear spread, landholders panicked. As one New South Wales Department of Agriculture officer, Brian Mansfield, told this writer, driving around and arriving unannounced to a property was dangerous. The visitor was likely to be met by the property owner holding a rifle.

Crump and Baker decided on another raid, to loot a house at Cessnock which one of them knew about. They did the break and enter, but on 13 November, driving away, they were spotted by police, who wanted to check them out. Crump and Baker sped off, firing at the police and hitting one of them, John Millward, in the head. A radio alarm went out and police came from everywhere. Crump and Baker abandoned their bogged vehicle at Woodville in the Hunter Valley, fired again at police, and were caught – by now themselves shaking with terror – on the Paterson River bank.

There always is, in these deadly duos, a leader and a follower, though the latter is often hardly less brutal. Crump was the one to crack – he told police what had happened. On his information, police found Virginia's body. Crump and Baker were tried for murder. Crump said from the dock that Baker had forced him to shoot Virginia. Baker said the decision to kill her had only been made late in the piece. Both were convicted and, on 20 June, 1974, sentenced to life imprisonment. Justice Taylor said: 'I believe that you should spend the rest of your lives in gaol and there you should die.' In the years since, Crump has applied several times for parole but has been rejected amid public uproar at the very suggestion of it. Mothers of both said publicly that they had wiped them.

Virginia Morse had made no mistake, done nothing dangerous, except being in an unlocked house in the isolation of the countryside, living with the normal assumption that Australia is a civilised place. Lauren Barry and Nichole Collins had been selected at random. They had just been in the wrong place at the wrong time – surfers taking a dip in a mild piece of ocean where a Great White happened to be cruising.

So it was as well for two nursing trainees, Lorraine Ruth Wilson, then aged 20, and Wendy Joy Evans, 18, from Sydney's St George Hospital. They had begun nursing in 1973, and on 21 September, 1974, embarked on a six-week holiday, which took them, on 29 September, to Goondoowndi on the Queensland–New South Wales border. Their borrowed Volkswagen broke down. The girls hitchhiked to Brisbane and, on 3 October, hitchhiked back to Goondiwindi to pick up their car. Someone undoubtedly gave them a lift. Twenty-one months later, on 25 July 1976, a bushwalker found the girls' skeletons on a cattle property at Murphy's Creek, near Toowoomba. The two had apparently been bound with cord and raped. They had been bludgeoned to death, probably by two lumps of wood found near the scene.

Several girls disappeared around that time, including Gabrielle Jahnke and Michelle Riley. Another woman from the Gold Coast, Margaret Rosetta Rosewarne, 19, disappeared while she was hitch-hiking. Her body was found at West Burleigh on 21 May, 1976.

In July 1976, Katherine Pamela Graham, 18, was found raped and murdered near Townsville. They came in spates elsewhere too: in Newcastle, for example. On Sydney's north shore just after midnight on 25 June, 1978, an 18-year-old, Trudie Adams, disappeared after leaving a surf club at Newport. She is said to have caught a lift and to have got into a beige-coloured panel van. She was never seen again. There would not be a part of Australia without a history of disappearing women.

Police, confronted with the fact that up to 30,000 people are reported missing in Australia each year and that some 99.8 percent come back home within a week, have to be circumspect about how they commit their limited resources. They are simply not to know, in the initial stages of most disappearances, whether they have been confronted with a family spat, a misunderstanding, or a tragedy. But lurking behind every disappearance is a tragedy. Sometimes the bodies are found. Sometimes the murderers are caught and convicted. Sometimes not.

Two events rocked the public in New South Wales, one involving a Sydney Hospital nursing sister doing nothing more exceptional than returning home after work; the other concerning a 20-year-old bank clerk going to a railway car park in southern Sydney to collect her car.

The nursing sister was Anita Lorraine Cobby, 26, a prefect at Blacktown's Evans High School in 1977, the 1979 Miss Western Suburbs, and an entrant in the 1979 Miss Australia Quest. Married, but separated amicably and living at that time with her parents, she had been on duty on the Sunday 2 February 1986. After work, she visited a Lebanese restaurant in Redfern with two work colleagues, one of whom drove her to Redfern Station. She caught a train to Blacktown at 8.45 pm and, arriving there half an hour later, started the short 20-minute walk to the home of her parents, Mr and Mrs Garry Lynch, in Sullivan Road.

She did not make it. Instead, in Newton Road she was spotted by John Raymond Travers, a 19-year-old youth with tattoos on his penis. He was in a car with four other men. Having contributed nothing to society so far, this pack of young men was about to tread into the mud this beautiful flower, the pride of Sydney's outer west, the beauty queen from a region so often put down as a cultural desert. They were about to commit a series of acts which would end her life, shatter her family and earn each of them incarceration, probably for the rest of their lives.

Travers was a violent criminal wanted for questioning about sexual assaults in Blacktown and Seven Hills and, apparently, in Western Australia for homosexual assault. He was the product of a wretched background. His father was a drinker and had deserted the family. The mother, a woman unable to handle the demands put on her, had struggled to bring up seven children. Travers, by his late teens had become known for excessive cruelty to animals. He was known to have slaughtered lambs as a party trick, had already built up a criminal record, including convictions for possession of marijuana, illegal use of a motor vehicle, car stealing, possessing housebreaking implements, receiving stolen goods and possessing a shortened firearm. With a dominating personality, he was able to tell the four with him – all with criminal records – what they should and should not do.

Michael Patrick Murphy, 34, the oldest, and, like the two brothers who were with him that night, the product of a tough upbringing, had convictions for stealing a motor vehicle, breaking, entering and stealing, offensive behaviour and escaping from lawful custody. He had escaped from Silverwater Correctional Centre where he was serving 24 years for armed robbery. Gary Stephen Murphy, 29, had a record of theft convictions and not long before the murder had been in Parramatta Gaol for non-payment of fines. Leslie Joseph Murphy, 23, had convictions for sexual intercourse without consent, stealing, illegal use of a motor vehicle, and break-ing, entering and stealing.

The fifth member of the group, Michael James Murdoch, 19, had convictions for smoking and possession of marijuana, malicious injury to a motor vehicle and being an accessory after the fact to breaking, entering and stealing. He, Travers and probably Michael Murphy had stolen an HG Holden sedan in Seven Hills on 28 January and Gary Murphy had repainted it from its original green to an undercoat grey. The group had gone out in that car that evening and were up to no good. For hours, they had been drinking and smoking marijuana. Any control any of them had wanted to place on themselves was gone. Taking a trip to Windsor where Travers was going to drop in on a friend, some of the group believed they were going to steal a tractor, or a car and trailer for the purposes of stealing the tractor.

As the group drove back through Blacktown, they were running low on petrol and saw Anita Cobby. Murdoch, according to Leslie Murphy, said: 'Pull over and I will grab her handbag.' Travers, according to Gary Murphy, had 'seen that Anita walking down the street... John just saw her and wanted her.' Michael Murphy, who was driving, wheeled the car round, Travers grabbed her arms and Michael Murdoch her legs. They dragged her into the car and started hitting her in the face to quieten her. Weighing only 52 kilograms, she did not have the strength to assert herself, certainly not against five men. Her screaming as they dragged her into the car attracted the attention of a resident, Linda McGaughey, who saw the abduction and was able to describe the 'dirty white' colour of the vehicle. Her brother John saw the car driving off without lights. Two other neighbours, Dale Stephen Dunn and Stephen Hodgeson, heard the screams and went out searching.

In the car, Travers produced a knife. Michael Murdoch said later: 'John and Mick Murdoch started ripping her clothes off as soon as she got into the car and both raped her.' They did pull into a service station at Prospect, and Travers threatened Anita with a knife to stop her crying out. They used $20 of her money to get petrol, then drove to an isolated spot, Sheen Road, Prospect, where she was taken from the car and pushed through a barbed wire fence. Michael Murphy said later: 'I think she was unconscious because she had been punched round a bit. We threw her over the barbed wire fence. I had a hold of one of her arms – she sort of walked down in the middle of the paddock, she was staggering.'

The group stopped at a point 70 metres from the road. Les Murphy said: 'All of us were just staying things like, "We are going to f*** the pants off you". I said it myself and others said similar things.' They raped her and subjected her to gross indignity, experimenting, they said, with different types of intercourse. Gary Murphy, on his later account to police, said he had oral sex with Anita while Michael Murphy was having vaginal sex with her.

Paul McGaughey came home just after 10 pm, heard what had happened, and went off driving looking for the vehicle described to him. He actually found it, parked and empty, in Preen Road, but it was not quite the vehicle he was looking for and he drove on. In the paddock, the rapists – Travers, Murdoch, and the Murphy brothers – heard a car and decided it was time they left. Murdoch and the brothers Murphy, when questioned by police, said they just walked away and that Travers had gone back. Michael Murdoch said that Travers joined them in the car and said: 'I am going to cut her throat. She has recognised the whole lot of us.' Travers said there had been a consensual agreement that he should be the one to kill her. He cut her throat.

At his home at Tich Place, Doonside, he showered the blood off and the others burnt her clothing in his backyard. All except her shoes, that was. Gary Murphy wanted them.

Anita's parents were initially not disturbed about Anita's failure to return home. She had occasionally stayed overnight with friends in the city. But when the hospital rang the next afternoon to ask why she had not turned up for work, the alarm was raised. On the Tuesday, John Cobby, a fellow nurse Anita had married and from whom she had been separated since Christmas, thought she had gone to Wollongong to visit friends and started driving there. That day, a cattle farmer investigating something in his paddock which was obviously disturbing his animals, found the body. News of the discovery of a woman's body at Prospect went over the airwaves and John Cobby heard it on the way to Wollongong. He rang his parents-in-law and a detective answered the phone.

A force of 25 police was put together. Information came to the police on a number of people, many of whom were charged with unrelated offences such as drugs, sexual assaults, theft and housebreaking. John Travers was in fact nominated as someone known to carry a knife and who was capable of committing such a crime. But there was then no other information on him. On Thursday 6 February, the then Premier Neville Wran offered a reward of $50,000 for information leading to the conviction of the killer or killers. The following day, Travers poured petrol on the stolen car and burnt it.

The breakthrough came when an informant told police that Travers and Murdoch had been involved in the theft of a car days before the murder and that the car had been painted grey. Police were also told that special mag wheels that were on the stolen car had been taken off and put onto Les Murphy's car. As well, a woman who had been a girlfriend of Travers offered to assist police by having herself wired up and getting incriminating statements from Travers. She did get the story of what had happened. The help shortened the police inquiry to just 22 days. The five culprits were arrested and, amid scenes of high hysteria, presented before court. Travers pleaded guilty but the other four did not. Their trial began on 16 March 1997. There was a hiccup when a media report led to the aborting of the trial but it started again on 23 March. The four were found guilty. On 6 June 1997, Justice Alan Maxwell in the New South Wales Central Criminal Court sentenced all five to life imprisonment.

They disappeared into the bowels of the New South Wales prison system. This writer spotted Travers in a court case in July 1997, when, aged 32 and filled out considerably from the scarecrow figure who featured in the news photographs during the case, he was acquitted on a charge of attempting to cut his way out of a prison van en route from Goulburn Gaol. Then he went back into the living hell of long-term, perhaps permanent, incarceration.

The abduction and murder of Janine Balding, a bank clerk, followed a similar pattern. That occurred on 8 September 1990, when she went to the Sutherland Station car park after work to collect her Holden Gemini. Waiting for her was a gang of teenagers, led by a stunted, dwarf-like young man by the name of Stephen 'Shorty' Jamieson, 22. With him were boys aged 14 and 16, and a mildly retarded 17-year-old girl who had been living on the streets for years. She had in tow her 15-year-old boyfriend.

Patricia Dawson, a self-appointed confidante of Sydney street kids, told this writer that Jamieson had a hangup about his physical size. 'Everyone knows that if you have a rotten time early in your life and you are a runt, the odds are stacked against you... he's very vicious... he got the young ones into this,' she said. 'One night they were up at The Wall [a male prostitution spot in Darlinghurst], bumming money off people. Jamieson saw a wino and decided to smash a bottle and slash his face. Vickie who was with him tried to stop him, but she got slashed too.'

The group had initially been out spraying graffiti. They had taken a train from Central Station to Sutherland. They had a knife. And on this occasion, their aspirations went a little further than vandalism. They tried once, unsuccessfully, to abduct a 19-year-old, Kristine Mobberley. Then they surrounded Janine, and although the confrontation was spotted by someone who took the trouble to alert police, they got her, and her Gemini, and sexually assaulted her in the car as they drove west. Pulling to the side of the F4 Freeway at Minchinbury, three of the gang took her, tied, 100 metres into a paddock and drowned her in shallow water in a dam. Arrow and her boyfriend stayed back to neck in the backseat of their car. The gang later used Janine's credit card to get $300 from her account.

Some of the group talked, and word quickly got back to police. Police made arrests on 18 September, 1990; Jamieson and the two who were with him were gaoled for life, their papers marked 'never to be released'. Justice Newman, sentencing them, said the murder had been 'surely one of the most barbaric murders committed in the sad history of this state'. The mildly-retarded girl eventually got a minor sentence for credit card fraud and theft and her 15-year-old boyfriend a maximum sentence of nine years and four months after pleading guilty to abduction, four counts of unlawful sexual intercourse, robbery, receiving stolen goods and receiving money by deception.

Anita Cobby and Janine Balding were just in wrong place at the wrong time. Revelle Balmain, who disappeared in November 1994, at the age of 22, had gone into a profession – prostitution – which carried inherent risk. That did not mean she deserved what happened to her; it just meant that such an event was a little more likely. Revelle was not up-front and blatant about what she did. In the early reports of her disappearance, she was described as 'a fashion model and dancer'. She was the daughter of a ballet teacher, Jan Balmain, from Soldier's Point on the New South Wales Central Coast, and she had indeed travelled overseas and performed at cabaret shows at large Japanese hotels. On Monday 7 November, Revelle was due to go on another dancing tour for six weeks in Japan. Only later did the darker side of the life of this attractive young woman become more apparent.

On Friday 4 November, Revelle met her best friend, Kate Brentnall, who said later that she appeared 'happier than she has ever been... really happy about getting out of the industry, going to Japan. She had died her hair from platinum blonde to a softer, more natural blonde, more like her own colour. I thought it was symbolic. I remember thinking she had never looked so beautiful.' It may well have been, as was later suggested, that Revelle intended that weekend, or indeed the Saturday, to be her last day working in the escort industry. Jan Balmain had been looking forward to a special lunch with Revelle on the Sunday. She travelled to Newcastle to meet Revelle as she got off the train that morning. When Revelle did not turn up as scheduled, and was not on the following one, Jan Balmain rang Revelle's friends and Sydney hospitals. But there was no trace of Revelle.

When the alarm was raised, detectives found her passport and an airline ticket to Japan in a packed bag on the floor of her bedroom. The only clues were her platform shoes, found in a rubbish bin, and a set of her keys found in Kingsford Street, with her diary and the plastic holder for her pager lying in the gutter. As days grew into weeks, and the weeks months, it became clear that Revelle had met with foul play. Jan grieved, as any mother would. She said she saw her daughter in her dreams. 'She floats past me and I cry out, "Where are you, Revelle?"' As revealed in an inquest before the New South Wales Deputy State Coroner, John Abernethy, she had been working as a prostitute. Police discovered that quickly enough, broke the fact first to her father, Ivan Balmain and, when they considered the time was right, to Jan, who eventually said, in an undoubtedly heartfelt statement: 'She lost her way for a little while. A lot of people do. Most of them escape it, but Revelle was unlucky.'

Revelle had been working for the escort agencies VIP Hostesses and, following that, Select Companions. Select Companions was owned by husband and wife team Zoran and Jane Stanojovic, who used a pager system to tell her where her services were wanted. Revelle normally worked during daylight hours, taking taxis to and from appointments. Because of her attractiveness, she enjoyed lavish treatment from wealthy clients. Jane Stanojovic said Revelle had not been their most reliable employee, sometimes failing to return work calls, or refusing engagements. But she had always paid the money she owed the agency. According to Detective Sergeant Graeme Mulherin of Rose Bay police, who led the search for her, she was 'very choosy' about the people she accepted as clients. She avoided 'old, ugly' men and men who had homes in 'funny areas'.

On the day of her disappearance, Saturday 5 November 1994, Revelle had a number of engagements lined up. One, from 4 pm until 6 pm, was with Gavin Owen Samer, whose live-in girlfriend, Michelle Oswald-Sealy, had flown to Brisbane to spend the weekend with her aunt and uncle. Revelle was due for another appointment at 10.30 pm that night, with a group of Yugoslav men, whom Zoran Stanojovic wanted to give a special treat, as they were friends and fellow nationals. Jane Stanojovic had impressed on Revelle that the appointment was special and said, 'Don't you go disappearing on me!'

Revelle rang the agency at 3.50 pm to say she was on her way to the Samer job. Samer wanted Revelle at his place at Kingsford, and to get the necessary funds, he pawned his girlfriend's clarinet for $250. He won the other $150 on card machines at the Red Tomato Inn near his home. He later told the coroner's court that he paid Revelle for another hour's service. This was known in the industry as moonlighting, doing work on the side with all the money going to the prostitute and none to the agency. Revelle did ring the agency again at 5.50 pm, saying she had finished the job and was moving on. But she might not have been intending to move on at that time at all.

At 7.15 pm, Revelle rang Kate Brentnall, saying she was with a client and that she would ring her from home in an hour and they would meet to have 'a few beers' at the Royal Hotel, Paddington. Samer said he dropped her at the Red Tomato Inn between 7 pm and 7.20 pm. Select Companions sent beeper messages at 8.17 pm, 8.24 pm and 8.31 pm, all of which went unanswered. She did not answer a message from her boyfriend at 7.53 pm. Samer said he had gone home, watched 'Hey Hey It's Saturday' (which went from 6.30 pm until 8.30 pm), gone to sleep, then woken for the Rugby League telecast. When police checked the story about dropping her at the hotel, they could find nobody who remembered seeing her, and the publican said: 'Look at the people we have got here. If a woman like that walked in, the whole place would stop.'

There was much gossip in the industry. One of her wealthy clients, who admitted using escorts and said he had been paying Revelle $500 to $1000 a week, was dragged into the witness box to suffer the glare of the most unwelcome publicity. He said that he had heard rumours of deep and dastardly motives by unnamed persons for doing her in, but they remained only rumour. At the time of writing, the mystery of Revelle Balmain's disappearance had not been solved.

Paula Brown, a lively Sydney hairdresser who had a sense of adventure and liked to dance the night away, had accepted perhaps a little risk on the last night of her life. New Zealand-born, aged 29, Paula had completed her School Certificate at Onehungra High School in Auckland and trained in hair care. She moved to Australia in 1985 and met David Rayner at a hairdressing convention at the Dee Why RSL Club, on Sydney's northern beaches. According to a friend, it was 'love at first sight', and they stayed together, eventually becoming engaged. They lived as husband and wife and planned to marry. In early 1988, Paula met friends Margo Hendricks and Jennifer Titmuss and the three joined up to go into a haircutting business, Cutting Remarks, at

Wynyard station in central Sydney. Jennifer Titmuss said later: 'She was just cheery and hyperactive.' Margo Hendricks said: 'She was really friendly. She would walk up and start talking to people. If someone said, "Come here", she would go, not in a bad sense, I mean, but she would have conversations with lots of people. She was a very trusting, loving person.'

In 1991, Margo Hendricks appointed Paula manager of the Future Cutz salon in Sydney Future's Exchange. Paula became very popular with clients. Ms Hendricks said: 'She had so much patience with people and would always remember their names and what they were doing the last time they were there. Nothing was too much trouble. Around 75 per cent of her clients were men and Paula had me put in a barber's chair in there. Clients loved it and her personality really helped the business.' Paula's mother, Norma Brown, adored her daughter. At the time she disappeared, Paula was planning a joint birthday party to celebrate her 30th and her mother's 50th birthdays.

Ms Hendricks said Paula liked to go out at night and let her hair down. 'Often she would get plastered and I would have to ring David up and tell him to come and get her,' she said. One night, very much under the influence, Paula had refused to get into a taxi and had spent the night at Ms Hendrick's home in Kirribilli. David Rayner said: 'Paula and I had a routine where if she went out like that, she tried to get the last Jet Cat to Manly at night. She always drank champagne, she always liked to drink socially with friends. But she knew she could not stay out until four or five in the morning and turn up home blind.'

On the morning of Friday 3 May 1996, David Rayner went off to work knowing that Paula would go out drinking that night. It was a regular monthly thing for the girls at the salon and this night Paula was celebrating Ms Titmuss's birthday at the Burdekin Hotel in Oxford Street, Paddington, though Ms Titmuss herself was unwell and did not attend. David Rayner said: 'The last thing I said to her was, "Please get the last Jet Cat. Don't get too drunk."' David Rayner said. Paula was still at the hotel in the early morning hours. She was seen talking to a man unknown to her friends. At some point, she must have got into a taxi, which did not surprise Ms Hendricks, who thought she would have been going home. For some reason, she left her jacket behind.

The next morning, David Rayner rang Ms Hendricks to see whether she was there. There was no trace of her. The alarm was raised. Paula Brown's body was found on 12 May in thick bush near boat ramps opposite the Patrick Stevedores terminal. She had been murdered. A taxi driver came forward to say that at 2.45 am on 4 May, he had taken Paula and a 'tall, lean, handsome and well-groomed man' to Port Botany in Sydney's east, and dropped them at the entrance to the Patrick Stevedores terminal. There was much comment about the circumstances of Paula Brown's death. Radio commentator Alan Jones said on air that she should not have been in a taxi at that time of the morning heading for a place like that. If she did, he said, she was looking for trouble. David Rayner sprang to her defence, saying that she would not have agreed to go out like that had she been of a sound mind. 'Something could have been put into her drink, we just don't know,' he said.

With suspicion falling on merchant seamen, police looked at what ships had been in Port Botany at the time of her disappearance. The Liberian-registered *Columbus Canada* had left on 4 May, en route for Honolulu. It had a crew of 24, comprising nine Germans and the remainder from the Pacific island of Kiribati. The ship's captain, Peter Hartmann, contacted by radio telephone by a Sydney newspaper, said sailors did bring women back to the ship. 'Why not?' he asked. 'We have a lot of friends there [in Sydney].' There were five ships at Port Botany the night Paula disappeared. The *Columbus Canada* and another ship, the *Anro Gower*, manned by a Singaporean Indian crew, were moored at the Patrick Stevedores terminal. The tall, lean, handsome man, if there were to be a choice between the two ships, fitted someone from the *Columbus Canada*. But it was hardly evidence against an individual. Police planned to interview crew when the various ships docked in foreign ports, but unless hard information came – such as someone informing – their chances of getting cogent evidence became more and more remote.

As with the disappearance of Revelle, at the time of writing this crime had not been solved. Life, of course, rolls on, and young girls continue to backpack, walk along neighbourhood roads at night, dance the night hours away and get picked up by handsome men. But others are doing nothing risky at all – they are in their own kitchens, or leaving suburban shopping centres, or going across the road to catch a bus, or going to their car after work. All of them are entitled to think and assume that they are living in a civilised community. But it is not, or not quite. Within its dark alleyways, predators roam.

THE MONSTER OF
BELANGLO

*My thoughts are crowded with death
and it draws so oddly on the sexual
that I am confused
confused to be attracted
by, in effect, my own annihilation.*

Thom Gunn
English poet

The ghastly spectacle of the Backpacker Murders, 1989–1992, when seven young people were abducted, ravaged, murdered and left to rot in a State forest, left many people sad and soulful. An idyllic place like this, with eucalypts swaying in the breeze beneath scudding clouds on mild autumn days, had become a chamber of horrors. People innocently pursuing their path through life had been chosen by fate to be in the eye of someone else's storm. Unsuspectingly, they had equated the sunlight, the busy highway, the people's smiles, the laid-back nature of Australians, with safety.

For those who had even noticed it, or taken the trouble to turn off and make their way along dirt tracks to the unspoilt parts of the Belanglo State Forest, an hour's drive south of Sydney, the bush might have been attractive. To this writer, it did not seem so pretty any more; innocuous, dreary even, turning up for searchers the odd bits of debris – false teeth, money and discarded garments. I had stood there for days, frustrated and morbid, waiting behind the rope being used as a police cordon, which was laid out in mid-forest by a Chief Inspector Fred Brame to keep the media in their place.

D.H. Lawrence, in his novel, *Kangaroo*, expressed his feelings about the Australian bush through his character, Richard Lovatt Somers: 'The vast, uninhabited land frightened him. It seemed so hoary and lost, so unapproachable. The sky was pure, crystal pure and blue, of a lovely pale blue colour: the air was wonderful, new and unbreathed: and there were great distances. But the bush, the grey, charred bush. It scared him... so phantomlike, so ghostly, with its tall pale trees and many dead trees, like corpses... and then the foliage so dark, like grey-green iron. And then it was so deathly still. Even the few birds seemed to be swamped in silence. Waiting, waiting – the bush seemed to be hoarily waiting. And he could not penetrate into its secret. He couldn't get at it. Nobody could get at it. What was it waiting for?'

What was it waiting for indeed!

Called in to assist in reporting the search, I had talked to cement factory workers on the one hand, and TV personality Graeme Kennedy (at his country retreat) on the other. These were normal people. But the bush itself, that tangle of nothingness, was a chasm capable of perplexing anybody exposed long enough to it.

Beyond the bush, things did look better. The settled and cultivated part of the Southern Highlands was beautiful. Always had been. Old-world, almost English in atmosphere and attitudes. My grandfather had served as a Methodist minister at Robertson and at Bowral. I had courted my wife here, cuddling her amid the tulips. But the upgraded freeway had brought the city closer, as had the railway, linked with the electrified metropolitan network – good for commuters and antique dealers, but it also gave people of less harmless bent easier access. The Backpacker Murderer, or Murderers, could have come this way, but they could also have been natives to the area. Who knew?

Ivan Robert Marko Milat, born 27 December 1942, fifth-born in what was to be a family of 14 children, was a problem from his earliest years. Given Catholic schooling in Liverpool in Sydney's far south-west, Milat right from his earliest years was disruptive, wagging school and not paying attention to lessons. Growing up in the depressed south-west, first at Rossmore, then Moorebank and Guildford, Milat was surrounded by other bored, socially inept young men looking for kicks. His father, Stijphan, a Yugoslav migrant – honest, hardworking but poorly educated – was not able to handle his large and unruly brood.

Milat's mother, Margaret, a good woman who did the best she could for her children, arranged for Milat, at the age of 13, to go into Boys' Town, a centre for wayward youth run by the Salesian Brothers. He was there a year, and left school at 14 to work for a fruit and vegetable merchant.

Milat almost certainly stole firearms from his first employer, and jewellery from that employer's wife. He also persuaded the employer to guarantee a loan for purchase of a motor car, then skipped off with the car. Milat appeared before the Liverpool Children's Court at the age of 17, charged with stealing from a dwelling. He appeared again on 27 August, 1962, on another offence, and this time earned himself a stint at the Mt Penang Juvenile Institution on the New South Wales Central Coast. By the time of his release he was 18, and ready to be an adult criminal. He took part in smash-and-grab raids, in company with mates, including one or other of his brothers.

Les Kennedy and Mark Whittaker, in their definitive work on the Backpacker Murders, *Sins of the Brother*, relate how in 1963, after a smash-and-grab raid at St Marys near Penrith, Milat and mates took off at high speed.

'Lots of people had seen them and now they were running scared out in the open, full throttle back towards home. Nought to a hundred in no time flat. No one could catch Milat's brother, Boris Milat's Ford. But sure enough, a car swung in behind them, and was closing in. Boris pushed it up to maybe 115 mph with a red light staring at them as they hit the Great Western Highway. There was no time to do anything. They shut their eyes and shot straight across the busy intersection. F*** it was a buzz.

'They hammered down Mamre Road, sure they had got away clean, but then the other car appeared through the intersection, closing in. They started throwing all the stolen gear out: tape recorders, cameras, watches. All the evidence. The pursuit car was bearing down quickly.

'"What the f*** are the cops driving?"'… As the car drew up with them, everyone's guns came up. All except Ivan's. He was sitting beside Boris in a prime shooting position. The only thing that saved the guy was that the others weren't in as good a spot. Before anybody could get a shot off, the guy saw all the guns, shit himself and hit the brakes.'

It was pretty hairy stuff. Not the sort of behaviour you'd expect from a well-brought-up lad from next door. Milat's mother despaired, but was fiercely defensive of him, and turned to an up-and-coming lawyer, John Marsden, for help. Marsden was good, but even the most brilliant lawyer has to concede facts. On 29 October 1964, Milat was convicted and sentenced to 18 months' gaol for safe robbery. He did the sentence, but on 8 November, 1965, appeared before Liverpool Local Court charged with larceny of a motor vehicle. He celebrated his 21st birthday in remand and was given a two-year sentence, part of which he served at the then notorious Grafton Gaol.

After that stint, Milat was employed by the Department of Main Roads (DMR), but was still busy getting up to mischief. He came to the notice of the then New South Wales Police Criminal Investigation Branch. By his mid-twenties, his record consisted of two juvenile and six adult convictions for offences including theft of a motor vehicle and break, enter and steal. He had spent a total of five years and three months – a fifth of his young life – behind bars. But from his behaviour, it appeared he did not mind the prospect of more time. There were even darker, more malevolent aspects of Milat's personality surfacing. He was fascinated by firearms. He loved the power they could give him, and the tough guy image. He loved knives, and big, flashy, powerful motor cars. Of average height, he was strong, and he enhanced that strength by regularly working out on weights. And he was into sexual kicks.

On 10 April 1971, Milat gave two 18-year-old girl hitchhikers, Margaret and Greta, a lift in his Falcon V8. The girls, who were undergoing psychiatric treatment, could have done without this. Taking them off the beaten track near Goulburn, Milat produced two knives and said: 'Either one of you have sex with me or I will kill you both.' Greta tried to escape and Milat caught her and tied her up. He said: 'You know what? I am going to kill you! You won't scream when I cut your throats, will you?' Margaret agreed to let him have sex with her, provided he then let them go. After satisfying his lust, Milat asked Margaret to buy them soft drinks at a service station. Once released, Margaret called for help. Greta, untied, made a break for it and Milat took off at high speed. He was caught after a police chase and a roadblock.

Charged that he did 'without her consent ravish and carnally know' the girl, Milat was nevertheless granted bail. But he was soon back in trouble again, charged with having, on 23 July 1971, armed with a sawn-off rifle, robbed a man and woman at Revesby in Sydney's south-west, and with having, the following day, robbed the Canley Heights branch of the Bank of New South Wales, while armed with the same rifle.

Milat appeared on the rape charge at Central Court of Petty Sessions on 13 October 1971. His bail continued, but he absconded, going to New Zealand. Not that that solved the Milat family problems. In March 1972, Michael Milat went before the Central Criminal Court at Darlinghurst, where he pleaded guilty to four counts of armed robbery and one of wounding.

Ivan Milat returned to Australia in late 1974, and on 12 December went before Central Criminal Court over the rape. Represented by Marsden, he had the benefit of confused and contradictory testimony from Margaret and he was acquitted, as he was also on the armed robbery charges.

In October 1975, at the age of 31, driving trucks and living with his mother at Guildford, Milat met Karen Merle Duck, 16, who was six months pregnant to another man. In 1977, he started living with her. But despite the possibility of domestic bliss and fatherhood, his evil streak remained, just below the surface.

It transpired years later, that two 18-year-old girls, Therese Tran and Mary Tregillas, hitchhiking on the Hume Highway at

Camden in 1977, were offered a lift by a man they later tentatively identified as Ivan Milat, who drove them into bushland and announced his intention to rape them. The two escaped, evading their attacker, who drove up and down the road looking for them.

Milat's brothers, Alex and Wally, shared his passion for firearms. They went shooting at Wally's place at the Wombeyan Caves on the Southern Highlands, and at Alex's place at Buxton, also in the Southern Highlands, blazing away, using various rifles and thousands of rounds of ammunition. Milat worked again for the DMR. A workmate at the time, Ross Jackson, noticed how fond Milat had become of firearms magazines. Another workmate, Noel Wild, said that while there were never any complaints about Milat as a worker, he was definitely a loner, carrying with him a huge Bowie knife.

Milat adopted Karen's son, Jason, and in 1981 bought a house at Blackett near St Marys in Sydney's far west. There was enough about his behaviour for Karen to have had some doubts about him. In 1983, he took Karen and Jason into the Belanglo forest, where he shot a kangaroo, then horrified her by walking across and slitting its throat. Milat and Karen were married on 20 February 1984, but from the outset Karen realised she had made a mistake. Milat was domineering and bullying, physically and sexually, denying her any personal freedom.

Karen took note of the fact that Milat kept a revolver either in a wooden case under his bed or wrapped in a sock under the driver's seat of his car, sometimes sticking a revolver down the side of his boot. She would say later: 'Ivan was gun-crazy… he would shoot anything he could find… these were a target on a tree, cans, anything he could see. Ivan was shooting a revolver and running round like a cowboy, calling himself "Texas."' At one point Milat asked his niece's boyfriend, who was a security guard, to get him a pair of handcuffs.

On St Valentine's Day 1987, while Milat was away working, she walked out, moving with her son to a secret address. A furious Milat went to see her parents in Newcastle to bully them into revealing her address. They refused. In February 1988, a fire in their garage destroyed their car. It might or might not have been coincidental. Divorce proceedings began between Milat and Karen.

Milat went to work for Sweeping Services, a company in western Sydney, signing on as 'Bill Milat', saying he was using the name because of a 'domestic situation'. He resigned from there in November 1988 and went to work for BHP Plasterboard at Camellia, western Sydney, again using the false name. He took solace in the company of a former wife of one of his brothers, but that ended acrimoniously in 1989. His divorce was finalised in October 1989. It has been said that Milat, cut off from such outlets for affection, went looking for his kicks elsewhere.

In December 1989, Victorians Deborah Everist and James Harold Gibson, both aged 19, wanted a quick post-Christmas break. Deborah, an arts student at Melbourne University, and James, training to be an artist, planned to be away for a week. James was particularly anxious to be back for his sister's wedding. On 29 December, Deborah rang her mother saying they had arrived in Sydney. 'I knew you would be in a panic until you heard from me,' she said. 'We are fine, don't worry. I will send you a postcard and I will ring you tomorrow.'

On 30 December, Deborah and James left Sydney to hitchhike south to Albury for an environmental rally, and disappeared.

On 25 January 1990, British backpacker Paul Thomas Onions, 24, from Willenhall near Birmingham, was making his way across Australia. He heard there was money to be made picking fruit at Mildura in the State's south. He took a train to Liverpool, walked some distance, and dropped in at Lombardo's shopping centre at Casula for a drink. He was pleasantly surprised when a man with a four-wheel drive vehicle offered him a lift.

In the vehicle, turning south onto the freeway, the man introduced himself as 'Bill', said one of his parents was from Yugoslavia, he came from Liverpool, he had recently divorced and he worked on the roads. He also made some off-putting remarks about Northern Ireland and Asians. Beyond the Bowral turn-off and 900 metres from the entrance to Belanglo State Forest, 'Bill' pulled up, reached under his seat and produced a pistol, saying:

'This is a robbery!' A startled Onions unbuckled his seat belt, but 'Bill' told him to do it up. When 'Bill' produced rope, Onions decided it was time to split anyway. As he sprang from the vehicle, abandoning his belongings, 'Bill' called out: 'Stop or I will shoot!'

Onions heard a shot but kept running. After several attempts to flag down vehicles, and at one time physically struggling with 'Bill', he forced a van driven by Joanne Berry of Canberra to stop. She was reluctant, but Onions pressed his case. He got in, blurted out his story, and she drove him to Bowral. 'Bill' sped off, it was presumed, in the opposite direction, taking with him Onions' possessions, including a 'Next' brand shirt. At Bowral, Onions gave details to Constable Louise Nicholson, including the fact that 'Bill' had a 'Merv Hughes-style moustache', and that the four-wheel drive was white, with a spare wheel mounted on the back and lambswool seat covers. Joanne Berry said the vehicle had had a red band along the side. A description of the assailant was broadcast. The police gave Onions $20 to get back to Sydney.

In the meantime, nothing had been heard from Deborah or James. Their families became increasingly worried. In March 1990, a backpack was found in Galston Gorge, north of Sydney. The name had been cut off the top, but James' name and address had been written on the bottom of the bag.

Simone Loretta Schmidl, 21, an office worker from Regensberg, Germany, was next. Her father, Herbert, bought camping equipment for her, including a pink, lilac and black backpack, and a gas burner. He saw her off and remembered loading her blue day-bag onto the train before she left for Frankfurt Airport. Simone had a green plastic water bottle which she inscribed with her pet name, 'Simi'. She visited Canada, Alaska and New Zealand before arriving in Australia on 19 January 1991.

Simone went to Guildford where she had friends – Jeanette Muller, who had hitchhiked with her in New Zealand, and Christine Murphy, whom she had befriended in Alaska. Simone wanted to hitchhike straight away to meet her mother, Erwina, in Melbourne. Christine warned her of the dangers of hitchhiking and Jeanette offered her money to take a coach. But Simone dismissed the concerns, saying: 'Don't worry about it. I am quite safe.' She agreed to stay overnight and leave on Sunday 20 January.

Jeanette accompanied her to the railway station, where Simone caught a train to Liverpool. Simone was not heard from again.

Almost 12 months later, Garbor Kurt Neugebauer, 21, and Anja Susanne Habshied, 20, students at Munich University, decided to travel, promising to keep in touch with their devoted families. They arrived in Sydney at Christmas, 1991. Anja telephoned her parents telling them that she and Gabor were travelling to Darwin and then to Indonesia. Gabor's family sent a parcel containing 'cookies and some vitamins' to Darwin for him to pick up. The two left their hotel in Sydney's Kings Cross on 26 December, 1991, to make their way south, and disappeared.

Joanne Lesley Walters, 22, a trained nanny, left her home in Maesteg, Wales, in May 1991 and travelled to Australia, where she worked as a waitress and a crew member of a yacht. She linked up with an English girl, Caroline Jane Clarke, 21. They were both well fitted out. Caroline included in her luggage a green and white Benetton top. She carried a sleeping bag with a small tear in it, repaired by a label.

The two hitchhiked in Victoria in February 1992, reached Sydney, then hitchhiked to Mildura. There they befriended an Englishman, Stephen Wright. Wright had a large tent, which he had damaged slightly with a fruit knife. The three went hitchhiking to Tasmania, where Stephen swapped his large tent for Caroline's smaller one. Caroline and Joanne returned to Sydney. Joanne rang her mother, Gill, who said later: 'She was very, very tired but she was in good form. She was going to stay a few days to get over her tiredness and then start her travels again.' Caroline and Joanne decided to return to Mildura to pick more fruit and departed on 18 April 1992. They were not heard from again.

All these disappearances were reported, and in August, 1992, police noted similarities in the disappearances of six foreign tourists in New South Wales and Queensland.

In the meantime, the Milat family had its share of worries. Michael was in gaol. A sister, Margaret, was killed in a car accident and another brother, David, was seriously injured in another car accident, which left him brain-damaged and unable to use one arm.

In June 1992, Ivan Milat met Chalinder Hughes, an Indian-born woman, a registrar at the Commonwealth Human Rights and Equal Opportunities Commission. The two struck up a relationship. As was noted afterwards, there were no more Backpacker Murders after this time. But there were still glimpses of Milat's darker side. Once, while driving past Belanglo with a workmate on the DMR, Anthony Sara, Milat said: 'You would be surprised what is in there.' Sara said: 'What, snakes and kangaroos?' Milat did not reply, and Sara, who had often heard Milat talk about hunting and shooting in places they passed, let it drop.

On 19 September 1992, two orienteers, Keith Siely and Keith Caldwell, on an exercise through the Belanglo, smelt decay and found the remains of Joanne Walters pushed into a cavity under a boulder and covered with leaves and branches. They contacted police, who arrived late and continued searching the following day.

Police found an area of vegetation that had been flattened some time previously, consistent with a woman having been raped on that spot. Joanne had apparently been gagged with a Gloweave men's shirt, size 41. She had been sexually assaulted and stabbed 14 times in the chest and neck and one of the knife-thrusts had severed her spinal cord. It was apparent that the person using the knife must have had enormous strength.

Twenty metres from Joanne, police found the remains of Caroline Clarke. Her T-shirt was bunched up to expose her stomach and chest and buttons of her jeans had been undone. Her head was wrapped in maroon cloth and 10 bullets had been fired into it, two of them remaining embedded in the skull, another four inside the skull casing. It seemed the killer, or killers, had used the head for target practice. Near the body, police found cartridges consistent with a 10/22 Ruger, made before 1982. There were six cigarette butts, indicating that the killer might have lingered.

The discovery of the bodies was communicated to Joanne's parents, Ray and Gill, who had travelled to Australia to search for their daughter. There was nothing to suggest that, however gruesome, this was anything other than an isolated double murder, where the bodies had been dumped in convenient bushland. From the last century, the Blue Mountains west of Sydney had been a dumping ground for bodies.

In February 1993, Milat moved with Chalinder to a house in Cinnabar Street, Eagle Vale, in Sydney's south-west. Just what was going through his mind, nobody knows. He could hardly have missed the news of the murders. Nor were the Milats as a family escaping attention. Richard Milat, another brother, also a 'gun freak', attracted the attention of workmates at the Boral plant at Camellia in Sydney's west by saying: 'They haven't found the Germans yet', and that 'stabbing a woman is like cutting a slice of bread'. Richard, who lived in Hilltop, a village in the southern tablelands, had a habit of combining alcohol and cannabis, which made him talk non-stop, perhaps letting things slip out.

On 5 October 1993, a local potter, Bruce Pryor, worried about the murders, had an impulse to search a piece of scrubland that had escaped everyone else's attention. He found the skeletal remains of Deborah Everist and James Gibson, 600 metres apart. Deborah had had her skull fractured in two places and her jaw had been broken. The zipper of her fly was down, though the top button had been done up. James appeared to have been stabbed through the spine, at a point where the thrust would have paralysed him. Other knife thrusts had marked his ribs and breastbone.

Now, with the clearest indications that a serial killer, or killers, had been at work, police stepped up their inquiries. The Liverpool police commander, Superintendent Clive Small, was assigned to the case. On 12 October 1993, a task force was formed, code-named 'Air', and a search of the forest was organised, using cadaver-sniffing dogs, capable of picking up the scent of decaying flesh. The police divided and cross-gridded the area. Reporters waited impatiently. Bowral residents resented the media invasion.

Alex Milat, an older brother of Ivan, one-time local miner and member of the Bowral pistol club, approached police with strange information. He said that 18 months before he had passed two vehicles going into the Belanglo and that in them were several men and two gagged women. He gave specific descriptions not only of the types of vehicles but also of the people inside them, even down to the tattoos on the men and calluses on their hands. He said he had not reported it earlier because men often took women into the forest for a good time. His story sounded inherently improbable – driving past vehicles would not have given him time to absorb such detail. But the fact that he had come forward at all was to acquire significance – given who he was.

At 3.15 pm on 1 November, police found the remains of Simone Schmidl. Around the remains of her head was a purple headband with the word 'Compactomat' printed on it. She had been stabbed once in the base of the neck, in a spot where such a wound was likely to have paralysed her, and seven times in the chest. She had shorts on, but no underpants, and her singlet was bunched around her shoulders.

Three days later, police found the skeletal remains of Gabor Neugebauer and Anja Habschied, 60 metres apart. Anja's skull was nowhere to be found, an indication that she may have been decapitated with a machete, perhaps, or a sword. Gabor had been gagged with a length of floral cloth. His hyoid bone, at the base of his tongue, had been fractured, suggesting he may have been strangled. He had been shot six times in the head. Because no projectiles were in the ground beneath his head, it was concluded he had been shot at some other place.

Some 165 metres away from Gabor's body, police found something in the order of 100 cartridge cases which, through ballistics examination, they were later able to link with the cases found near the body of Caroline Clarke, and thence with a 10/22 Ruger. Also near Gabor's body, police found a packet that had contained Winchester .22 calibre rounds. The packet had the batch number ACD1CF2. Police found a packet that had contained Eley brand ammunition, batch number J23CGA. Midway between the bodies and the cartridge cases they found a tangled mass of white sashes, electrical tape, part of which was formed into two loops, and brown leather straps.

A metal detector turned up a broken silver necklace and its clasp, remains of an 18th birthday present to Anja, evidence now of what must have been Anja's last, grim struggle for her life, as she tried to push away the murderer, or murderers. The bones spoke mutely of the horrors, the extent of which could only be imagined. But at least the bush was giving up some of its secrets. At work, Richard Milat again raised eyebrows when he said to workmate Richard Butler: 'I know who killed the Germans.'

Police took away an array of items: bones, bullet fragments, cartridge cases. Ballistics examination showed that at least some of the bullets found in Caroline's skull had been through two barrels, one of them a silencer. The job ahead of police was tracing the ammunition and firearms. Some 55,000 Rugers of the type they were looking for had been distributed, and the Winchester batch number ACDICF2 belonged to 320,000 rounds. Police visited gunshops, including that of Peter Arbela at Horsley Park in western Sydney. He had been a regular supplier, at least of ammunition, to Ivan Milat.

Of the items police had taken from the forest, one category was noticeable by its absence: backpacks, tents and other camping equipment. Very few personal items had been found. It was presumed that the murderer, or murderers, had taken them.

The task force called on the public for help. The public responded with information so vast that the computer system could scarcely cope with it – there were more than 5000 calls in the first 24 hours. Much of the information went nowhere, but buried in it were some gems. One woman had said she did not know whether it would help, but she knew a man who owned a property near the Belanglo State Forest, who drove a four wheel-drive vehicle, had a lot of firearms and was a keen shooter. His name was Ivan Milat.

Peter Bradhurst, a forensic pathologist at the New South Wales Institute of Forensic Medicine, pointed to the obvious fact that killing people who were travelling in pairs could be accomplished more easily by more than one person. It was also obvious that if the killer were able to inflict a disabling wound on one person, overcoming the other would not be so difficult. In fact, two of the victims had been shot and three had had paralysing stab wounds to the base of the neck.

On 13 November 1994, Paul Onions rang from Britain saying he had read the news reports of the murder inquiry and had realised his story might be relevant. Richard Milat's workmates reported Richard's strange remarks about the murders. In terms of frequency of 'hits' – using Internet jargon – that was another occasion on which the Milat name had come up. Another had been Alex Milat's information about two vehicles going into the forest.

In mid-December 1993, Small called on the services of forensic psychiatrist Dr Rod Milton and social anthropologist Dr Richard Basham to try to profile the person they were looking for. The two came up with a profile of a man in his forties, probably in trouble at school, perhaps in trouble with police as a teenager, not good at close relationships, probably good at holding a steady job. He would probably have had a four-wheel drive, was knowledgeable about firearms and knives, and had had access to these items.

By January 1994, police had 1.5 million items of information. And again, some of it was invaluable. Joanne Berry, who had picked up Paul Onions, contacted police and was interviewed on 6 February 1994. Police turned up the notes of Constable Nicholson, and the police occurrence pad entry on the attack on Onions, together with Onions' description of his attacker and the vehicle.

Police attention was being directed not just onto the Milat family, but onto Ivan. Arbela had confirmed that Ivan Milat had been his customer. Then Detective Paul Gordon went into Milat's record and came across the 1971 rape charge. He discovered that until September 1992, Milat had driven a silver-white Nissan four-wheel drive vehicle.

In February 1994, police mounted a surveillance operation on Milat, using station wagons and tradesmen's vans. Their presence in Eagle Vale did not go unnoticed by the locals, or by Milat himself. Police also made inquiries of Milat's workmates about Milat, despite the risk of that getting back to him. They made inquiries of his employers and discovered that on each occasion when backpackers had disappeared, and on the day Paul Onions was attacked, Milat had not been at work. Milat got wind of the inquiries and rang Wally, who, like Richard, lived at Hilltop, asking whether he could store rifles and ammunition at his home.

According to Wally, Milat said that his sister, Shirley Soire, who shared the house with him, was 'upset' at having the firearms around the house. Milat had also said police had been around 'asking people about a threaded rifle or something'. Richard Milat later recalled him saying: 'I had the rifle threaded at Readmix and I have problems with that.' Wally, together with Richard, helped Milat move the firearms, taking them to Wally's place, where they were put into an enclosed space below the house.

In March, a former workmate of Milat's, Ross Jackson, visited him. Milat asked him what he thought of the backpacker murders, whether police had 'been around'. Milat was getting edgy.

Therese Tran and Mary Trengillas approached police about the incident, where the man who gave them a lift had stated his intention of raping them. Therese, who had been sitting in the back seat and had only seen Milat's eyes, picked out two men from a photo board whose eyes matched. One was Milat. Mary, who had had a better view, picked out a picture not of Ivan Milat but of Richard, who was taller but otherwise looked similar to Ivan.

Onions was flown to Australia, and on 5 May, 1994 was shown a video containing photographs of 13 men. He identified Ivan Milat as his attacker.

Police decided on one coordinated operation, in which a total of 250 of them would descend on ten properties related to the inquiry, including two properties in Queensland, and others at Guildford, Hilltop, Buxton, Bargo, Ulladulla on the south cost, and a property at Wombeyan Caves. The first raid was on 21 May on the home of Alex Milat and his wife Joan at West Woombye, north of Brisbane, a place they had moved to in 1992. Joan volunteered an item she said Milat had given her and Alex some time after Easter, 1992, before they left for Queensland. It was the pink, lilac and black backpack, matching the one Simone Schmidl had had.

In the early morning of 22 May, police moved on the rest of the properties. They surrounded the home of Ivan Milat at Eagle Vale.

A police negotiator, Detective Sergeant Wayne Gordon, rang the home and a sleepy Milat answered. Gordon said he was to be interviewed in relation to an armed robbery, that his home was surrounded and that police had a search warrant. Milat was to walk out with his arms stretched in front of him. Milat agreed, but several minutes later, when he did not appear, Gordon rang again. Milat said he had thought workmates were playing a joke. Gordon rang a third time. Chalinder answered, saying he would be coming out but he had lost his keys, as he 'always does in the morning'.

Milat did leave the house, some 14 minutes after the first call, and was promptly arrested and handcuffed. Gordon, grabbing Milat, felt the size of Milat's muscles and realised the enormous strength of the man. He said in his mind: 'We've got him.'

Police had enough evidence to charge Milat over the armed robbery of Onions. They were hopeful that they would get more evidence from the house. What they found exceeded their expectations. There were indications that, after the first telephone call, Milat had made hurried attempts to hide things. They had heard a car door open and shut in the garage, consistent with Milat having gone there to collect the pistol under his seat. Inside the house, a police officer noticed that the washing machine out of alignment and slightly raised off the floor. Under it, he found a .32 calibre pistol.

Stuffed into a boot in the hall cupboard, police found a black Ruger receiver, a casing for a bullet. In a loungeroom wall cavity, police saw a white plastic bag containing items. Retrieved with difficulty, it was found to contain a metal trigger assembly, bullet, firing mechanism and a magazine which had apparently been part of a Ruger. In the ceiling, police found a rifle bolt, and in a spare bedroom, a cartridge case, and a German-made wood-handled knife. Under Shirley Soire's bed they found a rifle, and in between the two mattresses, a box of rapid-fire bullets. They seized tens of thousands of rounds of ammunition, shotgun cartridges, a telescopic sight and air-rifle pellets. They found a box of Eley brand ammunition whose batch number matched that of the box found in the forest. And they found a home-made silencer.

The literature they found included copies of the shooting magazines, *Sportsman's Gun Annual* and *Lock, Stock and Barrel*, and *Violent Crimes that Rocked the Nation: Unsolved*. Police turned up an application to join the Shooter's Party, a manual for a Ruger rifle, and a map of the Belanglo. They found a camera, made in Malaysia and exported to England, which was identical to a camera that had been owned by Caroline Clarke, and a postcard from someone in New Zealand starting 'Dear Bill'.

In a walk-in wardrobe, police found a green and purple Salewar brand sleeping bag stuffed into a garbage bag. It matched the description of the one Simone Schmidl had had. They found a plastic water bottle with something scratched out on it, New Zealand currency that Simone might have been carrying, a cooking set and tent which she might have had, and around the tent a Compactomat headband, similar to the one that had been found with Simone's remains.

In the console box of Milat's car, police found a 20-pence English coin, which might have been carried by Caroline Clarke or Joanne Walters. In the garage, they found a pillow slip later identified as belonging to Milat's mother. Inside it, they found sash cord stained with blood.

At Wally Milat's place, police found a huge array of weapons and ammunition. Inspector Paul Couch said the weight of ammunition they found there came to at least a tonne. They found a Winchester rifle and an Anschutz rifle. The Anschutz had a threaded barrel suitable for attaching a silencer. The rifle's bolt was wrapped in red-checked material, which matched material found at Ivan's place. Winchester ammunition boxes recovered had the same serial number as the empty box found in the forest. Police found items of camping equipment, including a blue day-pack matching Simone's.

In a garden shed at Richard Milat's place, police found a sleeping bag with a small tear repaired by a label, and a bedroll and tent which matched those Caroline Clarke had had. In a cupboard, they found a sleeping bag that matched Joanne's. At Milat's mother's home at Guildford, police took from a locked container a rifle inscribed with the name 'Ivan'. They found a sword. And they found a 'Next' brand shirt, matching the one Paul Onions had left behind in his flight for his life more than four years before.

At the Bargo home of William Milat, another brother, police looked at a photograph album which had a picture of a silver Nissan Patrol. It was labelled with the words 'Mac's Truck' or 'Towing Mac In'. 'Mac' was Milat's nickname. The vehicle had a bullbar, as Onions said his attacker's vehicle had had, and appeared to have lambswool seat covers. It had a red stripe along the side, matching Joanne Berry's description. Police found a photograph of Chalinder Hughes wearing a Benetton top strikingly similar to Caroline Clarke's.

At Alex Milat's former home at Buxton, police excavated a private firing range and recovered spent shells and bullet fragments to see if any matched what had been found in the forest. The total number of items seized amounted to more than one thousand, including 60 firearms.

Ivan Milat was confronted with a mass of incriminating evidence, even down to the size of the shirts he wore. His shirt size, 41 or 42, matched the size of the shirt apparently used to gag Joanne Walters. But he denied any knowledge of the disappearance of the backpackers. For that matter, so did all other members of the Milat family. Ivan Milat said he did not own a firearm and when shown the rounds recovered from the house, said he had borrowed a rifle occasionally to go shooting at Wally's property. Shown the Ruger parts, he said he 'would not have a clue' about them, and added: 'I presume youse had them.' Asked about the attack on Paul Onions, he said: 'It wasn't me.'

On 31 May 1994, Ivan Milat appeared before magistrate Kevin Flack in Liverpool Local Court, charged with the armed robbery of Paul Onions, and with the illegal possession of a silencer, a paint-ball gun, a 12-gauge shotgun, a crossbow, two Chinese barrels with silencer, a Ruger .44 calibre revolver, a .32 calibre automatic pistol, a 4.10 double-barrelled shotgun, two .223 calibre Ruger riles, a 12-gauge Winchester shotgun, a 12-gauge double-barrelled shotgun, two air rifles, a .22 calibre Ruger rifle, a .22 calibre rifle, a 30/30 calibre rifle, a Chinese SLR rifle, and ammunition.

Ian Lloyd QC, Crown prosecutor, told the court that the firing pin in the Ruger firing mechanism, found secreted in Milat's wall panel, had a distinctive crescent-shaped mark which it left on cartridges. That mark had been found on cartridges underneath Caroline Clarke's body. It had been used to fire the 47 rounds of cartridges found near the bodies of Neugebauer and Habschied. The Anschutz rifle had been test-fired and the spent cartridges matched some of those found at the same place. Lloyd said there were similarities between the camping equipment recovered in the raids and the equipment the murder victims were known to have had. It had been 'clear from the naked eye' that something had been scratched out on the plastic water bottle, and infra-red photographic techniques had revealed the letters 'SIMI'.

On 26 June 1994, Milat sacked Marsden for reasons he did not make clear. Milat claimed the police were framing him. 'I am stuck in gaol and they have not got one iota of proof,' he said. 'They are making it all up as they go along.' Another lawyer, Queenslander Andrew Boe, took over. Lloyd opposed Milat getting bail, saying, among other things that Milat had been arrested in 1971 for the rape of a teenager. He omitted to say that Milat had been put on trial and acquitted, something which he corrected soon after. Milat was remanded in custody.

Police travelled to England and Germany to interview the families of victims and get them to identify items of equipment. The DNA in the blood found on the sashcord in Milat's garage was found to be consistent with that of Caroline Clarke. When the blood of Caroline's parents was tested, it was found that only one couple in 96,000 could have produced a child with the DNA found on the sashcord.

The brief police put together comprised some 300 statements, some 600 photographs and more than 400 pages detailing the physical evidence and results of ballistics examination. Milat was charged with the murders of all seven backpackers. On 20 October 1994, he appeared at Liverpool Local Court before magistrate Michael Price. Price heard from 170 witnesses over five weeks. Another 331 statements and more than 600 exhibits were tendered.

Boe arranged for counsel Cate Holmes to represent Milat. On 14 November, Milat sacked her. At one point he erupted, accusing a detective of having put his initials on the backpack handed over by Joan Milat.

Boe engaged another counsel, Terry Martin. But changing lawyers did nothing to slow the pace of the hearing. Clive Small said the description Onions had given of his attacker could have fitted several members of the Milat family, but he did not think any others had had a vehicle like that and he did not think that anyone in the family would have borrowed the vehicle, because Milat was 'extremely jealous about it'. Stephen Wright, who had exchanged tents with Caroline Clarke, was shown a tent and started rummaging around in the lining. Lloyd asked what he was looking for. Wright replied: 'I am looking for the hole I made in the tent with my grape-cutting knife.' Lloyd asked: 'What have you found?' Wright replied: 'That hole.'

Price had no hesitation on 12 November, 1994, in ordering Milat to stand trial. After a long delay caused by arguments about the amount of legal aid Milat was entitled to, the trial started in the Old Banco Court in Sydney on 25 March, 1996, before Justice David Hunt. Crown prosecutor Mark Tedeschi QC said in his opening address that Milat had committed the murders 'for his own psychological gratification'. He said the Crown was not able to prove that he acted with one or more accomplices, but would contend that if he acted alone, he committed the murders, and if in company, then he was completely responsible.

Milat maintained his complete innocence and claimed he had been framed. He conceded that it was 'a reasonable inference' that the camping equipment found in his home and the homes of relatives had belonged to the backpackers, but suggested a conspiracy to set him up. When Tedeschi asked him on 18 June about Simone Schmidl's multicoloured backpack having been found at the home of his brother Alex, Milat said: 'Well, obviously somebody's trying to make me look real bad.'

Milat maintained that rifle parts found at his home had been planted, and that the Ruger parts in the wall cavity of his house had also been planted. The Anschutz bolt at Wally's home had been wrapped in the same red-checked material that was used to make a shirt found in the spare bedroom of his home. Milat had no explanation, but thought it possible that somebody might have got access to Wally's home to plant items there that potentially incriminated him. Pressed by Tedeschi, he said that if it came to the crunch, it was indeed 'sheer coincidence' that the rifle parts were painted with the same camouflage paint he had used on his weapons. Milat had no explanation for the bloodied sashcord found in his garage, nor for the identical batch numbers on the ammunition found in his belongings and on the boxes found in the forest. Tedeschi said: 'What I am suggesting is that you were the person at the deaths... and that you alone or with another or others left those boxes in the forest, thinking they could not be traced.'

Some of Milat's relatives were defensive of him. Chalinder Hughes agreed she had been photographed wearing a green-and-white Benetton top but said the picture would have been taken about 1994. Tedeschi rebutted that by referring to a date on the back, which was 1992. William Milat said Ivan had been at his mother's home all day on Boxing Day, the day Neugebauer and Habschied disappeared. But there was no corroboration.

Milat agreed that the evidence of Onions and Berry implicated him. But he seized on Onions' statement that the four-wheel drive had had a spare wheel mounted on the back. He could prove that his vehicle had no such wheel in that position at that time. He also disputed that he had what Onions said was a Merv Hughes-style of moustache. His was droopy at the sides, unlike Hughes', which 'sweeps back a bit'.

But others of his answers were far from convincing. Why had he had the silencer? His reply was that he had wanted one 'just to see how they go'. Why had he asked his niece's boyfriend to get him a pair of handcuffs? 'They just seemed interesting, that is all.'

Milat conceded that someone in the family must have been involved in the murders, but asked why he should have been singled out. He claimed he was innocent, but that Richard, and to a lesser extent Wally, were criminally involved. Martin took up the argument, telling the jury in his final address: 'If there was more than one, it could well be Richard Milat with Walter Milat or Richard or with a friend of Richard's or in combination.'

The jury was unimpressed and pronounced Milat guilty on all counts on Saturday 20 July, 1996. In his remarks on sentencing, Hunt said: 'In my view, it is inevitable that the person was not alone in that criminal enterprise.' He accepted Tedeschi's submission that Milat had killed for his own psychological gratification. He said: 'Whatever the actual cause of death may have been in each case, it is clear they were in each case subject to behaviour which, for callous indifference to suffering and for humanity, is almost beyond belief. They would obviously have been terrified and death is unlikely to have been swiftly applied.'

He sentenced Milat to life imprisonment.

On 4 November 1997, Milat, representing himself, appealed his conviction. It was the first time this writer, covering the appeal, had seen him. Clean-shaven and surprisingly bright and perky, even smiling, he seemed hardly the monster he had been portrayed as. He made a spirited submission on the points he had chosen: that the prosecutor in 1994 had severely prejudiced his case when initially omitting to say he had been acquitted on the rape charge, and that Onions' description of the spare wheel had not tallied with his vehicle.

But the court, which had set aside only one day for the hearing, quickly concluded that it was not enough. The then Chief Justice, Murray Gleeson, asked how, if Milat had not been the attacker, Onions' Next brand shirt been found at the home of Milat's mother. He said that if there had been a conspiracy, then that conspiracy must have gone back to the time Onions was attacked.

His appeal dismissed, Milat went back into the prison system. His name surfaced again when he was apparently involved in a conspiracy by convicted killer George Savvas to break out of Maitland Gaol, a plot which was foiled. In 1999, Milat made headlines claiming that he could identify who was responsible for the murders of two backpackers in the Gold Coast hinterland. The name or names he had in mind were not reported, but it was interpreted as an attempt by an embittered Milat to get back at brothers Richard and Wally.

On 30 September the same year, Jason Milat, Ivan's adopted son, pleaded guilty in the Hobart Supreme Court to attempted robbery. What chance Jason Milat ever had is a moot point. His early years were dominated by Milat. His mother had had to go into hiding. The publicity surrounding his adopted father's homicidal violence must surely have affected him. And he was cursed with the Milat name.

Milat undoubtedly had a sexual motive for the killings. He could hardly have got anything else out of it. The total value of camping equipment he took from the murder scenes would have only come to a few thousand dollars. Had he thought to protect himself at all, he would never have touched it. He need never have distributed it. He had had a chance, once he got wind of the police closing in, to get rid of incriminating evidence. But in the muddled brain of Ivan Milat, nothing much made sense.

The traumatised families returned to their lives. Caroline's parents arranged for the development of a special species of rose to be named after their daughter. Joanne's parents left a bouquet of flowers at the boulder where her body was found, and a card that read: 'No birthday card today Joanne. Just the love we have always had. Love always, Mum and Dad and Janet.' In time, the physical reminders of the grief, and of the slaughter, and of the police operation, would be swallowed up, and the great grey-green shroud of the Australian bush would envelop everything, returning to a state that had suggested such mystery and fear to D.H. Lawrence. But then, the fear did not emanate from the bush; it only seemed that way. The real source of such misgivings was, as it always is, humankind.

THE MURDER OF COLIN WINCHESTER

What the detective story is about is not murder
but the restoration of order.

P D James
English crime writer

One summer's evening in Canberra, 10 January 1989, an unseen assassin coolly fired two well-placed shots into the head of an unsuspecting assistant commissioner of police. The nation was shocked and quickly the cry went up: surely this was the work of organised crime. Who else could have stalked a high-ranking police officer, and then shot him dead in the driveway outside his Canberra home, and escaped undetected? Who else but a professional criminal could have identified his target's car approaching in the dark, watched it pull into a neighbour's adjoining driveway and, within eight seconds, slipped from the shadows and fired into the back and side of his victim's head?

The first shot was designed to kill; the second was just to make sure. Apart from two spent cartridge cases – identified as having come from a silenced .22 calibre self-loading Ruger rifle – the killer left no sign of his presence. No one saw him or his vehicle. With the exception of the victim's wife, no one heard anything, though a number of nearby residents reported hearing a V8-type vehicle leaving the area close to the time of the shooting.

Years later, a very experienced New South Wales crime intelligence operator, the former Detective Sergeant George Slade, would describe the killer of Assistant Commissioner Colin Stanley Winchester – aged 55, third-ranking in seniority in the Australian Federal Police (AFP) – as either a professional or a 'very, very lucky amateur'. That opinion was shared by many others, including some in the AFP itself.

But specific information came to hand soon after the murder. Within 24 hours, an informant contacted the AFP claiming that a Sydney horse trainer and private investigator, then in his early forties, had told him that a police officer was implicated in the murder, and that it had been carried out because Winchester was about to give evidence in a drug case that would expose corrupt police involved in drug dealings. What was most noteworthy about this tip-off was that it was so close (in time) to the murder itself.

At that stage, it was not well-known at all that Winchester was a key player in the drug-related committal hearing scheduled just three weeks away in the Queanbeyan Local Court. As police said at the coroner's inquest that followed, Winchester's link to the Bungendore crops was not a matter of general knowledge or media speculation. Allegations of police corruption were about to flow. If the story were true, someone was exceedingly well informed.

The informant's story was that five days after the murder he was told by the horse trainer that Detective Commander Ric Ninness, the joint head of the AFP murder investigation team, would be the next to die. He even gave the surname of the prospective killer, apparently a man of Lebanese extraction. The identities of these people could not be revealed publicity, due to suppression orders by the Australian Capital Territory's Coroner's Court in 1989.

The informant apparently happily admitted that he was a middle man in a drug distribution syndicate operating in Canberra, and that the horse trainer headed the ring. Police intelligence suggested there might be some truth to this claim. The fact that he was sticking his neck out for no apparent benefit to himself made police immediately sceptical. Nonetheless, they spoke to the horse trainer. He said a New South Wales police officer, whom he would not name, had told him that Winchester had been killed because of his involvement in the Bungendore case. But he had never heard of Ninness or his proposed assassin.

Police set out to trace the name of the would-be killer. They came across four men of that name, all brothers, all of whom might have fitted the bill. But all four had the perfect alibi: they were in gaol at the time of the murder. They identified a fifth man with the required name. He was nominated as someone linked to the heroin trade in the Australian Capital Territory. The informant's story was looking pretty reasonable.

There was understandably widespread disbelief when the AFP finally identified the prime suspect not as a mafioso, drug dealer or other such underworld figure, but a 44-year-old, overweight, myopic, former public servant, David Harold Eastman. Eastman seemed the most unlikely of hitmen, but was ultimately convicted and gaoled for life by the Supreme Court of the Australian Capital Territory. An appeal to the Federal Court in 1997 failed. Eastman has since launched a two-pronged High Court challenge in a bid to secure a retrial. His first attempt, based on a constitutional challenge to the trial judge's appointment, failed in September 1999. The second leg, based on a claim that he was mentally unfit to go on trial, was dismissed on 25 May 2000. Undaunted by the High Court's decision, Eastman immediately called for a judicial inquiry into the case. At the time of writing, Eastman was expected to lodge a request for this with the Australian Capital Territory's Supreme Court.

Shortly put, the case against Eastman centred on his one-time ownership of, and continued interest in, the same type of weapon as was used in the murder; a sighting of him at the home of the man who sold the murder weapon; death threats he made against Winchester; the discovery of gunshot residue in his car which was indistinguishable from that found at the murder scene.

There was one other significant fact. Less than a month before the killing, Eastman had obtained an interview with Winchester and had lobbied unsuccessfully to get an assault charge against him withdrawn. The meeting had been less than amicable. Winchester had refused to drop the charge. Written confirmation that the AFP would not do as Eastman wished might have been received by him on the day Winchester was shot.

Eastman went on trial in 1995 and the evidence, while overwhelmingly circumstantial, was arguably quite strong. It has often been said that a strong circumstantial case can be more compelling than one with more direct evidence. A jury can hear only so many coincidences before it is convinced beyond reasonable doubt. Eastman's explanation to the jury for his ongoing interest in purchasing a Ruger was most unconvincing. His inability to recall his movements on the night of the murder a mere 18 hours later was even less believable given his normally photographic memory.

Eastman's behaviour during his trial was bizarre. He abused the judge, Justice Ken Carruthers, and the prosecutor, Michael Adams QC in the most foul and intemperate way, often in front of the jury. He sacked four legal teams between May and November 1995. The most enduring and long-suffering, led by Sydney criminal trial specialist Winston Terracini, was dismissed more than a dozen times. Representing himself, Eastman refused to cross-examine all but two of the Crown's witnesses. On one occasion he did a superb job. On the second, he nearly hung himself in a performance which moved Terracini to later inform his client that he was 'a turkey'. Eastman allowed crucial witnesses, most notably his nemesis, the then Detective Commander Rick Ninness, the investigation chief, to come and go without challenge. If Eastman were ever going to defend himself successfully, he or his lawyers had to grill Ninness. But to do so could have backfired easily.

On the seventieth day of the 87-day trial, Eastman sacked his lawyers one more time, peremptorily terminated the defence case, and declared that he would not even address the jury before it passed judgment on him. Within a week, he was crawling back to his lawyers and begging them to return to the cause. Somewhat surprisingly, they agreed. But the damage had been done. An exasperated Justice Carruthers would only permit a limited re-opening of the defence case and would not allow into evidence material the defence team would have argued was consistent with Eastman's innocence.

Eastman was found guilty, and if he was innocent, he was the victim of one of the greatest failures of the Australian criminal justice system or one of the most comprehensive frame-ups and cover-ups imaginable. If he was innocent and there was no frame-up, just a monumental failure of the system to get it right, Eastman had largely himself to blame, because of the way he conducted himself during the trial. There were, however, many who remain sceptical. They were not just conspiracy theorists who wanted to believe that the system had conspired to frame an innocent man to protect powerful interests of some description. The sceptics included lawyers, journalists, former police and a good number of Canberrans, those who knew Eastman and those who did not.

But Eastman was to remain his own worst enemy. As late as June 1999, while awaiting the outcome of his High Court appeal, Eastman sacked another team of lawyers. He sacked his lawyers again in March 2000, simply to lodge his own supplementary submission to the High Court, one that didn't have to be made.

There were two key matters which might have come to light if Ninness had been cross-examined. One might have helped Eastman's lawyers construct a scenario consistent with the guilt of someone other than Eastman, and which the jury might have found more than vaguely interesting. This related to the theory that Winchester had been murdered by, or at the behest of, members of a Calabrian-style organised crime group known as 'Ndrangheta or The Honoured Society. In this regard, the contents of a semi-secret AFP report on the possible involvement of 'Ndrangheta had to be presented to the jury. An Australian Bureau of Criminal Intelligence (ABCI) report, which nominated Italian organised crime as probably behind the murder, might also have proved useful. But the jury never heard about these documents.

The second matter which might have emerged from the quizzing of Ninness was the existence of a large number of confidential reports prepared for the AFP by a Sydney forensic psychiatrist, Dr Rod Milton. While Eastman's lawyers sought to rely on these during High Court proceedings in 1999, his defence in 1995 was desperate to keep the Milton reports a million miles from the jury, so prejudicial were they to Eastman's cause. Reading the reports could quite easily have led a juror to believe that Eastman was a very dangerous man and more than capable of committing murder.

The Milton reports had another relevance, one which would counter the suggestion that Eastman had only himself to blame for the outcome of his murder trial. If Milton's diagnosis was correct, Eastman had long been suffering from paranoia, and this might have explained his outrageous and self-destructive conduct both prior to and at the trial. The Milton reports, coupled with his diagnoses of paranoid schizophrenia, would support the theory that Eastman had no control over his behaviour and was, therefore, not fit to plead to the charge or to instruct his lawyers. In other words, he was not fit to defend himself and should not have been put on trial. That proposition was at the heart of his High Court appeal.

So, what did the jury not hear that might have helped his cause? There were a number of matters his lawyers wanted to present to the court but were unable to because of an act of 'forensic suicide' on Eastman's part in sacking his lawyers and in other ways mishandling his case.

One thing the defence wanted to do was call as a witness a former near neighbour of the Winchester family. This witness's evidence, it was said, might have suggested that the killer had an accomplice, a possibility never remotely hinted at by the Crown in its case against Eastman. Not a lot would ever be known about what the reluctant witness might have said, because Terracini had not been able to convince the judge that this witness should be ordered to attend court from interstate. Several years earlier, in the months following the Winchester murder, the woman had complained that police had not taken her story seriously. She said that very close to the time of the murder, she had heard the footsteps and voices of two people on the gravel driveway outside her home office, shortly before they had departed in a vehicle. The driveway, lined with large conifers, had been directly in line with the point where an assassin, fleeing the Winchester home through rear yards, would have emerged in the adjoining street.

On its own, the woman's report to the police in 1989, was inconclusive. However, some years later, she apparently thought she might have been able to identify two men who had been outside her home within minutes of the murder: a man subsequently jailed for large-scale drug trafficking in Canberra, and a criminal associate of that man, from Melbourne. The first man could certainly have been placed in the area very close to the Winchester home some months after the killing. The woman's evidence might have pushed his links to the area back to the fateful day. Independently of the woman, this man had been nominated as a suspect in the murder and his alibi had been doubtful. But the investigation into him went nowhere. The idea that a major player in the Canberra drug scene, and one with indirect links to police, had been known to frequent the area in which Winchester lived, and may have actually been there on the night of the murder, never saw the light of day. Nor did the fact that the man owned a V8 vehicle. V8 vehicles figured in the evidence on more than one occasion. Apart from the drug dealer, two other people of some interest to police in this investigation apparently owned, or had access to, a V8 vehicle.

The case was perplexing. Though there was sufficient evidence to convict Eastman, the notion of darker forces, a conspiracy, a contract killing of the type that had taken away Griffith anti-drugs campaigner Don Mackay, was alive and well. Police investigating the horse trainer had discovered in his diary a reference to a notorious former New South Wales detective. That detective had been nominated independently as being corruptly involved in the Bungendore plantations. As recently as April 1999, the horse trainer and the ex-detective were linked at a New South Wales Police Integrity Commission inquiry. Once again, suppression orders imposed nearly a decade ago prevent identification of these figures. The credibility of the informant who told police about the horse trainer might have improved further when police learned that the horse trainer drove a V8 Ford LTD. But the investigation apparently went no further. Federal police accepted their New South Wales counterparts' opinion that the informant was no more than a 'clever and manipulative liar'.

In police evidence presented to the coroner's inquest into Winchester's death, there was specific reference to the fact that Frank Patrick Barbaro, one of two Canberra men who had provided an important alibi on the night of the murder, had access to a V8. Barbaro was the son of Pasquale Domenico Barbaro, a person nominated to police by two of their many informants as being in on the plot to kill Winchester. The inquest also heard that a Riverina man, also called Pasquale Barbaro, but much younger, had been stopped at a police roadblock early on the morning following the murder, test-driving the V8 he had obtained from his cousin Frank's residence.

More important to the defence case was material prepared by the AFP which, it was suggested, pointed to Calabrian-style organised crime as the source of the killer. Some of this material had been published before, well before Eastman's trial. But some of the most compelling material remained totally secret until midway through the trial, and never made it into evidence anyway. The material Terracini wanted to present was contained in an AFP report entitled 'Suspicion of Calabrian Organised Crime Involvement in the Murder of Assistant Commissioner Colin Stanley Winchester', prepared by Commander Bob McDonald, head of AFP operations in New South Wales and an expert in Italian organised crime. Roughly one third of McDonald's report was released in 1991 as an appendix to the report of the coronial inquiry into the Winchester murder. But the remainder was suppressed. During Eastman's trial, defence lawyers sought to get the whole report into evidence. This was opposed by the AFP and the National Crime Authority (NCA) for reasons relating to police operations and the protection of sources. Ultimately, Justice Carruthers declared that roughly another third of McDonald's report was protected from disclosure on public interest immunity grounds. The remaining third was not so protected, but Eastman's lawyers never got to use it.

The Calabrians were an integral part of the story because of their cannabis-growing activities during 1981–83 in the Bungendore district, east of Canberra. After one of their group, Canberra supermarket proprietor and Labor Party member Joe Verduci, approached police with information, Winchester became head of AFP operations. The plan was to allow the crops to be grown, in an ambitious bid to identify the financiers and controllers behind them. Later evidence strongly suggested that those responsible for the crops thought Winchester and his deputy, Detective Sergeant Brian Lockwood, were being paid off. They may well have assumed that New South Wales police were also in their pockets. There was no evidence to support such assumptions, but the entire operation, known to New South Wales Police as Operation Seville and to the AFP as Operation Sanctum, was ill-fated and in many ways a fiasco.

The alleged participants in the Bungendore crops were arrested by NCA officers months before Winchester was murdered, although years after the crops themselves had been harvested, ripped-off or destroyed. The proximity of the committal proceedings against the Bungendore cultivators to the murder of Colin Winchester was, superficially at least, compelling. But there was more to support a conspiracy theory than that. The edited McDonald report contained a claim that the decision to have Winchester murdered was made at a meeting in Canberra attended by two interstate police officers and three Italian criminals. Following the meeting, the assassination was carried out by a mysterious Ukrainian hitman known only as Jabranov.

The sources of that information were two men: Mario 'The Fox' Cannistra, who had moved from Canberra to the western suburbs of Sydney, and a Sydney private investigator, Joe Sassine. Cannistra, one of those charged over the Bungendore crops, was of Calabrian extraction. Sassine, of Lebanese extraction, was described by McDonald as 'supposedly' associated with the criminal element and corrupt New South Wales police. McDonald's view received some support many years later when a Sydney detective told the New South Wales Police Royal

Commission that he had had a corrupt relationship with Sassine, who was known as a 'Mr Fixit' between police and ethnic communities. The detective, codenamed WS14, told the commission that Sassine had been 'pretty connected' with Task Force One, a key investigative group within the New South Wales Drug Enforcement Agency. Cannistra told AFP investigators about Jabranov four months after the killing. He claimed the Ukrainian had been flown to Australia to do the hit. One of the Italians allegedly involved had been Pasquale Domenico Barbaro, a long-time Canberra resident who was murdered outside his Brisbane home in 1990. He had also been shot, but not seriously wounded, in April 1989, three months after the Winchester killing.

The story told by Cannistra and Sassine was a bit of a many-headed monster at times. While hearing that the murder had been arranged by corrupt police, presumably from New South Wales, and the Calabrians, AFP investigators also heard that the murder was tied in with what Winchester 'found out in Sydney' – whatever that meant – rather than with the Bungendore operation. Sassine later talked of unreported murders during the Bungendore operation and of other rip-offs of drug crops. Winchester apparently had found out about all this – in Sydney, perhaps – and was killed to shut him up. Verduci, the supermarket proprietor who was giving information to police, said that a worker on one of the Bungendore crops – one 'Frank of Turin' – had been murdered and buried on-site. A Calabrian from Sydney was named as the killer. Cannistra tried to push a line that the NCA had been established as a 'political cover-up' for the Bungendore operation, that Winchester had played a key role in its establishment, and that his murder was related to all of this. Such a nonsensical theory – Winchester had nothing at all to do with the NCA's creation – did Cannistra's credibility no good at all. Cannistra and Sassine also linked the murder of Winchester to the murders of three Italians, all of whom were involved in the drug trade. One, Giuseppe Monteleone, may have had an interest in the Bungendore crop before his execution-style murder at Narrabri in western New South Wales in 1982. He was reputedly an associate of Pasquale

Barbaro, but there appears to be no other link between the murders of the three Italians (and seven others between 1980 and 1984) and that of Winchester several years later.

It was only after Cannistra and Sassine had floated all these other theories about the murder that they came up with the Jabranov story. And to complete the picture, they dropped in the names of well-known but now deceased crime bosses Lenny McPherson and George Freeman, plus a once high-profile politician and an eminent Sydney QC.

So who are all these people that Cannistra and Sassine were dobbing in? Pasquale Barbaro, who was born in Plati, Calabria, in 1931, was the elder brother of Tony and Rocco Barbaro, both of whom had lived in Canberra. Tony Barbaro moved to Melbourne, Rocco to Hillston in southern New South Wales. Pasquale was alleged to be the top 'Ndrangheta man in Canberra in the early 1980s. Rocco Barbaro had two convictions for cultivating cannabis. In 1975, he had pleaded guilty to growing 15,000 plants on his farm at Tharbogang, near Griffith, a crop which in 1999 values would have retailed for $30 million. He had been given a suspended sentence, fined $250, and released on a bond. This outcome had outraged many Griffith residents, including anti-drugs campaigner Donald Mackay. In 1996, Barbaro was jailed for eight years over his involvement in a $16 million cannabis plantation at Yuleba near Roma, in south-west Queensland. The Queensland conviction was the end result of a mammoth NCA-led operation, codenamed Pegasus, which resulted in 13 arrests and the discovery of five plantations worth more than $60 million.

The Barbaro brothers were also charged over the Bungendore cannabis crops, as were Cannistra and several others. They were charged by the NCA rather than by New South Wales Police, several months before Winchester was murdered. A number of these men were also charged over a $40 million cannabis crop at Guyra, in central northern New South Wales. In addition, Tony Barbaro was prosecuted for a $500,000 cannabis deal in 1980 at One Tree Plain, near Hay, allegedly involving himself, a number of Italians from South Australia and Victoria, and undercover police.

The seized cannabis ended up at Flemington police station in Sydney, from where it was subsequently stolen by corrupt detectives and sold.

Committal proceedings, relating to Bungendore, Guyra and One Tree Plain, against 12 men, 11 Italians and a Greek commenced in the Queanbeyan Local Court less than a month after the Winchester killing. All charges were ultimately dismissed or withdrawn because of the failure of the principal prosecution witness, Joe Verduci, to give any worthwhile evidence against his former associates. Verduci clammed up at the committal hearing, ostensibly fearing he would suffer the same fate as Winchester. He told police: 'If Winchester could not be protected, why should I give evidence and face certain death?' Outside the courtroom, however, he was more than happy to continue talking to the media.

A second attendee at that alleged assassination meeting was said to be a 46-year-old South Australian of Calabrian extraction, Frank Spagnolo, sometimes known as 'One-Eyed Frank'. Cannistra and Sassine did not name him, but police worked out who they were talking about. Spagnolo had been linked to alleged members of 'Ndrangheta operating in Adelaide, and to a young Calabrian-born man, Bruno Musitano, who was once identified to the AFP by Italian police, the Carabinieri, as the possible Winchester killer. McDonald reported Spagnolo had been linked to 'Ndrangheta cells in Canberra and Griffith and was suspected of being involved heavily in the cultivation and distribution of cannabis.

A mere fortnight after the murder, the Carabinieri passed on the news that two of Musitano's brothers had been murdered in Italy and that Musitano had, just three months before Winchester's murder, travelled to Australia to perform a deed to 'redeem his family's honour'. Musitano travelled to Australia in October, 1988, in the company of another young man from Plati, Giuseppe Ielasi. Ielasi, a nephew of the Barbaro brothers, was in Canberra on the night of the Winchester murder. There is no evidence Musitano ever went there. Ielasi was subsequently investigated by police because of his relationship with the Barbaro family. For the night of the murder, he was provided with an alibi by Frank Barbaro, a son of Pasquale's, and Giuseppe Nirta, whose father had recently been charged over the Bungendore cannabis crops.

Spagnolo also figured in an earlier allegation to the AFP. An informer claimed he had delivered cannabis to Spagnolo on behalf of the one-time head of detectives at Queanbeyan, the late Detective Inspector Bill Cullen. This assertion, and broader ones of corruption, was emphatically rejected later by a former colleague of Cullen's, the then Detective Superintendent Mal Brammer, who went on to become the reforming head of the New South Wales Police Service operation in Kings Cross. Spagnolo's alleged role in the murder took on greater significance some months after the Cannistra/Sassine story was first told. Two men of considerable interest to police, Musitano and his father-in-law, Umberto Pollifrone, were seen visiting Spagnolo's Adelaide home on 9 September 1989. Musitano had already been identified as a possible murder suspect and Pollifrone and his son, John, were regarded by the AFP as 'Ndrangheta members. Earlier that day, police had raided the Adelaide homes of Musitano and his wife Caterina, her parents, Umberto and Maria Pollifrone, and her brother John, his wife Teresa and Teresa's mother, Caterina Trimboli. Four days later, a police bug recorded Musitano's cousin, Sam Catanzariti, telephoning Musitano and instructing him and Pollifrone senior to meet that evening at 'Uncle Frank's' home to discuss the raids.

The AFP was interested in Musitano when Italian police passed on the fact that he had been identified to them as the Winchester killer by an informant from within the Australian–Calabrian community. Its interest was further heightened during another Adelaide bugging operation. The translation of taped conversations from this operation strongly suggested that Musitano had killed a man who had betrayed 'Ndrangheta and had carried out the task at the behest of his father-in-law, Pollifrone. According to the translation, Musitano, speaking in Calabrian dialect, was heard to say, 'I had to shoot him in the head. I even have the gun here.' Later, he purportedly told his wife he did not want to kill any more and that her father promised 'that I would kill one who is against *omerta* (the code of silence). Now what else does he want from me?'

At about the same time, police bugged a so-called Calabrian organised crime summit in Adelaide and heard talk of the acquisition of a .22 calibre Ruger pistol. They would have noticed immediately that it was a .22 Ruger – probably a rifle but possibly a pistol – that had been used to execute Winchester on the eve of court proceedings which might have been regarded by the defendants as representing the betrayal of 'Ndrangheta.

As McDonald put it, once those involved in the Bungendore crops were charged, 'an act of treacherous betrayal on the assistant commissioner's behalf was perceived by this criminal group and a motive for murder tends to emerge, particularly when consideration is given to the code under which this criminal organisation operates.'

In short, within seven months of the Winchester murder, police were aware that Winchester had been intimately involved in a police operation involving 'Ndrangheta drug crops near Bungendore. He had been shot dead with .22 calibre Ruger three weeks before the participants in growing those crops, who apparently thought Winchester had been 'bought', were to face the courts. Australian–Calabrian crime figures had expressed interest in acquiring a similar weapon to the one that killed Winchester. Some of those involved in the Bungendore crops could be linked directly to Spagnolo, Musitano and Pollifrone in Adelaide. Musitano, who had travelled to Australia four months before the murder with a close relative of the Barbaros, was a murder suspect. Spagnolo had been identified as allegedly being part of the murder plot, as had another Barbaro brother. Musitano had been bugged while apparently discussing a murder carried out at Pollifrone's request. Is it any wonder, then, that the AFP team investigating the Calabrians thought it was onto something and identified the Musitano/Ielasi material as 'the most positive indication yet' that the Winchester murder had been an 'Ndrangheta hit?

It must be reiterated here that no evidence of any substance ever emerged that Winchester had been behaving corruptly.

But the whole scenario might have taken on a new significance a few years later, if anyone had still been interested, when Musitano was arrested on a $16 million cannabis plantation in the Northern Territory. The alleged mastermind of this was South Australian Domenic Perre, the man accused in 1994 of the fatal bombing of the NCA's Adelaide office. That charge was dropped but Perre was sentenced to a long gaol term for conspiring to manufacture amphetamines and for organising the Northern Territory crop. In September 1999, an Adelaide coroner declared that Perre was, in fact, responsible for the NCA bombing.

A lot of the steam went out of the Calabrian theory long before any of this though, back in 1990, when police arranged to have the Musitano tapes enhanced and re-translated. To their dismay, and subsequent embarrassment, an entirely new version of the conversation was produced. Gone was all reference to guns, bullets and shooting someone in the head. Gone was any trace of the distinctive Italian word, *omerta*. Instead, they were told that Musitano and his new wife had been involved in sexual activity and that had been the subject of their taped discussion. How so-called expert interpreters could get it so wrong is hard to fathom.

While the AFP seemed to lose interest in the Calabrian theory, the ABCI did not. More than a year after McDonald's report was prepared, the ABCI produced an intelligence assessment which proffered the view that on the balance of probabilities, 'Ndrangheta members had been responsible for the Winchester murder. The AFP rejected this proposition and told the Coroner for the Australian Capital Territory inquiring into Winchester's death, Ron Cahill, that the matter needed no further investigation. And that, it seems, was the end of the matter.

Little is known about the ABCI report. It has never been released publicly or admitted into evidence. However, Eastman dropped a few tidbits along the way after a copy was inadvertently given to his legal team. From these it can be gleaned that the ABCI had more than a passing interest in a former Canberra businessman allegedly involved in the drug trade and with strong links to 'Ndrangheta heavies in the Riverina and Canberra. Some years later, the businessman became the focus of New South Wales organised crime squad interest. The ABCI report apparently referred to a huge shipment of heroin that had arrived in Queensland shortly after the Winchester murder. An anonymous informant told police at the time that the shipment and the Winchester murder were somehow connected. The ABCI report apparently contains the suggestion that a link could, in fact, be found between one of those arrested for the heroin importation and the Canberra businessman. But none of this ever saw the light of day while Eastman's fate rested in the hands of a jury.

Some people might have had a motive for falsely implicating Pasquale Barbaro senior in a murder plot. He had become *persona non grata* within the Calabrian community for leaving his Italian wife and marrying a Filipina. It may have been this that led to his being twice shot, the second time fatally. Some years later, another member of the same extended family was shot and seriously injured for having an affair with the wife of a prominent Calabrian figure from the Riverina.

Barbaro was murdered outside his Brisbane home on 18 March 1990 by a young Italian man. He was shot in the chest with a .38 calibre pistol and had also been stabbed. Ironically, Barbaro had earlier told police that when a murder victim was knifed as well as shot, it was because the killer wanted to 'show the population who understand that this man was dishonest, he do something forbidden'. Barbaro was doing something forbidden in the latter part of 1989: he was talking to the NCA. He apparently told police something of the workings of 'Ndrangheta, while denying his or any of his immediate family's involvement, and he identified a number of men from the Riverina region as being behind the earlier attempt on his life.

As for Joe Verduci, the man who became Winchester's informant during the Bungendore crops saga, Barbaro described him as 'a cheat, a liar and a bastard' who had been involved with police from Canberra and had paid Winchester for organising a crop. But, said Barbaro, Winchester had 'changed the plans'. (It is not in contention that Verduci gave money to Winchester to give the appearance that he had corrupt police on side. The money was then paid into consolidated revenue.)

Very shortly after the murder of Colin Winchester, senior police briefed psychiatrist Dr Milton on their prime suspect, Eastman. Eastman was first spoken to by police 18 hours after the murder, once it had been discovered that he had seen Winchester in person less than a month earlier, and in less than cordial circumstances. Eastman was spoken to again a day later and, within the week, his flat had been raided and his car was impounded. From the very earliest days of the investigation, Eastman was at or near the top of the suspect list. It is remarkable, therefore, that it was not until December 1992, nearly three years after the murder, that he was arrested. Another three years elapsed before he was found guilty and gaoled for life.

Six weeks after the murder, Milton provided the AFP with the first of 13 reports. This detailed Eastman's personal and psychiatric history, including the fact that he had commenced psychiatric treatment at the age of 21, two decades before he shot Winchester. (Eastman's twin sisters had long been hospitalised with severe mental disorders.)

Eastman's condition had apparently deteriorated from about the age of 29. He started losing his friends, dropping out of social and sporting interests and, eventually, tossing in his job in an irrational fit of pique which, in a roundabout way, 12 years later cost Winchester his life.

Between 1977, when he resigned from the Treasury, and early 1989, Eastman went to extraordinary lengths, first, to get his resignation converted to a medically related retirement, then to prove himself medically fit to return to the Public Service, and finally, to obtain re-employment. He succeeded on the first two points but failed on the third.

A pivotal event took place in late 1987. Eastman was involved in an altercation with a neighbour and was charged with assault. He saw this as grossly unfair and, at the very least, believed the other man should have been charged, too. More importantly, he saw the prospect of an assault conviction as a major threat to his chances of getting back into the Public Service. He pulled out all stops to get the charge withdrawn, culminating in an interview with Winchester (accompanied by shadow attorney-general Neil Brown) on 16 December 1988. The interview went badly, and when Eastman made derogatory remarks about police, Winchester jumped down his throat. Milton thought this, and the occasion in 1977 when he was carpeted at work for leaking information to the media, were probably the only times in his life when people had stood up to Eastman. On the first occasion Eastman had destroyed his career. On the second, 'he might well have taken Mr Winchester's life'.

In 1976, after Eastman's parents returned from Mexico, where his father had served as Australian ambassador, Eastman began displaying violent tendencies and his parents had to seek police intervention. His psychiatrist commented that violence was characteristic of the paranoid person and that Eastman 'was out of control'. Milton thought Eastman had a severe paranoid personality behaviour, 'with a tendency to react towards others with great suspicion, to feel entitled to use aggression and violence against them in the furtherance of his aims and wishes, and to engage in endless efforts to prove himself right'. Milton concluded in that first report that Eastman was 'a typical, dangerous, paranoid personality', a textbook example of the condition.

Later, Milton expressed the view that Eastman's interview with Winchester in December 1988 had had a major emotional impact, both symbolically and in reality. These factors provided a probable motive for murder. Milton continued: 'His silence in the face of knowing he is a suspect, having his flat searched and being under surveillance, is extraordinarily uncharacteristic of him. If he believed himself to be innocent, his sense of outrage would be monumental... His failure to remember his movements on the night of the murder is unacceptable – paranoid, intelligent persons do not have lapses of memory of this type. His visit to the prostitute that night is not inconsistent with him having committed a murder, and, in fact, his heightened pleasure that night might well have derived from a sense of release and achievement at having just killed a powerful and very masculine person.'

During the first year or two following the murder, the issue of alleged police harassment was at the top of Eastman's agenda.

Never mind that he was being publicly touted as the prime suspect, that up to 30 detectives were working on his case, and that a very public inquest was proceeding and would ultimately lead to his being charged with murder. Rather, Eastman appeared to concentrate his efforts on exposing police harassment and having the incessant surveillance removed. When it was suggested to him that his own best interests would be better served by having a lawyer at the inquest to protect his interests, Eastman became abusive.

The supposed harassment became a significant public and political issue and, following media exposure, won Eastman considerable public sympathy. Eastman was able to photograph at close quarters members of the surveillance team and their vehicles, using a cheap throwaway camera. Some of his photographs, and details of his repeated sightings of unmarked police vehicles, appeared in the *Canberra Times*. The strong impression was of a patently overt surveillance operation designed to goad Eastman into a violent response justifying his arrest.

The Milton reports threw a different light on the issue. As early as February 1989, Milton told the AFP that continued surveillance was not only justified but necessary to protect the community. There was no way Eastman could be committed to an institution under existing mental health laws, and the only way to protect the public was through surveillance. Milton expressed surprise that Eastman had so far not baulked at the police presence. This was to change dramatically in the months and years to follow.

It was another year before Milton was called in once more to assist police. In January 1990, Milton was aware that Eastman had been linked to a rifle similar to the murder weapon and that he had listened to the output of a secret bugging operation which captured Eastman talking to himself at length. Milton was of the view that Eastman 'should now be regarded as psychotic [insane] and suspect he has been this way for a long time'.

This passage, and others like it, took on more considerable significance when Eastman's High Court appeal was heard in 1999. At that time, his lawyers were arguing that Eastman's mental condition was such that he had not been fit to plead or instruct his lawyers at his 1995 murder trial and that his conviction at that time should therefore be quashed.

Milton thought surveillance, both physical and electronic, should continue, to protect both Eastman and others. He suggested that Eastman might take his own life, a prediction which remained unfulfilled the best part of ten years later. He told Ninness to continue having direct contact with Eastman, both as a form of personal protection and also to provide Eastman with an opportunity to talk, something he felt Eastman greatly needed to do. And he thought Eastman admired and respected both Ninness and his authority, although his abusive remarks might suggest otherwise. His idea, that Eastman might be approaching the stage where confessing would be a relief, was also wildly inaccurate, unless Eastman's utterances to him are regarding as 'confessing'.

The following is the police version of part of an Eastman monologue secretly recorded in June 1990. This material was played to the jury at Eastman's trial.

Eastman was recorded as saying: 'Be the first of many people, and there's no doubt I had it in mind I should never have murdered, neglection of duty, in a police department. A famous evidence frame-up. To discover how common, this experience along life's rocky road is for everyone… I wanted you to straighten it, you're a cop. I'll go to the top okay, I warned you, straighten, straighten those men, straighten them, your officers, out. Let there be a murder trial, but remember those people, they find it very hard then to face the fact that you have killed.

'Make them remember the, remember the crime, relax… the bastards, but of all the menace… Minimise the reliance on medication, that's crucial you know. Now just think of it, c***, it's useless. I never wanted them to know, I think they know, that I killed Winchester and nobody in the projection room really knows what I've created. So sorry I had to kill him sitting down for you. And some of them will take great… it's going to make them feel… You wait for it, everything will be grey, and yet all it needs is someone to, everything is so different, the sky is great, the sun isn't, is that vital. Depression is one thing. Winchester is dead, do you think, why was I worried about that. Black or white now… the nature of the depression, that who is ah, you made the…

'If you could just keep that thought. I don't know the thing that I worry about. The depression is twaining in the making, in the making of, in the making, it's shrinking and it's magnified. I've just, I've killed, I've killed. If I could just, the pressure of making all these decisions. They're definitely, if I could just… just not make any sudden decisions.

'He was the first man. He was the first man I ever killed. It was a beautiful thing, one of the most beautiful feelings you've ever known, beautiful feelings… It's simple at the end of your life. You will never… not only that I doubt that when I doubt… You will… that's the husband, the man, the child and the parent.'

It is important to bear in mind that this was the police version of what Eastman was saying. There were several other versions, most prepared by phonetics experts from Australia and Europe and some dramatically different from the AFP version. For instance, where police had Eastman saying: 'I never wanted them to know, I think they know, that I killed Winchester.' British expert Dr Peter French believed the words probably were: 'I never wanted you to know that… I kept following her.' On the other hand, French tended to agree with the AFP's claim that Eastman had said: 'He was the first man I ever killed.' A second British audio expert, Christopher Mills, thought the tapes as a whole were of such poor quality that they should never been transcribed in the first place.

In mid-1990, Milton was exhorting police not to withdraw surveillance. While pulling out would reduce Eastman's aggressive behaviour, it might also give him the opportunity 'to express it in a more direct and malignant fashion', although only if he was, in fact, already a killer. Milton thought that if Eastman still had access to a firearm, as police suspected, he might well use it 'on one or more of an increasing number of people whom he perceives as having disappointed him or offended him'.

As it turned out, this was a timely warning. Within weeks of Milton's remarks being passed to the AFP, Eastman allegedly threatened to kill half a dozen people, and made threatening and abusive telephone calls to a score of others, all in a single day. According to evidence given in the Magistrate's Court of the Australian Capital Territory in 1992, Eastman had threatened to shoot several people, all of whom might well be seen as individuals in positions of power or influence who, to his mind, had let him down. The same might be said of Winchester, back in December 1988. Eastman has never been put on trial for making those death threats, and may never be. The charges were left pending in the Australian Capital Territory's Supreme Court until all proceedings relating to the murder charge were finally disposed of.

Police surveillance was called off in early August 1990. A week later, Eastman had a chance encounter with a detective on the Australian National University campus. He immediately assumed that surveillance had recommenced and became extremely angry. It was later that day that he made a string of threatening phone calls to politicians, senior bureaucrats, lawyers and journalists. He was also seen in a police car park, as he had been on the day Winchester was shot. Milton commented: 'It is of grave concern that he does not even attempt to conceal his homicidal urges now, but speaks openly of shooting people.'

Milton noted also that Eastman had frequently returned to an area of bushland where he had been seen a number of times, apparently searching for something. Police suspected that the murder weapon might have been concealed in the area but nothing was ever found. He concluded with the advice that surveillance should be resumed. Once Eastman was over his initial period of arousal and anger, he was more likely to once again direct his annoyance at police, 'rather than to a wide spectrum of people in positions of authority and influence'.

Three weeks later, Milton again recommended the resumption of surveillance. Eastman had been charged over the death threats and had 97 outstanding charges against him. He had received advice from the Public Service that he would never be mentally fit to return to work. He had become alienated from everyone and was being openly reported as the police's prime suspect. Even the 'comfort' of surveillance was no longer present. His situation 'becomes progressively more desperate', said Milton. Suicide was a distinct possibility.

Milton did not communicate with police again until early 1992. By then the coroner had returned an open finding into the murder of Winchester (it would be another ten months before the inquest was re-opened, leading to Eastman's arrest in December 1992). Eastman was then facing 90 criminal charges. He was also increasingly isolated. He had been banned from three Canberra hotels, youth hostels in Sydney and Melbourne, and had been kicked out of a local bushwalking club (after trying to push a walker's head into a camp fire) and the Labor Party. He remained in a birdwatching club and had started voluntary work with Meals on Wheels. He would also set his alarm for the early hours so he could wake and bang a saucepan on his neighbour's wall.

Milton thought Winchester's death 'could have represented the most successful and aggressive act in Mr Eastman's whole life'. But on the other hand, he said: 'it could have brought to the surface longstanding conflict regarding his wish for affection and recognition by his father, who had died in late 1987, as well as hostility and aggression towards that person.' Public safety remained a concern and Eastman was still 'a potentially very dangerous man'. He could decide at short notice to take violent action against someone he felt had particularly wronged him, such as Ninness or a prominent political, bureaucratic or legal figure.

Most significantly, Milton reported: 'Mr Eastman suffers from a serious emotional disorder and it is this which underlies his aggression and hostility. His disorder is sufficiently severe as to be likely to qualify for a defence of diminished responsibility were he to face trial for Mr Winchester's murder. The late Dr Macdonald, who treated David Eastman for a long while, considered that Mr Eastman would eventually require to be placed in an institution because of mental illness.'

Some months later, Eastman threw a jug of water at a Canberra magistrate but missed. During 1992, he had a number of run-ins with magistrates. One magistrate jailed him for seven days for contempt and another committed him for trial on assault and threatening phone call charges. Milton thought that at least one of the magistrates was in danger because he had appeared sympathetic to Eastman but had then 'betrayed' him. Eastman was bugged talking about the third magistrate and saying to himself, 'I'll go and get my gun and pay you a visit'.

As stated previously, Eastman's High Court appeal is unresolved at the time of writing. But rarely could a more convoluted and complex prime suspect than this have ever been found.

JAIDYN, THE BOY WHO NEVER HAD A CHANCE

*Far from being the basis of the good society,
the family, with its narrow privacy and tawdry secrets,
is the source of all our discontents.*

Edmund Leach
English anthropologist

Who killed Jaidyn Leskie, broke his arm, beat him to death and then stuffed the tiny body is a sleeping bag, weighed it down with a crow bar and threw it into deep water? What sort of person would do that to a 14-month-old child?

Many people, including members of the Victorian homicide squad, thought they knew the answer to that question. But the jury, which sat through the 1998 trial of the man charged with Jaidyn's murder, was not convinced by the web of circumstantial evidence the prosecution spun against him.

What probably influenced the jury was the possibility that the wispy-haired young man in front of them, the last person known to have seen the infant alive, had just been in the wrong place at the wrong time, and that another person, someone mysterious and malevolent, had seized upon an opportunity, slipped in and out of the house and then ended the child's life. Such things had happened before, and in the muddled, unhappy world from which Jaidyn's family came, it was at least a possibility.

And of his seemingly incoherent and rambling account of events? Well, so what? What rule-book is there that prescribes how people must react to traumatic events? There were many questions to be raised over the case, and many answers, none conclusive.

The story began in June 1997, in a town called Moe in Victoria's LaTrobe Valley. Before the events that followed, few people outside Victoria would have heard much of Moe, let alone been there. It took, until the burst of unwelcome publicity, a degree of local knowledge even to know how to pronounce the town's name, which outsiders were inclined to rhyme with 'toe', rather than 'toey'. Moe has been called a lot of things since – and because of – the child murder with which its name will be as inextricably linked as Snowtown is with the grisly mass murders revealed in 1999 in South Australia. Moe has been painted, with unblushing inaccuracy, as both a sleepy hillbilly 'hamlet' and as a ghetto gripped by a nightmare of unemployment, crime, drugs and catastrophic social breakdown.

Descriptions have veered from ribald images of hicktown inbreeding to solemn denunciations of urban decay inflicted by Thatcherite policies in the post-industrial, economic rationalist age. Neither sweeping generalisation is justified, though easy enough to understand. The truth is, Moe at the time of the events in this saga, was just a big country town fallen on hard times.

Moe is in the heart of the Latrobe Valley, at the western end of the brown coal fields once grandly described by the late Victorian Premier, Sir Henry Bolte, as 'Victoria's Ruhr'. It was one of a string of towns – the others are Yallourn, Morwell and Traralgon – which became big working class centres in the 1950s and 1960s, when the State Electricity Commission expanded rapidly to meet the power demands of post-war expansion. In the 1970s, the Latrobe Valley Hotel in Morwell was reputed to have the highest liquor sales outside Melbourne's enormous suburban 'beer barns', and local Holden and Ford car dealerships and television stores were a licence to make money.

But that was before 20,000 jobs were lost in 'The Valley', most of them in the 1990s. The towns came to share the problems of their New South Wales equivalents, such as Newcastle and Wollongong, where the old heavy industries were dying faster than anything could be established to replace them. Unemployment was high, real estate prices depressed, and there would hardly have been a street without several households relying on some sort of social security benefit. The same could have been said about Dandenong, an outer-eastern suburb of Melbourne, just an hour away by road, not to mention western suburbs like Sunshine and St Albans. For all that, the casual observer who bothered to drive into Moe from the Princes Highway by-pass was not immediately confronted by a provincial slum.

On the Melbourne side of Moe was 'Old Gippstown', a replica of a 19th-century bush town more like the real thing than a theme park. Opposite was the racecourse, one of the better provincial tracks close to Melbourne and home of the time-honoured Moe Racing Club. Nearby was the golf club, framed by a postcard backdrop of green paddocks and blue hills. The shopping strip running beside the railway line was clean and well-kept. Nature strips were mown. The railway station was freshly painted, neat and without the graffiti that blights most suburban stations. Many of Moe's public buildings were built in its heyday in the 1960s. One was the police station, a solid cream brick structure that got plenty of business most nights, especially on weekends and pension days.

At 5.15 am on Sunday June 15 1997, it was cold, dark and lonely. The buzzer, sounding at the station's front door, was answered by Senior Constable Farnham Molesworth, one of three officers on duty. When Sergeant Maxwell Hill looked up from his desk a few seconds later, he saw a couple talking agitatedly to Molesworth. The male had a slight figure with a gnomish face and thin, sandy hair worn long at the back and prematurely bald at the front. He recognised him as Gregory Nicholas Domaszewicz, 28, whom he knew as someone in a fringe group that regularly came to police notice. The young woman, who had bleached blonde hair, looked dazed and upset. He was soon to know her as Bilynda Murphy.

Hill got up and walked to the counter. 'Greg, what's happened?' he asked. There followed a bizarre exchange. Domaszewicz said:

'Her baby's been kidnapped, me window's been smashed and they've left a pig's head there!'

Hill: 'What?'

Domaszewicz reiterated: 'Someone's smashed me windows and taken her baby!'

'What's this about a pig's head?'

'Yeah, they've left a pig's head outside me window!'

'What, a real one?'

'Yeah!'

Domaszewicz was flustered and spoke so quickly he was hard to understand. Bilynda Murphy was crying, and obviously affected by alcohol. She managed to say her full name was Bilynda Robynne Murphy, aged 21, and that her child was Jaidyn Raymond Leskie.

She said: 'He's one – 14 months!'

Hill: 'Where's he gone missing from?'

'I don't know!'

She pointed at Greg Domaszewicz and said: 'He told me he was in hospital.'

Hill: 'What did he tell you?'

Domaszewicz cut in: 'They took him from my place in Narracan Drive!' he said.

Hill continued with Bilynda Murphy. 'What did he tell you about the hospital?' he asked.

She replied: 'He told me Jaidyn was in hospital.'

Hill turned to Domaszewicz: 'Is he in hospital or is he missing?' he asked.

Domaszewicz replied: 'He's been taken from my house. He's not in hospital.'

'Who's taken him?'

'I don't know.'

Hill, a policeman for 21 years, half of it in the Latrobe Valley, was perplexed. Domaszewicz, on his own account, had been the last identifiable person to have seen the child alive, and yet his version of events contradicted what Bilynda Murphy said he had told her only a short time before. Domaszewicz told him he had left Jaidyn asleep on the couch of his house at 150 Narracan Drive, Moe,

The funeral of Assistant Commissioner of Police Colin Winchester,
who was assassinated outside his home on 10 January 1989.

Following Winchester's assassination, police search the car that he was parking in his driveway when he was murdered.

David Eastman is arrested at his Reid flat on 23 December 1992, and charged with the murder of Colin Winchester.

Detective Commander Ric Ninness (right) and Australian Federal Police counsel, Brian Macquire, arrive at the Winchester inquest.

Gwen Winchester and her son Peter leave from the High Court of Australia after Eastman's failed appeal.

Jaidyn Leskie was 14 months old when he disappeared. His body was later found in a dam.

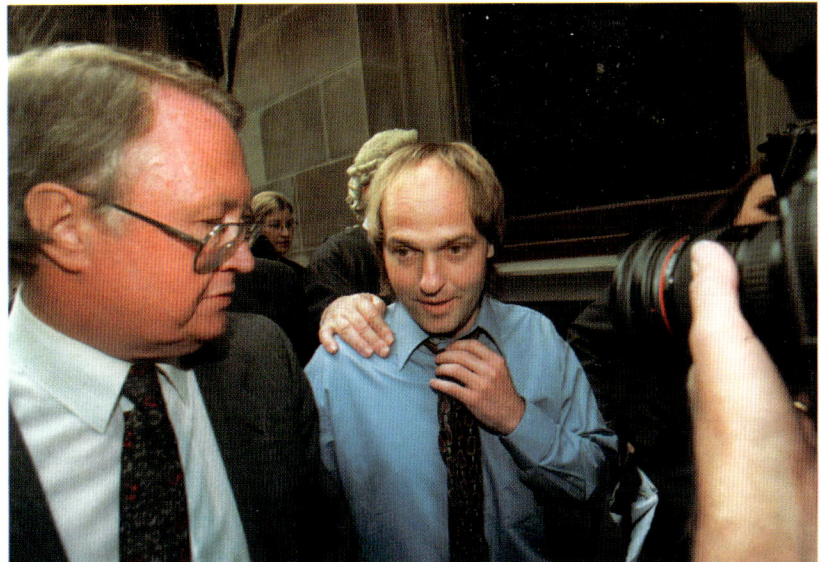

Greg Domaszewicz leaving the court during his trial for Jaidyn Leskie's murder. Domaszewicz was the last known person to see the toddler alive. He was acquitted of the murder.

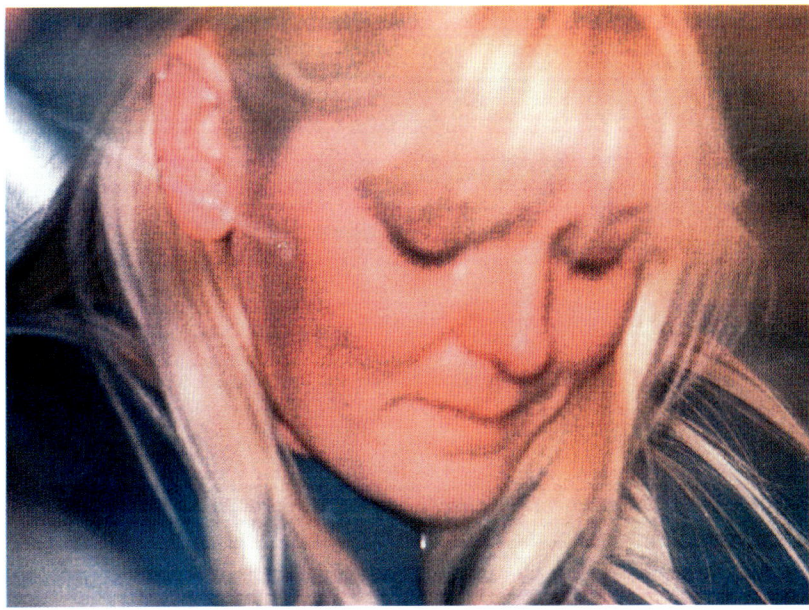

Bilynda Murphy, the mother of Jaidyn Leskie, leaves Moe Police Station in an emotional state after reporting her son is missing.

The funeral of Jaidyn Leskie. Bilynda is seen behind the coffin carrying her daughter Breehanna, born 15 months before Jaidyn.

Brett Leskie was married to Kadee when he struck up a relationship with her sister, Bilynda. Bilynda and Brett had two children, Breehanna and Jaidyn.

Kadee Leskie, sister of Bilynda Murphy, who was once married to Brett Leskie, Jaidyn's father.

Coffin Cheater leader Eddie Withnell arrives at Karrakatta for the funeral ceremony of Marc Chabriere.

Police officers display the mask and gun taken from Jeffrey Fowler. It is believed he was on his way to attack Nathan Piggott.

A police officer inspects the Toyota vehicle driven by Mark Doyle, its rear window shattered as it sits beside Maida Vale Road.

The Operation Gallipoli poster distributed by police during their crackdown on the bikie gangs.

Bikies form a procession towards Karrakatta cemetery for the funeral of
Coffin Cheater Marc Chabriere.

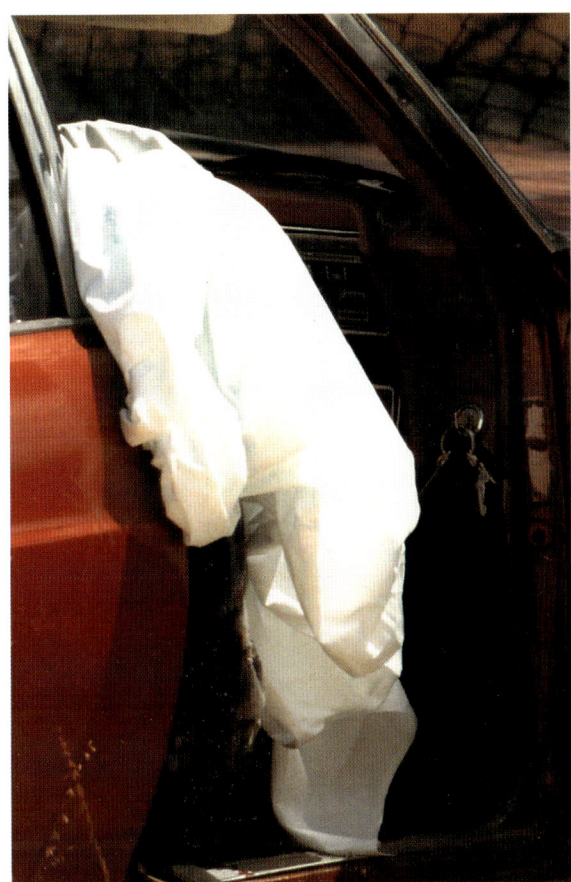

The body of one of the warring bikie victims after a revenge killing between Club Deroes and the Coffin Cheaters.

Below: John Watson, who initiated the 'Operation No-Tolerance' challenge to the bikie gangs, with WA Premier Richard Court.

Detective sergeants Tim Brums and Charlie Barham flew to Darwin to escort escaped criminal Brendon Abbott back to Queensland.

Victorian detectives escort Brendan Berichon back to Melbourne where he was facing two charges of attempted murder.

John Newman, the State ALP Member for Cabramatta, was shot outside his home on 5 September 1994, while putting a cover over his car to protect it from paint bomb attacks.

Tu Quang Dao outside Darlinghurst Courthouse during the John Newman murder trial.

Below: Ambulance officers tend to a man stabbed outside the Mekong Club in Cabramatta.

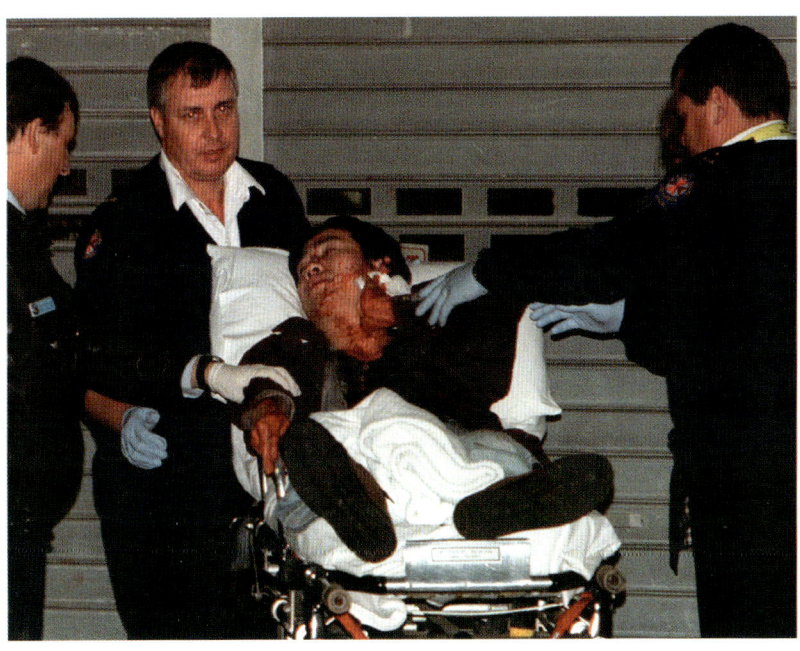

Cardiac surgeon Victor Chang's car was ambushed as he drove to work,
and he was murdered in a suburban street in Mosman.

while he went to pick up Bilynda from a hotel in Traralgon – two towns and about 25 minutes drive away. He claimed that would have been between 2.30 am and 3.30 am.

Hill: 'Why didn't you come here straight away?'

Domaszewicz: 'I don't know, I don't know. I went to Yvonne's looking… '

At this point, Hill quietly fetched a small tape recorder from the station storeroom and, hiding it, started taping Domaszewicz. The secret taping lasted 47 minutes. Later, at 10 am that day, Hill started a formal tape-recorded interview that did not end until 4.09 pm. In four hours and 39 minutes, not counting the four breaks, he asked 1733 questions. Hill wanted to get to the bottom of the baby boy's disappearance and, rightly or wrongly, felt that comprehensive interrogation of Domaszewicz would help him in that direction, even if he had to work around the clock.

When Domaszewicz later came to trial for Jaidyn's murder, Crown prosecutor Bill Morgan Payler conveyed to the jury that the initial investigators had been suspicious of Domaszewicz and that being 'sensible, practical competent men', their judgements could be relied upon. Defence counsel, Colin Lovitt, was to disagree, and in the process condemned the entire police investigation. 'It was a total sham,' he said. 'All you were doing was running a Spanish Inquisition on the accused man at that stage, weren't you?'

Gary Tippet, a writer for *The Melbourne Age* covering the case, a seasoned newspaperman with a gentle touch as well as the common touch, was one of the first reporters to go to Moe when the story broke. An intuitive operator – part knockabout, part poet – he quickly struck up a rapport with Bilynda Murphy and her family which gave his readers a window into their world. He was to write many thousands of words about the case, but none more telling, or more touching, than the opening of the retrospective piece he completed during the trial, 17 months later.

'The first time you see Jaidyn he is already gone,' he wrote. 'Walk down a broken concrete pathway to a dusty white Hardiplank home in Hawker Street, Moe. Blu-tacked behind the middle pane of the loungeroom window, highlighted by white curtains, is a small gallery of photographs of the boy, like a candle to light his way home. Here, on the left, he is newborn: displayed proudly in his now-gone daddy's arms, his new big sister at their side. Above, fat-bellied and naked, on his back on a blanket, little fingers in his little mouth. Higher still he sleeps, wrapped tight in the same blanket.

'Work clockwise and watch him grow. Over here in thick-knit jumper, intent on some toy; down there playing on a patchy lawn; now bath-time; and then those first stumbly steps. Inside, there are others: carefully snapped into his car seat and beaming a gummy grin; dressed up formal in dinky suit and skew-whiff bow-tie. A sook, some say later, but there's no evidence of that here. He looks so happily ordinary. Chubby and gorgeous, with a full moon face, wide, dark chocolate eyes and cornsilk hair. At times he wears a look of grave intent, at times a little devil cheekiness.

'And so to the baby becoming the boy. Tentative-brave, beside a smiling, boof-headed bull terrier, one of three belonging to mum's new boyfriend. Finally, in a photo from near the end, standing straight and handsome in checked flannelette in the boyfriend's lounge. Behind him, coincidence only, a poster says: "I want to believe". You need to see these. Here are his 13 months and two weeks, his entire history. Twenty-something snapshots of his short, stolen life. You need to see these and focus on the child.

'And this message, down at the bottom-most of those pictures, written in what looks like white-out pen: "Where are you, Jaidyn?" Exactly. Because the full story of this story is the double disappearance of Jaidyn Leskie: Not only did he vanish from that house at 150 Narracan Drive... but, too soon thereafter, you might think, from the calculations of all involved.

'From the start, Jaidyn Leskie was lost behind the bizarre circumstances of his disappearance, of pigs' heads and puerile feuds fought out with them; the neat coincidence and appalling humour of his babysitter's "prank" that he had burned himself and was in hospital. He was hidden behind the entanglements of his own almost Appalachian family history: of two sisters and the young man who wed one and fathered children by both.'

Let's put the question again. Where did it really begin, the pathetic story of Jaidyn Raymond Leskie? Not when he was born, although the portents were ominous enough: on April 30 1996, within two days of the Port Arthur massacre. Nor was it the night he disappeared from the house in Moe, starting a search that ran longer than the one for a drowned prime minister 30 years before. It did not end when the tiny body floated to the surface of a lake six months afterwards. Nor did it end with the sordid squabble over where – or whether – to bury the remains, so his disfigured, brutalised remains could be laid to rest.

The truth, elusive in all this, was that the black farce played out for 17 months was only the public part of a story that started years before – and which might not be finished. It was not only the story of a battered baby, but of where he came from; from a place of broken families, broken hearts, shattered trust and stunted dreams. It was an ugly soap opera with real blood and real bruises, a tragedy, a morality tale, and a love story gone wrong. Like all dramas, it turned on sex, betrayal and death. It went something like this…

Let's go back to the late 1960s. Pam Blackwood is a policeman's daughter in a mountain town in far East Gippsland. The man in her life then works in the timber mill, the district's only industry apart from sheep and cattle. If it is not love, it is near enough, even if her parents are not too keen on the idea. In 1970, Pam at age 19 is married in the old Presbyterian church in the main, and only, street of Swift's Creek – which, back then, is the sort of place that almost justifies smirking references, regardless of how unjust they might be, to inbreeding. Nearly two years later, she has her first child in the Omeo hospital. They call her Katie.

For Pam, married life is fine, for a while. To hear Pam tell it, as soon as she is pregnant things start to fall apart. The marriage, on her account, becomes a living hell, and her mother-in-law, having suffered the same sort of torment in her own marriage, tells her to get out of hers. But there are some reconciliations between herself and her husband. A daughter, Bilynda, is born three years after Katie, at Bairnsdale, then a son, Glenn. Babies do not make things better. Nor does the move, the first of many, to Myrtleford in 1977.

At Myrtleford her husband goes to work in the bush at 3 am on Mondays, and returns on Friday nights. But the marriage continues its erratic course. Pam Blackwood works in a motel at night to bring in more money, but the marriage is in serious trouble. She leaves him three more times, the last occasion a month before her tenth wedding anniversary. Her father moves her to Lakes Entrance, a sleepy fishing town on Victoria's east coast which swells into a bustling holiday resort every summer, and he warns her about continuing on in the marriage. This time, she listens. Years later, talking about her husband to her children, she is less than complimentary but does say that he 'always had a job', which is more than could be said for the younger generation.

Pam and her children are constantly on the move. In the fifth move, back to Myrtleford, Katie renames herself Kadee. At the age of 14, she leaves home for the first time. A rebel, she stays seven weeks with friends, then goes home because she says: 'Mum would buy me smokes, and the other people wouldn't.' Kadee turns 15 around the time they move to Heyfield, another Gippsland timber town. She leaves nearby Maffra High School in year nine, bolts down the coast to Lakes Entrance and lands 'the second best job I've ever had' in an old people's home. 'I got $75 a fortnight and thought I was rich,' she says. It lasts nine weeks, until, on her account, her boss argues with her grandmother on the golf course.

Kadee's favourite job is sorting rubbish in a recycler's yard, but that does not last long, either. In fact, the most constant thing in her life is the social security payments. They have been far more reliable than most of her men, and on that subject the family's big troubles start.

Kadee is 16 and living at Nathalia – after the family's eighth move in as many years – when she leaves home for the second time. She takes the train to Moe, where she has met a girl on a previous visit. 'Everything I owned was at my feet,' she says. 'I had nowhere to go.' She finds the girl, and arranges to stay in her flat. Three nights later they go to a party, armed with a flask of Jim Beam bourbon. 'We spotted three guys, gave them marks out of ten,' she says. 'One was gorgeous, and we gave him bonus points. Another got seven, but he was married.' They give only three points to the third – 'he was feral' – but when Kadee goes outside later, he follows and chats to her. His name is Brett Leskie. They form a brief relationship. Two days later he dumps her. A week later she gets back with him and takes him to Nathalia to see her mother.

Pam does not like the 16-year-old Brett, and, naturally, that is enough to make Kadee want to keep him. Even then, the streetwise Pam notices that Brett is paying undue attention to 13-year-old Bilynda, who is well developed for her age. Kadee and Brett return to the LaTrobe Valley and Kadee moves in with Brett's family, who then share a farm at Yallourn North, not far from Moe. She pays $25 a fortnight board, and helps milk the cows four nights a week and Sunday mornings. She and Brett also draw the dole.

It is a wonder it lasts five months. When the relationship does break down, Kadee forms a relationship with another man in Moe, who is violent towards her. Then she goes back to her mother at Nathalia. The family moves again, to Moruya on the far south coast of New South Wales where Pam suffers a stroke that paralyses her down one side and puts her in hospital for months. Kadee gets restless and returns to Lakes Entrance. She runs into Brett Leskie at the local speedway car races and tries to resume the relationship but he leaves and she does not see him for 18 months.

A few weeks later, she falls pregnant and a boy, Harley, is born in Moruya in late 1991. They all move to Sale: Pam, Bilynda, brother Glenn, Kadee and Harley. They stay with friends. It does not work. Kadee, carrying Harley in her arms, chances upon Brett Leskie in the street. Later, he comes around. It is pension day. Kadee buys a bottle of rum for the occasion. She says: 'I thought if we get pissed and get back on together, that's a start.' She becomes pregnant again. Brett's mother, Elizabeth Leskie, insists they marry. Kadee, happy, borrows a debutante dress that is too small and has it altered. The Leskies buy the rings from a pawn shop in Morwell and set a date three weeks away, 24 October 1992.

A Baptist minister marries them in the front yard of the Leskies' brick veneer on their new share-farm at Denison, which is on the flat irrigation farming country near Sale. The reception is a barbecue in the backyard. Kadee recalls spending the afternoon driving Brett and his mates around in her car, celebrating. Just another weekend, really. She says Brett has done a lot of celebrating and is in bed and out to it by 8.30pm. Kadee drives to Sale, buys beer and spends her wedding night drinking with a female friend.

The 'honeymoon' is spent on the farm putting a new motor in Brett's car. Not long afterwards, Kadee says that Brett's parents kick him out for 'doing donuts and burnouts' in front of the house. Brett and Kadee go to Brett's sister's at Morwell, then rent a house at Yallourn North. Brett, she claims, starts to 'dress up to the nines' and stays out late while she is home with her baby boy. She becomes unhappy and cries herself to sleep each night. She miscarries. She falls pregnant again. Kadee may have problems, but lack of fertility is not one of them.

She and Brett argue at their joint 21st birthday party in June 1993. They go to Lakes Entrance to try to patch it up. When she is eight months pregnant, Kadee, on her account, finds Brett embracing Bilynda, now 16, in a back shed. Brett insists there is nothing in it, but that night he tells her he has 'fallen out of love' with her. She abuses him and tells him to leave. He does so but takes Bilynda with him. Two weeks later, Kadee gives birth to his daughter, Shannan. But she is now alone, and the father who should have been celebrating the birth of his child and comforting her is off with her sister. Kadee vows revenge. If it takes ten years, she says, she will split up her husband and her sister. As it happens, it takes her only four.

Cut to early 1997. Brett and Bilynda, barely 21, have had two children. Breehanna was born on January 17, 1995, and Jaidyn in April, 1996. Bilynda has named Jaidyn after a guest on the 'The Rikki Lake Show' on television. Kadee, by this time, has a third child by another man. She is also coping with the knowledge that Shannan has leukaemia. But she is obsessed with Brett and the fact that he ran out on her. There follows a series of plots. Allegedly as part of that, Kadee picks one of Brett's friends as an accomplice. He is a self-taught mechanic and panel-beater who runs a panel shop with Brett in Moe under a Commonwealth employment grant scheme. She calls him 'Grishka', but nearly everyone else calls him Greg. Like most people, she cannot spell his surname – Domaszewicz. Sometimes they call him 'Doma'.

'I stooged Brett with his best mate,' she is to recall with characteristic bravado. 'I kept tipping Boo (Bilynda) off about Grishka. We had a code so I could tell her when he was down the street without Brett knowing. Brett would even mind all the kids while we went down the street. Grishka knew I was using them all as puppets, pulling the strings. I said to him, I didn't care if he stayed with Bilynda or not, as long as he split them [Bilynda and Brett] up.' Eventually, Brett Leskie rows with Kadee and leaves town, heading for Kalgoorlie and taking Breehanna with him. Bilynda carries on openly with Domaszewicz, who seems fond of Jaidyn, and often looks after him. For a while, Kadee is happy, or as close to it as she gets.

Two months later, Jaidyn goes missing.

From the minute Domaszewicz walked into the Moe police station on the morning of June 15, 1997, he had a credibility problem. The police only believed that something bad had happened to Jaidyn. For all the distraction of pigs' heads, broken windows and bad blood with old girlfriends, Domaszewicz was the person they most wanted to question.

And it is here we must mention the alternative scenario we adverted to above. Domaszewicz, on his account, had left the child alone in the house for a relatively brief period to go pick up Bilynda. Leaving a baby alone at any time is not wise, but it happens, and 99.99 per cent of the time nothing happens.

But every householder, especially women, have been startled at times by movements or odd sounds in the dark, perhaps in the backyard or the street at night. Again, many have an innocent explanation, but some do not. From the beginning of civilisation, society has been afflicted by wandering misfits, people of deviant or violent disposition, people frustrated, obsessed, or mentally ill, who wander, particularly at night. They end up in backyards, in pantries, in bedrooms. They watch and they wait. Then they see an opportunity such as a young woman asleep with the window open, a child unattended in a nursery… Such people do strike, and often there is tragedy. In some cases, an innocent person who is placed at the scene is blamed. And there are miscarriages of justice. In the late 1950s and early 1960s, Perth had its own monster, Eric Edgar Cooke, a hapless individual who over a period of years shot, stabbed and ran over people at night, usually women. He killed at least six people, for which he was hanged in 1964.

But two other men were charged and convicted over killings which Cooke might have carried out. One, Darryl Beamish, was convicted of murdering socialite Jillian Brewer and was sentenced to death. His sentence was later commuted to life imprisonment. Another, John Button, was seen in his car following his girlfriend and pleading with her. She was run over and killed soon after. Button served ten years for manslaughter. At the time of writing, following some brilliant sleuthing by enterprising journalist Estelle Blackburn, those convictions have been thrown into doubt and are now subject to review.

Of course, there is also the possibility that indeed someone was there in Jaidyn's house, but perhaps not a stranger. The social muddle in which Domaszewicz and Murphy moved could well have produced an individual who, for whatever reason, took advantage of the unguarded moment to harm the child. And, perhaps, Domaszewicz went into a blind panic when he found the child missing, telling people whatever came into his head, leading to his incoherent and contradictory manner which was held against him.

For the police, in order to try to discern whether it was Domaszewicz or someone else, it was necessary to find the baby, or as they believed, the body of that child. There were plenty of signals to suggest police thought they were dealing with a homicide. There was never a serious all-points alert for abductors travelling with a 14-month-old baby boy matching Jaidyn's description. Instead, there was a massive search of dams, swamps and waterways in and around Moe – and painstaking sweeps through local tips by hundreds of police.

Two days after Jaidyn's disappearance, Domaszewicz and Bilynda went to Melbourne to see lawyers, to begin custody proceedings to get Breehanna back from the Leskie family – Breehanna's father, aunts and grandparents – who, unsurprisingly, insisted on caring for her after Jaidyn's disappearance. For the pair to be concerned about that while strangers were scouring bush and watercourses for the lost baby struck people as odd.

But here again, it is important to introduce a note of caution. People can react in totally unpredictable ways to trauma. In the Azaria Chamberlain case in 1980, Michael and Lindy Chamberlain left Ayers Rock while the search for their baby was in progress. They said and did other odd things that told against them in the public mind, such as the extraordinary lengths Michael Chamberlain took the day after Azaria disappeared to get black-and-white film and take photographs at the behest of a journalist. But years later, following investigation, charging, conviction and a gaol sentence for Lindy, who was another 'obvious suspect', a royal commission exonerated both parents.

Returning to Jaidyn, the hunt in mid-1997 rapidly became the most sustained search for a body in Australia since 1967, when Harold Holt, Australia's prime minister, disappeared in the surf off Portsea. More questions were being put to Domaszewicz. On Thursday afternoon, June 19, he was interrogated once more in the cramped interview room at the Moe police station. In seven hours, he replied to 1872 questions put to him by Detective Sergeant Michael Roberts and Sergeant Stephen Fyffe. Domaszewicz said: 'I've told youse and told youse and told youse, yeah. That's all I know. That's it.'

The thousands of words in which Domaszewicz related his account might be condensed thus: it was a wet Saturday and he had got up late. After taking his usual Tattslotto numbers at the local newsagency he had driven around Moe, then to Bilynda Murphy's place to say 'hello'. She had been in her pyjamas talking on the telephone to Brett Leskie, so he had left. He had returned after midday. Bilynda told him she was going to a party that night and was having Jaidyn babysat by her sister, Kadee. He offered to take Jaidyn for a while, while he was working on his car. She had accepted, which was not unusual. She had been known to leave

Jaidyn with him for days at a time, despite an incident two months earlier when he admitted to hitting the little boy.

Bilynda's account included a description of how she had dressed Jaidyn in a disposable nappy, grey tracksuit pants with green trim and 'Baby Games' written on it, a green, long-sleeved shirt, a blue-grey windcheater with a hood, and red jacket. She had put four nappies, more clothes, a bottle, a muesli bar, a lollipop and an apple in a plastic shopping bag. She and Domaszewicz had put Jaidyn's baby seat in the green Ford and strapped the child in. Domaszewicz had dropped Bilynda at Kadee's. She had kissed Jaidyn goodbye and Domaszewicz had driven off in the Ford with Jaidyn strapped inside. She never saw her son again.

Domaszewicz said that on arriving home, he had worked on the car, 'giving (Jaidyn) stuff to hold, actually, like dirty bolts and that, you know…' The toddler had also played with Domaszewicz's three bull terriers, dug up some bricks in the back yard and played in the dirt. After dark, Domaszewicz told police he had washed the boy and had had a shower. While in the shower Jaidyn 'got a bit red on the bum from the gas heater.' Then they played Nintendo and watched television. Domaszewicz thought Bilynda had rung at about 10 pm from the party before she moved on to a local hotel. This did not quite tally with Bilynda Murphy's subsequent statement that she telephoned Domaszewicz several times that evening, between 5 pm and when she left for the party about 8 pm.

Domaszewicz's account was that he had told Bilynda that Jaidyn had burned himself slightly, and that he had taken him to hospital. For some reason, possibly because of the amount she had drunk, Bilynda Murphy had decided, or agreed, to stay at the party until Domaszewicz picked her up some hours later. Domaszewicz had repeated to her that Jaidyn was in hospital. When they went to the police just before dawn, Bilynda mentioned this. Domaszewicz hastily contradicted her, saying it had been a joke.

Why he had come up with the hospital story several hours earlier, as if to explain Jaidyn's absence at a time when, on his subsequent claim, Jaidyn had still been with him? This was never really answered. His mother claimed later that her 'Grishka' (as she nicknamed Domaszewicz) was a practical joker with a tendency to make up stories and talk rubbish. Poker-faced Detective Senior Sergeant Rowland Legg, not long in the Homicide Squad after years in intelligence work, was perplexed.

A week after Jaidyn's disappearance, Legg played a characteristically flat bat to media questions: 'The longer the investigation goes, the less chance of finding him alive.' At that moment, fellow police officers were preparing to drain Lake Narracan in Moe. 'We would have thought it likely had someone been caring for Jaidyn that they would have by now told us where he was, or at least that he was all right,' one of them said.

Police divers searched Narracan Creek and Moondarra Dam, north of Moe. A police spokesman said there was concentration on waterways because of 'information received'. On the twelfth day of the inquiry, June 26, detectives seized Domaszewicz's green Ford Fairmont sedan and sent it to Melbourne for forensic tests. The car was held for testing for five days. Nothing much was found and it was returned on July 1.

Acting commander Peter Blick said on the record that since Jaidyn has been missing more than two weeks, the chances of finding him alive were 'very remote' and that 'at this stage we are dealing with this as a homicide investigation. We have got to the point where we can eliminate all other possibilities.' Blick conceded that it is more difficult to make an arrest without finding the body, but said he expected the search to be scaled down.

The same day, Bilynda Murphy was fined $250 after pleading guilty to offensive behaviour – for challenging another woman to a fight outside the Moe police station. Such incidents flagged the cross-currents of violent ill-feeling between groups and individuals in the sub-culture in which the Murphy girls and Domaszewicz moved. Domaszewicz, as it turned out, had many enemies, a fact that happened to cloud what otherwise appeared to police to be another tragic case of child abuse gone wrong.

As if orchestrated by a malevolent deity playing a black cosmic joke, there was the startling coincidence of a pig's head being thrown through Domaszewicz's window on the night Jaidyn disappeared. Domaszewicz insisted that the person or persons who had thrown the pig's head through his window while he was driving to or from Traralgon must have taken Jaidyn. This loomed over the case, lending a bizarre twist that ultimately overshadows more prosaic facts. The so-called 'pigs-head team', meaning a likeable local thief called Kenny Penfold, his sister Yvonne, and associates Darrin Wilson and Dean 'Dumbell' Ross, was seized on by the media – and later by the defence counsel.

Domaszewicz had a connection with the Penfolds. He had lived for two years with Yvonne Penfold in a relationship marked by jealousy, spite and violence before their split which was followed by more of the same. After the split, he changed his locks and they both took out – and regularly breached – intervention orders against each other. In early June 1997, he rammed Yvonne Penfold's car with his. That was related to the 'pig's head' raid.

Penfold's antics did take up police attention. Police were obliged to investigate the possibility that the pig's head pointed to some sinister outside force, though from the outset there was no evidence that anyone had climbed through a window or forced the door of the Narracan Drive house. It did not take long for some people to raise the spectre of 'a cult'. The defence counsel explored the idea that whoever had perpetrated such a nasty practical joke on Yvonne Penfold's despised ex-boyfriend, Domaszewicz, might also have been capable of abducting and killing a child in his care.

The weight of public opinion in Moe, though, was clear enough. On 3 July, day 19 of the search, Domaszewicz's green Ford was sitting on his driveway. It was daubed with the words 'murderer, sinner, killer'. Police said they would investigate the incident, without success, apparently, as nobody has been charged.

Investigative journalists looked at the background of Domaszewicz. His Russian mother, Helen, had arrived with her family from Sinkiang, western China, in 1959, when she was 17. In 1966, she married a Polish electrician, Mick Domaszewicz, whose father had been killed in a German concentration camp. The couple had two sons in quick succession – Peter, then Greg who was born in 1968 in Newborough, which was really part of Moe.

Peter was a good student and won a scholarship to university. Greg never even got close to achieving what Peter did. He was badly affected, his mother was to recall, by his father's sudden death in 1983, at the age of 47. Greg left school at 15 and drifted from one dead-end job to another, spending most of the next seven years on the dole. When his mother remarried and moved away in 1989, he shifted into the little house the family had been renting in Narracan Drive. In 1996, he tried to start a panelbeating business, but it soon failed. He worked for a while with Brett Leskie, which is how he came to know Kadee and Bilynda Murphy.

'He always had friends, good and bad,' Helen Domaszewicz said years later. 'He had too many mates, I think.' She added, perhaps, tellingly: 'Not many people took Grishka seriously. He's a soft touch.' He was, in other words, the sort of person that even Bilynda Murphy was not keen to go out with in public – but all too willing to use as an unpaid babysitter while she conducted a hectic social life at pubs and parties. 'She probably thinks I'm very slow and that, I dunno,' Domaszewicz was to tell police in an awkwardly revealing moment. 'She always sort of complains about that.'

Police carried out a painstaking eight-hour search of his house. On July 16, 32 days after Jaidyn's disappearance, Domaszewicz was arrested for the boy's murder. A cynic might have thought the police stage managed the arrest, wringing every drop of drama from the situation, in the hope it would rattle Domaszewicz. If it had not been obvious that Domaszewicz was under constant surveillance before, it became painfully clear when a swarm of police vehicles suddenly surrounded his green Ford in a Melbourne street at 2 pm on 16 July. Homicide detectives handcuffed and took him to the St Kilda Road police complex, where they interviewed him for four hours. Or, at least, they tried to. This time, on legal advice, he said nothing. They charged him and took him before a bail justice in an out-of-sessions hearing in the Melbourne Magistrates Court.

Domaszewicz stuck to his story. Asked if he understood the charges against him, he said: 'They're alleging that I've done something I haven't done.' Later in the ten-minute session, when asked if he could put a reason why he should be granted bail, he said: 'I'm not guilty of any offence.' The inscrutable Sergeant Legg intoned: 'The person before the court is charged that at Newborough, between the 14th and 15th days of June, 1997, he did murder one Jaidyn Leskie.' Domaszewicz, dressed as usual in jeans and flanelette shirt, shook his head slightly at times during the hearing and closed his eyes when the charge was read to him a second time. He was remanded in custody and appeared again the next morning under tight security.

When reporters rang Brett Leskie, he said he was 'still getting his thoughts together'. Brett Leskie's father, Ray Leskie, a respectable and religious dairy farmer, said the family hadn't given up hope Jaidyn would be found safe. 'We've been praying that he is still alive,' he said. And Bilynda Murphy? She was reported to be staying with friends at Moruya in southern New South Wales, and could not be contacted.

New Year's Day, 1998, was warm and fine. Late that afternoon a reporter called the head of the Victorian homicide squad, Chief Inspector Rod Collins, about a murder case in the Albury area. The affable Collins took the call, but warned he could not talk long; a baby's body has been found near Moe. It was the break police had been waiting for. It had happened just after lunch. Sam Payne, 14, and his stepfather, grandparents and little brother were having a walk after a picnic at Blue Rock Dam, just a few kilometres from Moe. Sam had seen what he thought was a dummy in the sand, then what he first thought was a pillow in shallow water, before realising it was a bloated child's body floating face down.

Police divers found a sleeping bag tied to a crow bar. The stitching had rotted after six months in nearly six metres of water, letting Jaidyn's body float free. On the silt nearby was the white plastic shopping bag containing his clothes, bottle and apple. By chance, friends of Bilynda Murphy's saw the police arrive at the dam and alerted her. She arrived soon afterwards, but had to wait at the police roadblock set up to keep sightseers out. Five days later, she went to the Moe police station to see what had been found with her baby. She identified each item of clothing she had put on Jaidyn the last time she dressed him on that far-off winter day. 'And I recognised an apple,' she said. 'It was black. The apple was green when I sent it with Jaidyn.'

Finding the body did not appear to alter her public support for Domaszewicz, who had been refused bail repeatedly while in custody awaiting committal proceedings. She stayed in touch, travelling the 130 km from Moe every week to visit him in the Melbourne remand centre, all of which she later claimed was a sham to lull Domaszewicz into telling her the truth about Jaidyn's death. She complained she was treated like a suspect in the case because of her continuing association with him. 'The police don't tell me anything,' she told a reporter. 'It just makes me feel like this kid was never mine.' One thing they did tell her was that Jaidyn had suffered a broken arm before his death, then a head injury so severe it would have caused brain damage similar to that suffered in fatal car crashes. This posed a question often asked about the mothers of children battered by the men in their lives: what sort of deal do they do with themselves to put a sexual relationship above the suffering, or even the torture and death, of their own offspring?

An ugly and bizarre public quarrel raged over where, how, or even whether, Jaidyn would be buried or cremated. Bilynda had wanted Jaidyn buried in Moe. But Brett Leskie, by this time living back with his parents near Sale, insisted that he be buried at Sale – or otherwise be cremated and the ashes shared. This upset Bilynda. 'I just do not want him cremated,' she said. 'I couldn't imagine burning him after all he has been through.'

Tactful clergy managed to arrange compromise funeral arrangements, and the warring factions called a temporary truce. Seven months exactly from the night Jaidyn disappeared, mourners finally gathered at Moe. Perhaps it was the sight of the tiny coffin covered in white roses, irises and teddy bears in the Moe Baptist church that reminded everyone of the shocking reality lost in the seven-month circus. Ushers directed the Leskie family and their friends to one side of the church, the Murphys to the other.

There was a poignant moment when three-year-old Breehanna, Jaidyn's sister, sat first with the Leskie family – but, on spying

Bilynda across the aisle, jumped down, ran over to her and cried 'mummy'. For the rest of the half-hour service, mother and daughter clung to one another. By the time the Lord's Prayer was offered, Breehanna had fallen asleep in her mother's arms. Her grandmother, Elizabeth Leskie, had told the little girl the ceremony was to bury Jaidyn's body. Breehanna had nodded, saying: 'He needs a new body.'

The service did not draw the enormous local support some might have expected, given the intense speculation about the case. But there were about 400 people jammed in the church, with another 80 watching video screens outside. One group of locals had made a teddy bear from hydrangeas and pine needles and put it outside the church. A note tied to it read: 'We prayed you would be found... You were loved in our town.' Inside, a message read on behalf of Bilynda Murphy said that the day Jaidyn had disappeared she felt her heart had been ripped from her body. 'I would give my world to hear [your] little laugh again,' she wrote.

Afterwards, members of both families embraced each other, and Breehanna was passed from her mother to her father. And when the tiny coffin was lowered into the ground at Yallourn, ten kilometres away, Jaidyn's estranged parents briefly embraced each other as 50 coloured balloons floated into the sky. Then everyone headed to Moe for the wake.

Hundreds of thousands of words were spoken and recorded in the marathon trial that eventually unfolded in the Victorian Supreme Court in late 1998, grist to the mill of a story that had long since taken on a life of its own. New Moe jokes were coined every day, variations on the theme of moccasin-wearing white trash unsure of the paternity of their children. The cast of characters were known by their first names, even nicknames, in a thousand conversations. It was grotesque, tasteless, brutal, nasty, and fascinating. Highlights of each day's hearing were reported in detail and at length. Cameras and microphones bristled from the milling herd of media people jostling each other outside the 19th century sandstone courts. Inside, the press benches were packed. Of all the exchanges between the bar table and the witness box, none was more telling than a brief encounter between the defence counsel, Colin Lovitt, QC, an abrasive, persuasive streetfighter known, not always fondly, as 'The Embarrister', and Sergeant Legg, described by Tippet as a hunter 'who has seen too many bad endings'.

Lovitt asked Legg what sinister significance he placed on the white plastic bag found with Jaidyn's body. Legg replied: 'I was always interested in the fact that no-one else would have known to remove all trace of the child from the house... that you would remove those items that no-one else would know about.' Those items were exactly what was found: clothes, bottle, shoes, even the apple, that Bilynda Murphy had described to police the day after Jaidyn disappeared. 'And every item removed from the house ended up with the body,' Legg said.

The trial attracted intense media interest. One high moment was the evidence about the pig's head. It turned out, according to the evidence, that Darrin Wilson was a butcher, and was visiting his home town of Moe on June 14, 1997. He met Kenny Penfold, a friend, at a party. He heard that Yvonne Penfold's former boyfriend, Domaszewicz, had been beating her up and harassing her. 'Kenny said, "We're gunna give him a scare,"' Wilson said in evidence. They had gone to the railway track across Narracan Drive from Domaszewicz's home about 2 am. After Domaszewicz had driven off, Wilson and Penfold had gone to the house and thrown the pig's head through a window and had smashed other windows with rocks.

Lovitt told the jury it had been one of the 'bizarre coincidences' of this case. But then, he suggested, could it have been related? Might they have startled Jaidyn, by then asleep in the house, and panicked? 'One is left wondering if they took the child from the house, possibly injured, possibly in pain, upset and making a noise and needing to be quietened down,' he asked. No evidence was presented that could possibly have backed that up. But no evidence was presented either that conclusively linked Domaszewicz with Jaidyn's Leskie's death.

There was also a question of motive. Why would Domaszewicz want to do it? The evidence was that he had developed a close bond with 'The Boy', as he referred to him, liked to expose him to 'man-type' things such as working on the car and movies with Arnold Schwarzenegger in them. And he was 'a willing, unpaid babysitter', but on the evidence lacked the parental skills to handle a grizzling or crying child in an appropriate manner. That was not to say he had lost his temper with the child, gone too far, then covered it up? It could have happened, but it was mere speculation.

Lovitt felt obliged to say: 'We're dealing with some unusual people. We're dealing with people who don't think and act in the same way we expect most people to think and act.' Domaszewicz was 'a stupid, practical joker,' he said, on the evidence that might have caused critical communication problems the night Jaidyn disappeared. 'But,' said Lovitt, 'I am defending him for murder, not for being an idiot.' On December 4, 1998, after a trial lasting 34 days, Domaszewicz was acquitted of murder.

Despite warnings that his life would be in danger, Domaszewicz returned to Moe soon afterwards. Two months later, Bilynda Murphy obtained a two-year personal protection order against Domaszewicz, forbidding him approaching her. On 9 May 1999, Greg Domaszewicz re-stated his innocence on television, though conceding he should not have left Jaidyn alone. 'I have nothing to do with Jaidyn's disappearance and death,' he said. 'I've said that all along and I always will… I know in myself I've done nothing wrong, so that's that.' Bilynda, who had at times become equivocal in her public statements about Domaszewicz, eventually said she was taking him back into her life.

What really happened that night in Moe? Like that other celebrated Victorian mystery, now recast as the enduring myth known as 'Picnic at Hanging Rock', the truth behind Jaidyn's disappearance is destined to be buried in the mists of time.

THE CHOPPER'S MECHANIC

*Blown with restless violence
about the pendant world ...*

William Shakespeare
Measure for Measure

This is a story about an ambulance driver turned hit man, and a corrupt suburban detective who allowed him to prosper. It is about corruption that continued despite daily revelations from the New South Wales Police Royal Commission, 1994–97. It is about the murders of nine people, five of whom were not villains but innocent bystanders or anti-drug campaigners. It is also about the New South Wales Police Task Force Yandee, which worked covertly to solve what many regarded as unsolvable crimes at a time when public confidence in the ability of the force to deal with corruption within its ranks was shaken.

It began with the discovery of a body. In this case, it was that of Darren Anthony Spradbrow, 29. He had been found shot dead on the cattle property of his uncle, Brian Leslie Smith, at Yarrowitch, in the New South Wales mid-north coast hinterland 100 km north-west of Port Macquarie.

Spradbrow had lived on a hobby farm, The Falls at Yarrowitch, close to Smith's property, with his de facto wife and baby. Spradbrow had been a hard man, and he had many enemies.

Unemployed, he had been a local drug dealer and was believed to have pillaged the marijuana crops of others, which were growing in the dense mountain country nearby. He had disappeared on 2 March 1994. Police had been alerted and had begun a search for him. After a tip-off of mysterious origin, they found the body, covered in logs, rocks and dirt, on a track.

There was talk that Spradbrow had been giving information to police about rival drug dealers and that bikies were after him. Talk was that it had been some sort of payback. Police were anxious to interview Spradbrow's uncle, Smith. Smith, a rodeo rider and horse chiropractor, lived with his de facto wife Pauline Landrigan in Wauchope but ran one hundred head of cattle on the unfenced mountain terrain.

Spradbrow's stepfather, Victor John Bridge, was to tell police he had been on Smith's property on the day of the shooting. He said he had been feuding with Spradbrow, who had moved into Bridge's Yarrowitch farm some months earlier and kicked him and Spradbrow's mother, Carol Bridge, out of the house. But he had also been partners with Smith and a local tradesman and rouseabout from the Yarrowitch area, Peter Dykes, in a marijuana crop.

On 1 March, Bridge had gone into the mountains to return a car he had fixed for a woman, and to look for stray cattle. On that day, he had run into Smith and Dykes at Smith's homestead. Smith had wanted Dykes to build a verandah extension onto the homestead. After a cup of tea the three had gone in search of stray cows coming into calf, and to check on one hundred marijuana plants.

Bridge's evidence was that on that day, Smith had gone into a 'rage', that he had 'lost his banana' over something that Spradbrow had done and was ranting. Bridge had spent the night on Smith's farm. The next morning, Dykes and Smith had prepared to go out in Smith's Toyota Landcruiser to search for the cattle. As Dykes got into the front passenger's side, he had seen a handgun on the seat and had brushed it aside.

When they returned from the search Smith started 'spewing' about Spradbrow, saying he was going to 'bash' him. 'He was saying what he was going to do and what he wasn't going to do. He was going to kill Darren. It [the ranting] went on probably for an hour and a half, two hours. He got worked up and said he was going to get him, going to get him,' Bridge later recalled.

Dykes, in his account, could not be sure of the exact date, but he recalled it was a Wednesday that he had been on Smith's property, and that he and Smith had encountered Bridge. He also said that Smith had blown up about Spradbrow. They had sat on Smith's verandah and had smoked a 'bong' but that had not settled Smith down. Dykes said that he and Smith had gone off in Smith's four-wheel drive towards Spradbrow's property and that Smith had told him he was going to assault Spradbrow. But halfway there, Smith had dropped Dykes off in a paddock that had been used by crop-dusters as an airstrip.

Dykes had then sat down and lit a cigarette as he watched Smith drive off towards the Spradbrow farm. Some time later, he had heard two shots, and he thought they had come from a gully at the bottom of the airstrip, near Spradbrow's place, although he could not be sure. He had taken no particular note; the odd rifle shot out there came as no surprise.

About 30 minutes later, Smith returned and picked Dykes up. According to Dykes' later evidence, as he got into the vehicle he caught sight of a human leg in the back. It had an old canvas army boot attached. It had been a nervous drive back to Smith's home, with very little conversation. When they arrived, Smith had seen Bridge and told him to get the tractor started.

According to Dykes, the tractor had a tree-clearing tool attached and was difficult to get going. But Bridge did get it started and Smith had taken over the tractor from Bridge and had driven it towards the mountains. Dykes got into the Landcruiser to follow. But first he took another look at what was in the back of the landcruiser. The leg belonged to Spradbrow, who was lying there dead. Dykes, on his account, had followed Smith, and at a gully, Smith had dragged the body from the Landcruiser, put it on the ground, then used the tractor to push logs and dirt on top of it.

They returned to the house. Dykes said that he had seen a small amount of blood in the back of the Landcruiser, and that Smith had taken a bucket of water and flushed it away. Police charged Smith and Dykes with murder. Dykes made a deal with the police, offering to give evidence against Smith in return for a chance to plead guilty to a lesser offence: concealing a serious crime. Police acceded to that.

Smith, aged 45, was committed for trial at the Newcastle Supreme Court in July 1995. He indicated he would plead not guilty. In June, he served notice that he had an alibi: he could not have done it because on 2 March 1994, he had been in Sydney on business. He had wanted to buy some fancy cowboy hats and rodeo gear after competing a few days earlier in the national horse-cutting titles in Tamworth. He had also gone to the Burwood Hotel in Sydney's mid-west that day to hunt down 'a bloke called Lindsey' as a favour for Dykes, who wanted to know whether he could off-load 2.5 kilograms of marijuana.

To corroborate his story, Smith produced two witnesses: a knockabout standover man, private inquiry agent and one-time ambulance officer, Lindsey Robert Rose, 39, and a detective senior constable from Canterbury in Sydney's inner west, Michael 'Clag' Thomas (not to be confused with Michael Thomas, who at the time of writing is a serving police officer). Smith also produced a statement from the chief of Earlwood and Canterbury detectives, Detective Sergeant Alan Robert Thomas (no relation to constable Michael Thomas).

There was something inherently suspicious about the sudden appearance of the alibi evidence. It was at least possible that Smith had cooked all this up, and that the three individuals he had selected to back him up were all in on it. The New South Wales Police Integrity Branch (PIB) launched an inquiry into the two Thomases and the alibi.

There was other disturbing information as well. In an unrelated operation, police had been inquiring into suspect city and mid-north coast drug dealers in New South Wales. This entailed the installation of listening devices. During this surveillance, police picked up a conversation about what appeared to be a conspiracy to establish a false alibi. When Smith went on trial in the Supreme Court of New South Wales, sitting in Newcastle, on 25 July 1995, and members of the PIB were there, listening with intense interest.

Dykes and Bridge gave evidence against Smith. Rose, for the defence, said that on 2 March 1994, he was drinking with Smith at the Burwood Hotel, in Sydney's mid-west. Constable Thomas then said he had gone to the same hotel to look for Sergeant Thomas, who had left work sick, and had spoken briefly to Rose. But when questioned, Constable Thomas could not recall the exact date he had done this. Nor could he recall ever having met Smith.

Dykes could not recall Smith telling him on 1 March, 1994, that he intended to go to Sydney the next day on business, or asking him to find a potential buyer called Lindsey for marijuana that was coming into harvest. He said he had never met or known of Lindsey Rose.

Smith's trial began on 25 July 1995. He stuck by his alibi. His lawyer said that Bridge had had more motive to kill Spradbrow, because Spradbrow had evicted him from his farm. Smith said Bridge owned a number of firearms and had lied about them to police. He said he had met Rose at Dykes' request on 2 March, 1994, and later that afternoon he had driven from Sydney to Wauchope. He said Dykes had supplied drugs through an intermediary to buyers in Newcastle and the Central Coast, and that the intermediary had told him to contact 'Lindsey' in Sydney. Dykes denied Smith's claim. Smith would later deny on oath any involvement in cannabis growing.

On Monday, 21 August, the jury was sent off at 2 pm to consider their verdict. They sat on it overnight and did not return with their verdict until 11 am the following day. After considering the matter for only four hours, effectively, the jury brought in a verdict of not guilty, and Smith walked from the court an undoubtedly very relieved man. Within half an hour of his acquittal, Smith had settled in the front bar of the Grand Hotel opposite the Supreme Court, and was enjoying a soft drink, surrounded by relatives and his legal team. But his elation was short-lived. Spradbrow's mother, Carol Bridge, and her daughter, Deborah Schneider, appeared and rushed at Smith, screaming: 'Murderer, murderer!'

The women tore Smith's shirt. Smith's lawyers and other drinkers tried to intervene and were pushed away. Smith's wife, Pauline Landrigan, and daughter, Corina Ylias, got involved. Punches and kicks were exchanged and glasses were smashed to the floor. Pool cues were raised as both women continued to swear and make threats. Spradbrow's brother, Chris, and hotel staff finally broke it up. But the insults continued out on the street. The bar-room brawl was snapped on film by a newspaper photographer, and its publication brought the case to public notice at a time when most eyes were turned towards the Police Royal Commission rumbling away 150 km south in Sydney.

That, however, was not the end of the matter. By late 1995, a police task force, code-named Yandee, had been formed with a reference from the Police Royal Commission to probe three murders on the mid-north coast believed to be linked to marijuana growing cartels protected by corrupt police. Although the three cases were unrelated to the Spradbrow murder, that case was drawn into the investigation, and Smith, Landrigan, Rose and both Thomases were questioned over an alleged conspiracy to provide a false alibi for Smith. Landrigan had been intercepted on the telephone talking about the apparent conspiracy to another man, Michael Simeon, an informant of Alan Thomas and a partner with him in a racehorse.

According to information Landrigan later gave Yandee investigators, she paid Simeon $35,000 and later $100,000 to enlist the aid of Alan Thomas in helping Smith beat the murder charge. She said she had retained her belief in Smith's innocence and believed others had committed the crime. Paying the money was the only way he could get justice, she believed. Like Smith, she denied any knowledge of a conspiracy to provide him with an alibi. She and Smith told investigators they thought the money handed over to Thomas had been to pay the legal costs of a new defence team. Smith said he believed Thomas and Simeon had ripped off his defence money and was angry about not getting it back.

Alan Thomas, confronted with telephone intercepts, told

investigators that he alone had dreamed up the alibi. He had done so because he believed Smith had been set up and thought the only way Smith could get a fair trial was to even the odds by 'squaring up' the brief against him. He had paid Rose about $4000 to participate, and Rose had been true to his word. Michael Thomas denied any involvement in the conspiracy and repeated his account that he had gone to the Burwood Hotel to look for Sergeant Thomas. He said he had seen Rose there, but could not recall being introduced to Smith.

News of Alan Thomas' arrest prompted a convicted drug grower, Errol James Wright, to contact Police Internal Affairs. Wright claimed Alan Thomas had extorted more than $35,000 from him. Wright's farm in Goulburn had been raided in April 1995, and as a result he had been charged with cultivating 1500 marijuana plants. Alan Thomas, who was on the raid, had told him that if Wright paid him the specified sum, he would help Wright beat the charge. Wright had paid the money, and Thomas had told him to blame an Asian man, whose name Thomas provided.

In May 1996, police investigating the false alibi in Smith's case charged Smith, Langrigan, Rose, Michael Thomas, Alan Thomas and Simeon with conspiracy to pervert the course of justice. Alan Thomas, a 46-year-old father of two children from two marriages, who had led a relatively obscure life as a senior detective, was in a spot of real bother. Not only was he confronting the conspiracy charge, but he was also confronted with Wright's claim, and he knew that he had no chance of beating the latter. He decided to 'roll over' and tell all, an act from which he would derive benefit – probably indemnity against prosecution and witness protection, though, as it turned out, not involving the same publicity that the other rollover policeman at the time, Trevor Haken, received for appearing before the Police Royal Commission.

Thomas' story was of a drunken policeman milking suburban crims of every dollar he could squeeze. He also delved into more serious matters. He told Internal Affairs he knew of at least one double murder committed by Lindsey Rose. He said Rose had been his drinking mate and collected bribes for him, ostensibly as payment for fixing trials that, for one reason or another, never came about.

Thomas, who liked to be called 'Chop, Chopper' or 'Choppy' after the notorious Victorian criminal, Mark 'Chopper' Read, confessed to numerous offences. He had once handed a criminal several bags of marijuana to sell on his behalf but the criminal had not given him any money, so he had executed a search warrant on the criminal's home to recover the bags. Thomas had tried, unsuccessfully, to extort money from a leading Sydney jockey. But his main game was taking money from criminals facing serious charges and willing to pay large amounts of money to avoid them.

Thomas' lapses as a police officer had not gone unnoticed among his workmates. Many colleagues called him, behind his back, the 'invisible man' or the 'wandering minstrel'. Thomas was often hard to find when he was supposed to be at work, and had become a heavy punter. Many knew, however, that a check down the pub would likely find him imbibing. His record at the track and on the pokies was at times spectacular and at other times disastrous.

Among Thomas' few staunch drinking mates was Lindsey Rose. Rose, born Lindsey Robert Lehman on 2 May 1955, a man with fair ginger hair and spectacles, fitter and turner by trade, had grown up in Sydney's inner western suburbs. His mother had remarried when he was a young child and he had adopted his stepfather's name. Rose had had many jobs. He had been a volunteer in the State Emergency Service and a member of the Army Reserve. He had been unsuccessful in joining the police service because of his poor eyesight. He became an ambulance driver and on 18 January, 1977, had been off-duty when he heard of the Granville rail disaster. He got into his uniform and offered his services. He spent all night there, enduring the horrors, was deeply affected and suffered a back injury. The back injury forced his resignation from the ambulance service that year.

And by the mid-1980s, he was on the wrong side of the law. He worked as a private inquiry agent but much of his work was on the downside of that industry. With thick neck and barrel chest, he was a strong man who liked to drink, though he normally spoke to people with disarming courtesy. He preferred to be called 'The

Mechanic'. When introduced to people and asked what he did for a living, Rose would say: 'I'm a mechanic and not in the normal way, but in the true meaning [implying that he was a hitman, someone who 'fixed things'].' He would brag that he had 'gone all the hard yards' as a private inquiry agent, anything from being a VIP guard to a brothel minder, not just knocking down people with his fists, but 'knocking' them in the homicidal sense of the word. People did not take him terribly seriously; they thought it was more the alcohol talking.

The Chopper thought as much. Lindsey, as far as he was concerned, was talking drunken gibberish, although he knew the Mechanic would take a cut in a bit of illegal cash if any were on offer, and that he liked firearms. He knew Rose could be tough, but did not think Rose had the toughness to kill. The drunken words had been uttered over long, late-night drinking sessions. The two had become so close that there were times when they were both as broke as each other and hungry for money. The cop and the PI, the Chopper and the Mechanic, called it being on the 'bones of their arse'. Any offer of a quick easy earn, no matter how illegal, was snapped up.

Throughout those talks with the PIB and Task Force Yandee, Alan Thomas maintained that for the most part his actions had been 'noble cause corruption' – breaking the law, certainly, but doing so to put criminals away and make society a better place. This had included fabricating evidence in 1984 against an Asian man who was charged with murder and convicted and sentenced for manslaughter. It also included fabricating and giving perjured evidence against a man charged with shooting a police officer, a case in which, Thomas said, he had been so upset he would have shot the offender himself. Both men pleaded guilty anyway, served their sentences and left the State. But in yet another case, in which Thomas admitted to fabricating evidence, a man who had served three years of a seven-year sentence for armed robbery was released and pardoned.

Asked about Rose, Thomas told his interrogators of the Mechanic's occasional bragging about having knocked five people.

He told them that Rose had sometimes said there were many more, but had always come back to the figure of five. Thomas said he had been sceptical for a long time, but had taken the talk far more seriously after the murders of prostitutes Kerrie Pang and Fatma Ozonal at the Kerry's Oasis massage parlour at Gladesville on Valentine's Day, 1994.

A week after those murders, Rose had come to him and asked him to sell a pistol for $500. Rose had taken him to the Burwood RSL carpark, taken the weapon from the boot of his car and handed it to him. Rose had told Thomas that night that he had killed the two women, but Thomas had still thought the Mechanic was kidding him. He sold the pistol for Rose. On two more occasions, Rose had told Alan Thomas he had committed those murders, the last time in a Parramatta restaurant, where he complained about Mark Lewis, the West Ryde-based private inquiry agent who had been Kerrie Pang's estranged husband. He said Lewis had promised him $20,000 for the hit but had then disappeared.

Thomas said that at that stage he had himself been very short of money, having been burdened by bills and by maintenance payments for his son to his ex-wife. He had been trying to raise cash for a house, but the money just kept slipping through his fingers. He had thought he would soon die from colitis. His drinking and punting were out of control. Money had been owing for stable fees for the racehorse he had an interest in. In these circumstances, he had accessed the police computer and driven to Lewis' new address at St Marys to get that $20,000. Lewis had not been at home, so Thomas had cruised the streets and at a nearby shopping centre had seen his car. Lewis had been with relatives and in the end he did not approach him.

Thomas continued his debriefing for months, enjoying the mixed blessings of special protection. Every time he told them something, the brief around Yandee grew. In late 1996, 12 Yandee investigators and five from the PIB had been working together. Initially, they were operating from a one-man police station at Gladestone, a tiny village 18 km south-east of Kempsey on the mid-north coast of New South Wales. From there they covertly probed other suspects and known drug dealers for clues to outstanding drug murders.

The investigators came to call their targets 'deer hunters' and their turf the 'green triangle' – a vast tract of heavily timbered and picturesque rainforest country stretching from Port Macquarie to Coffs Harbour on the coast and inland to the mountain country of Dorrigo. But the remoteness of many of their targets and close-knit community ties both worked to defeat their efforts.

Thomas knew nothing about the north coast drug dealers; his area of graft was confined to the suburbs. He had learnt of Smith's plight through a relative who drank at the Burwood Hotel.

He told Yandee of another time, years earlier, when Rose had come into the pub and had seen a story about unsolved murders in a newspaper. Rose had taken exception to the fact there was no mention of the Pang and Ozonal killings. He had also pointed to the murder of another couple mentioned in the article.

'I did them.'

Thomas said his unspoken words in response had been 'Yeah, sure, bullshit,' and that everyone present had thought the same. Two more murders were the last thing Yandee expected. Their terms of reference had gone from four murder inquiries to possibly two more unsolved double homicides. Eight murders were the last thing they expected, and if Rose's bragging about being responsible for five killings was correct, they were looking at nine homicides.

But alcohol and poor health had addled the Chopper's brain. For the life of him, Alan Thomas could not remember the names of the two other victims Rose had pointed to in the paper, only that it was a man and woman, and that the man had been an interstate truck driver and some kind of druggie. He recalled that it had happened in the 1980s and that the man's name might have begun with the letter K.

Detective Inspector Rod Baker, a veteran investigator from the Drug Enforcement Agency, and Yandee's chief investigator, knew that the information from Alan Thomas, as it stood, was not enough for the police to lay charges against Rose. He needed better evidence than that. 'You've got to give us something better to go on,' Inspector Baker said. 'Something that only the killer would know. Something that hasn't been reported in the media. Did he tell you anything about what happened?'

Thomas racked his brain. All the booze, plus his colitis, had taken its toll. 'Was one of the women shot through the eye? I remember he said something about shooting one of them in the eye.' It did not seem much, but when the case files on the murders were opened it showed that Kerrie Pang had been stabbed at least 21 times, bashed and shot through the right eye. Ozonal was shot three times in the upper body and head.

With investigators afraid that too much information had been made public about the murders back in 1994, the mention of the bullet wound to Ms Pang's eye was tantamount to turning up a gem. It was one of the few details that had never been disclosed.

Rose had worked for more than ten years on and off as an investigator for the inquiry firm run by Pang's husband, 59-year-old Ryde businessman Mark Lewis. Lewis had long been the prime suspect in the murder and had claimed that in the hour preceding the killings he had received an anonymous call from a person threatening to kill her.

Rose, following his arrest on 18 April 1996 for his part in the conspiracy to pervert the course of justice over the Spradbrow murder, had been required under the terms of his bail to report three times a week to Task Force Yandee. He had kept conscientiously to his bail conditions. But the possibility of a double murderer walking around free sent alarm bells ringing. Rose had to be pulled back in and interviewed. The Chopper gave the police the excuse they needed. He told them he had given Rose a .22 Mark 1 Ruger pistol in May 1995 as a birthday present.

On the morning of Saturday 29 June, 1996, Rose was being heavily dogged by surveillance officers from the PIB, backed by members of the State Protection Group. They were watching a flat in Sellwood Street, Brighton-Le-Sands, where he had spent the night with a new girlfriend. They saw him leave at 6.45 am and return a short time later with a newspaper. Rose emerged from the block of flats at 7.43 am carrying a blue travel bag, and walked to a station wagon. As he was trying to start the vehicle, police moved in. Searching the travel bag, they found a fully loaded pistol. Under the driver's seat they found a small plastic bag containing 11 grams of cannabis leaf. On the way to the Sydney Police Centre, Rose told the officers he also had a .303 rifle at his home at Jersey Road, Wentworthville. Police went there and took possession of the rifle and ammunition.

Interviewed at the Sydney Police Centre, Rose said he had bought the pistol for $1000 at the Burwood Hotel from a man known to him only as Mick. Then he said Alan Thomas had given it to him for his birthday. He said the .303 belonged to Thomas and he had borrowed it a few months earlier. He did not know where the dope had come from.

Rose was charged with being in possession of a firearm without a licence and with being in possession of a prohibited drug. He appeared in Central Local Court in Sydney and was refused bail. Later that afternoon, Detective Sergeant Gary Williams and Detective Senior Constable Perry of the State Major Incident Group, told him they wanted to question him about the murders of Pang and Ozonal. Rose refused to be formally interviewed, but did admit to having been present when the murders occurred and having been involved. He said he would give a statement only by inducement, which meant that the evidence could not be used against him in a prosecution.

The police notified the New South Wales State Crime Commission, which was practiced at taking statements on inducement. Its chairman, Phillip Bradley, called together a small team for a special Saturday evening hearing. Rose told the commission how he killed the women, and that Alan Thomas had been there at the time. He spoke calmly and matter-of-factly about it all. It was a spiteful act on Rose's behalf. Naming Alan Thomas was the only lie, but nobody at that stage disbelieved him.

Alan Thomas, now under suspension from the police service, denied being present at the murders. He expressed surprise that Rose had put his name up at all. He had had no involvement apart from failing to report his suspicions. The police could not use the evidence Rose had given under inducement about his own involvement, and they did not have enough other evidence to charge him. Alan Thomas said there was a man Rose knocked around with at the time of the Pang and Ozonal murders, a man Rose referred to as his 'apprentice'. Police went to find that man.

As police expected, Rose got bail. He walked free from Central Local Court on Monday 1 July 1996. As part of his bail conditions, he reported to Task Force Yandee that day and the following Wednesday, and was meant to have reported again on the Friday.

It was felt that now that he had put his hand up for the Pang and Ozonal murders, Rose might abscond. A surveillance team was put onto him. But the surveillance police were new at the job and not very good at it. On Thursday, 4 July the surveillance team tailed Rose from Brighton-Le-Sands to a hairdressing salon at Burwood. They watched as he had his hair dyed dark brown and cut short. He replaced his prescription pebble lens spectacles with contact lenses. Then he slipped down a crowded shopping mall and the surveillance police lost him.

That night police quizzed Alan Thomas, who said that on 30 June, Rose had told him he planned to abscond and go to his parents' home in Queensland. Police also interviewed Rose's girlfriend. She told him he had gone off that day to see his solicitor. He was then to have been interviewed by police about an unrelated inquiry. He had told her he would be back that night and had left his mobile phone. The next morning, 5 July, she had discovered he had stolen American currency (the amount would convert to $A2000) from her home.

This is what, in fact, did happen on that day. Rose had hired a rental car and, using his birth surname of Lehman, had driven to Adelaide, where he abandoned the car at the airport. For the next six months, he was to live in Adelaide, working under the name of Lindsey Lehman. He would apply for a South Australian driver's licence under that name and give a correct address for where he was living. From November 1996, he would live in a boarding house at 18 Eleventh Avenue, Bowden, near a red-light district, paying $60 a week. He would hang out with local prostitutes and frequent the Gaslight Tavern, where patrons would describe him as a 'happy-go-lucky fellow'. Police put Rose's name on a wanted circular. They included the name Lehman among his aliases and sent the circular to police in Queensland, Victoria and South Australia. Because Rose obtained a licence in South Australia under the name Lehman, it would have been a simple enough exercise for the South Australian Police to have done a computer check. But it was never done.

In the meantime, a separate team of investigators tried to identify the second double murder which Rose had mentioned to Alan Thomas. They undertook a painstaking search of newspaper archives and struck pay dirt. On 20 January 1984, Edward Cavanagh, a truck driver who had connections with the Griffith Mafia in southern New South Wales, and Cavanagh's de facto wife, Carmalita Lee, had both been shot four times in the head in their home at Hoxton Park in Sydney's south-west. The information roughly squared with the recollection of Thomas, that one of the victims had been a truck driver and his name had started with a K.

The case files on the Cavanagh-Lee murders were dusted off and Detective Sergeant Matt Appleton was assigned the brief. Cavanagh was a brute of a man who often handled problems with his fists. At the time of his death, he was believed to have been running marijuana interstate for the Mafia boss, Robert Trimbole. Cavanagh had been found dead at the foot of his double bed. Lee had been on top of the bed, naked and bound by telephone cord, and the home had been ransacked.

Police also investigated another matter that might have been related to Rose. That was the disappearance of his uncle, Maxwell Smeal, 43, a chronic asthmatic, from Smeal's home in Burwood in July 1990, a time when Rose had just finished serving a gaol sentence in Queensland over a stolen car racket.

On 10 April 1997, armed with a warrant from the Crime Commission, police began tearing apart a shed at Wentworthville, where Rose had lived on and off. Under the concrete floor they uncovered a hidden bunker. In a smaller padlocked shed they found the remnants of a hydroponic cannabis farm and some bags of cannabis. A warrant was issued for Rose's arrest. On the night of 10 April, police went on television appealing for information as to Rose's whereabouts. They said Rose was wanted for questioning over the murders of Pang and Ozonal. Police allowed a photograph of Rose to be televised. A drinker in the Gaslight Tavern in Adelaide spotted the similarity with another man in the bar. He rang the police. At 5.40 am the next day, as Rose was about to start a shift at the Patawalonga dredging project at Glenelg, he was approached by South Australian Police and he surrendered to them without resistance.

While New South Wales Police prepared to fly to Adelaide seeking Rose's extradition, South Australian Police questioned him on a matter of their own: the murder of Brompton prostitute Susan Bobridge, whose body was found in sandhills at Tennyson Beach on 10 January, 1997, with four gunshot wounds to the head. Ultimately, that went nowhere but, on the day of his arrest, Rose appeared in the Holden Hill Magistrate's Court charged with the murders of Cavanagh, Lee, Pang and Ozonal. He was remanded in custody.

Rose was being held at South Australian Police headquarters on 15 April when Inspector Baker and Sergeant Appleton arrived to question him. They questioned him for two days about the four murders, and about other crimes. 'When we first spoke to him he knew that we had him, but he was playing a bit of a game, seeing how much we knew,' Appleton said. 'Once he knew that we had quite a bit on him he decided to spill his guts. He was getting it off his chest. He seemed happy to tell us about it.'

Appleton, questioning Rose about the Cavanagh and Lee murders, laid his cards on the table as to the evidence they had connecting him with the killings. At each winning hand, Rose replied to the effect: 'Well, you've done your homework.' Finally, he said: 'Well, I'll tell you about it.'

Rose, according to his account, had killed Cavanagh 'because it's a righteous thing to do'. A friend, David Norton, had been badly beaten by Cavanagh some years earlier. As far as Rose was concerned, Cavanagh had to be paid back (though Norton was not party to any retribution). On the day of the shootings, Rose had gone to Cavanagh's home with a mate, Peter Francis. Francis had helped Rose in repossession jobs when Rose was working as a private inquiry agent in the Australian Capital Territory, and on this occasion thought he had gone along just to rob the place.

Rose revealed another gem, an item of information that only the killer would have possessed. When Rose shot him, Cavanagh had dropped a bottle of oysters which smashed on the verandah of his home. Despite the macabre nature of the interview, Rose spoke as if he was having a 'normal conversation' with a friend. Said Appleton: 'He was always very calm, very well spoken, nothing out of place in his manner. He came across as educated, the sort of bloke you'd enjoy having a beer with.' Rose said he only had two regrets: the killings of Lee and Ozonal. Kerrie Pang, Ozonal's employer, had been 'a job to do', 'business', but the others – Lee and Ozonal – had not been part of the deal. He had not liked killing them, because they were innocent. Yet they had to die. They had seen everything, including him. Of Lee, he said: 'I had to kill her – she was there!' Questioned about Cavanagh, he said: 'Shot him.'

'Then?'

'Shot her.'

To Rose's way of thinking, as came out in the interview, Cavanagh and Pang had been 'righteous' killings. He had attacked Lee, but that had only been to immobilise her while he waited for Cavanagh to arrive home. He had tied her naked to the bed but at no time had he molested her. He wanted it to be known that there had been no sexual overtones in any of the murders of the women. He was a man of dignity, at least in his own mind; he would never molest a woman.

Rose, giving an account of the sequence of events in each murder, said he always got to a point where he would start to shoot, and from then everything would become 'a robotic blur', like watching a video clip in fast-forward mode.

He had entered the brothel in 1994, to kill Pang and Pang only. He had taken with him a one-time tattooist, Ronald Lewis Waters, whom he regarded as his 'apprentice' in the crime business. Waters had posed as a customer to get past a security lock. But only Ozonal had been there, sitting on a white leather lounge. He had made her sit at gunpoint while he waited for Pang. About half an hour later Pang had arrived in company with Mark Lewis. Rose had shot Ozonal, then turned his attention to Pang, stabbing and shooting her, with Lewis urging him on. The stabbing frenzy had become another blur. The silencer he made for the firearm had come off in the struggle and his glasses had been smashed.

Rose could remember setting fire to the premises in a bid to cover his tracks. Then he had found himself sitting in his car. Though he had blood on his clothes, other things had seemed normal. With Waters giving directions, he had driven off, half blind. Waters would later tell police that when Rose had murdered Pang and Ozonal, a glazed look had come over his face and his eyes seemed to roll back. The acts had been violent and frantic, followed by a retreat to the car and a return to normal behaviour.

Rose, continuing his account, confirmed that Waters had been present at the shootings, but Alan Thomas had not been. Rose had only made up the story about Thomas being present to get his own back for Thomas informing on him. He said Lewis had offered him a $20,000 contract to kill Pang. Lewis, who had afterwards reneged on paying him, had wanted Pang killed because she had been stealing girls and trade from his other brothels. Rose had once had an affair with her and hated her for the way she had treated Lewis.

After three days of recorded interviews, Rose was extradited to Sydney, arriving at the airport under heavy guard. His appearances in court were always marked by an escort of at least six prison officers, and Rose's wrists were manacled to a thick leather belt around his waist, from which a chain dangled, linked to more manacles attached to his legs.

Over the ensuing year, Rose confessed to many crimes, including ones totally unsolved and others where there had been arrests. The crimes included drug growing and dealing, home burglaries and, in December 1982, the hijacking of a truck, in which there had been $600,000 worth of cigarettes. He had stolen another truck and driven it to Queensland, where it had been stripped and the shell buried. He had been tipped off that certain elderly people were wealthy and he had broken into their homes to steal from them. He had done a break-and-enter on a gun shop and had robbed an amusement parlour. A number of crimes could not be identified by police because Rose could not remember precise addresses or dates. But with each confession, Rose agreed to give evidence against any co-accused.

Throughout all this, Rose did not identify the fifth person he was supposed to have murdered. He emphatically denied responsibility for the disappearance of Max Smeal. In August 1997, Inspector Baker and Detective Sergeant Stephen Tedder confronted him with the allegation that the fifth victim had been 44-year-old Reynette June Holford, an executive secretary with the Waltons retail chain and a society hostess who had been killed on 20 January 1987.

Holford's body had been found at 7.40 am that day by her de facto husband, millionaire property developer and racing identity, 78-year-old Bill Graf, with whom she had been living since her twenties. Holford's body had been lying on the floor in the upstairs bedroom of their mansion in Winbourne Road, West Ryde, a quiet tree-lined street overlooking the Parramatta River. She had been gagged with a stocking and bound up. Her killer had punched her several times, then stabbed her 32 times, mostly in the arms and head, using a screwdriver and a kitchen knife. One thrust had pierced her left lung. She had put up a struggle.

Police had found a bloodied knife in a sink. A towel had been found near the front door and a fly wire on a window had been cut. Sitting on the floor in the middle of the lounge room had been a wine flagon that belonged in the house. It had looked like a burglary gone wrong, though some aspects of the case were contradictory. A $10,000 ring Graf had given Holford was missing, but thousands of dollars of other jewellery had not been touched.

When Yandee investigators spoke to Rose, there were grounds for suspicion that Graf had been involved in Holford's murder. On his account, he had been asleep in an adjacent room with the door wide open, but had not been disturbed. Graf had suffered a stroke earlier that year and Holford had been looking for a new place to live. There had been talk that she had been planning to leave him because his condition had restricted her access to family and friends. In the coroner's inquest in 1989, evidence had been given that Holford feared Graf might die and had been looking for a new place because she would not be able to bear to live in the same house after Graf died. Evidence was also given that in the weeks before her death, she had thought on several occasions that somebody had followed her home.

Graf died the month before the inquest without ever being able to defend his name. Even so, police and the Coroner believed he was a prime suspect, if not for doing the killing himself, then for commissioning somebody to do it.

In probing Rose's past, Yandee investigators had discovered that Rose had worked as an investigator in 1987 with a private inquiry firm run by Mark Lewis. Apart from accepting a commission from Lewis to murder Pang, Lewis had also got him to do an arson so that someone could collect the insurance money. Lewis had also run a printing business in Victoria Road, West Ryde. The offices had been leased from Graf, who had acquired and built at least half the West Ryde business centre, and had had a street named after him. So was it possible, given all that, that Graf, hating his de facto wife for disloyalty, had commissioned Rose, directly or through Lewis, to do her in?

Asked about Holford, Rose confessed. Yes, he had done it, but it had not been a commissioned hit; it had been a bungled housebreaking, and he regretted what he had done. He had learnt of Graf's fortune from listening to Lewis talk about the man dubbed 'Mr Western Sydney'. He had not told Lewis he planned to rob Graf; it had been an opportunistic crime of his own.

He had cased the home in advance and had gained entry through a partially opened garage door, then found a key to the front door in the glove box of Graf's car. To prove that he was telling the truth he told the investigators about leaving the wine flagon in the middle of the room, something that police had never revealed publicly. Holford had woken, realised there was an intruder, and as Rose had walked past her door, had jumped at him with a pair of scissors. Taken by surprise, Rose had stabbed her with the screwdriver he was carrying and 'thumped' her several times to stop her from screaming. He then tied her up and gagged her.

As he had left the house, he had cut the fly wire and interfered with a window to make it look well and truly like a burglary. He had tried to fence the stolen ring but had given up after being given a cheap valuation. When he had left the house, he had not thought she would die. His training as an ambulance officer had indicated to him that she was not sufficiently injured. He did not think he had stabbed her 32 times, nor did he recall using a knife.

Lindsey Rose's cooperation with police was argued as a point in his favour by both police and his counsel, Stuart Littlemore QC, when he pleaded guilty to the homicides before Justice Levine on 28 August 1998. Littlemore said Rose had been noted for 'meritorious conduct' in the aftermath of the Granville Rail Disaster. He had helped police solve a number of crimes and had pleaded guilty to the murders. These were some of the principal reasons, he said, why Rose should not be gaoled for life.

Crown Prosecutor Mr Chris Maxwell QC said the murder of Cavanagh was an act of revenge for his having beaten up a friend of Rose. Lee had been shot because he 'couldn't have any witnesses'. Holford's murder had been a 'robbery gone wrong and she got in the way'. Ozonal had also got in the way.

Forensic psychiatrist Dr Bruce Westmore said Rose's crimes involved extreme violence. Rose had an 'adult anti-social personality', with schoolday memories of being a 'small bullied boy' who did not seem to fit in. He changed jobs and careers regularly, and had developed a technique of revenge against society which, as an adult, became murderous.

Westmore had taken particular note of the remarks attributed to Rose as he watched a television report showing Pang's grieving son. Rose had reportedly said: 'I wonder if he knew what a bitch she was.' Westmore said: 'It's a fairly cruel and callous sort of statement. His [Pang's son's] mother is dead at the hands of this man and even in death he denigrates her.' He said Rose's adult antisocial disorder was a condition that commonly affected professional criminals such as contract killers and major white-collar criminals, and Westmore doubted whether the condition would change much with age.

Maxwell said Rose faced life imprisonment or a minimum term which he suggested could be 40 years. Levine said he could not excuse Rose's actions, murders which he said had been of 'horrific seriousness'. Levine said Rose's confessions and other help to police were not enough to justify a lighter sentence. 'On all the material, I find it impossible to reconcile a compassionate concern as an ambulance officer for the sanctity of human life and the saving of it with the cynical, violent and cold-blooded destruction of human life involved in the five homicides, and thus am unable to attach weight to this component in mitigation of the penalty to be imposed,' he said. 'There is simply no warrant for leniency in this case.' On 3 September 1998, Levine sentenced him to imprisonment for the term of his natural life.

In August 1999, Rose refused to give evidence at the Campbelltown District Court trial of Brian Smith, Michael Thomas and Michael Simeon, all of whom pleaded not guilty to the charge of conspiring to pervert the course of justice by providing a false alibi in the Spradbrow trial. All three of the defendants were found not guilty.

Landrigan, who had separated from Smith, pleaded guilty to the conspiracy charge but maintained Smith's innocence. Acting Judge Joseph Kevin Ford sentenced her to 250 hours of community service. Rose had already been sentenced by Judge Dodd in December 1998 to a fixed term of eight years after pleading guilty to his part in the Spradbrow alibi conspiracy.

Alan Thomas, who also pleaded guilty to the alibi conspiracy charge, was sentenced by Judge Flannery in June 1998 to seven years, with a minimum of three years to be served. The sentence also incorporated other crimes that he pleaded guilty to.

On 9 November 1998, Justice Greg James, sitting in the Supreme Court, ordered a jury to find Peter Francis not guilty of being an accomplice with Rose in the murders of Cavanagh and

Lee, despite Francis admitting being present when Rose shot the couple. James said that in his view the evidence against Francis was not sufficient to establish his guilt of either murder, and Francis was accordingly acquitted.

On 19 November 1999, a Supreme Court jury found Mark Lewis, 62, guilty of the murders of Pang and Ozonal. Ronald Waters, who gave evidence against Lewis, was found guilty on 28 August, 1999, of being an accessory after the fact to the murders and was sentenced to 18 months' periodic detention. Michael Thomas was dismissed from the New South Wales Police Service under the 'loss of confidence' powers of the Police Commissioner, Peter Ryan, though subsequently he was acquitted on a charge of conspiracy in the Spradbrow matter.

Alan Thomas, and Rose, went into strict protective custody in prison. There was reason enough for that. During the course of the Yandee investigation, and through admissions from both Rose and Alan Thomas, 58 people had been arrested and charged with more than 220 offences, from robbery to extortion, and including drug offences and conspiring to pervert the course of justice.

part four

THE
GANGS

the Western Australian bikie wars

the escapade of Brendon Abbott

gangs, Asian style

THE WESTERN
AUSTRALIAN
BIKIE WARS

... into their land to murder and to ravish...

William E Aytoun
Scottish poet (1813–1865)

On 30 September 1998 a thin, scruffy man sauntered into the yard of Golden City Motors in Western Australia's goldmining town of Kalgoorlie and casually looked over a 1984 model Ford Falcon. The vehicle was a slightly metallic bronze S-pack sedan with orange stripes on the sides. The man, 168 cm tall, was clean-shaven, sandy-haired and aged 30–35 years. But he was hidden behind wraparound sunglasses and gave a false name and address. So-called Michael Armstrong of York Street, Boulder, Western Australia, closed the deal and drove off.

The bikie gang, Club Deroes, one of the four major outlaw bikie gangs in Western Australia, had just acquired another cheap car for a crime spree.

Eight hundred kilometres away in Perth, Marc Chabriere, engaged in his sandblasting business, was driving through the city's eastern suburbs in his brown Fairlane. A caring father of two children, Jack and Chantal, Chabriere, who had previously worked in the mining industry in Africa, was well respected in his business dealings. He and his wife, Helen, had bought Sandblasting and

Industrial Coating Pty Ltd in February 1996, and had recently moved to premises in Cullen Street, Bayswater. The Fairlane was for work and family use.

But when it came to his own time, there was a transformation. Then Chabriere chose a bright shiny Harley-Davidson motorbike, lovingly stripped and modified into a 'chopper'. Proudly straddling it, he wore the jeans, red club shirt, leathers and patch of Perth's biggest and longest-standing bikie gang, the Coffin Cheaters. To his bikie mates, he was known as 'Shabs'.

As so often happened in bikie-land, the Coffin Cheaters, in September 1998, were involved in a long-running feud with Club Deroes, another of the four major outlaw bikie gangs in Western Australia. The feud had started over the activities of one man, Kevin 'Mick' Woodhouse. More of him later. In the preceding six months, violence had been escalating.

At the outset, clashes had been marked by brutal bashings with batons. People on the receiving end normally suffered injuries such as broken arms and legs and fractured skulls. But in the interim period, secretly, the gangs had built up stocks of high-powered rifles and flak jackets.

It's 10 o'clock on the morning of Wednesday 14 October, and Marc Chabriere is at the wheel of the Fairlane, chatting to passenger 'Big' Mick Anderson while they drive along Kurnall Road in the industrial area of Welshpool. They are driving past Hampton Transport when a metallic bronze Falcon speeds up behind them and starts to overtake. As it draws alongside, a masked man in the front passenger seat aims a high-powered rifle at the Fairlane and sprays it with bullets. He gets seven in before the Falcon overtakes the Fairlane and speeds off. Three bullets strike the Fairlane's door. One smashes into Anderson's arm, shattering his elbow. One goes straight through the window, hitting Chabriere in the head. The Fairlane slews out of control and crashes into fencing. Chabriere is dead at the wheel. Mick Anderson crawls out of the car, in agony, as he clutches the bloodied mess of his arm, and struggles to Hampton Transport's fence and slumps against it, the image of the killer's eyes through the balaclava still before him – cold, determined, deadly, unforgettable. Eyes he didn't know but would recognise if ever he saw them again.

Shocked workers, finding a badly wounded man and a dead one, called the ambulance. The paramedics arrived at 10.20 am to give emergency treatment to Anderson and speed him away to Royal Perth Hospital for surgery and recovery under police guard. For the moment, Chabriere was left where he had died, his body covered with a white sheet. Speeding away, the assassin and his driver pulled off their balaclavas. They drove to a bushy hideaway and torched the car, then celebrated the success of their ambush.

The Coffin Cheaters could not believe Shabs was dead. Four of them, big and burly, demanded to see the body inside the area cordoned off by blue and white tape. They scuffled with police, who were blocking their way. The four included Woodhouse and a high-ranking Coffin Cheater with an impressive record of violence and lawbreaking, Eddie Withnell. The police held the line. But the surrounding area was a hive of activity, swarming with journalists and photographers, on foot and in helicopters whirring overhead. One-and-a-half hours later, at 3.40 pm and after much negotiation, police allowed Withnell through to see the proof. He viewed the body of his slain comrade, his brother-in-arms. Three hours after the shooting, police found the burnt-out shell of the getaway car. They commenced a massive search operation, an operation which would net two guns, a loaded firearm magazine and cannabis, when seven Cheaters were searched in a Mandurah car park one hundred kilometres away.

The Coffin Cheaters' members liked to refer to themselves as 'bikers'. To the general public, whose terror and loathing they enjoyed and encouraged, they were 'bikies'. To the public, the term denoted a gang of drunken louts, involved in drugs and organised crime, intimidating standover men. They were feared – and as glamourised – as the Mafia. They were the 'one-percenters', taking pride in the label given by the American Motorcycle Association in 1947. That association had described the bikers who caused a riot at a Californian rally as 'the one per cent deviant fringe' the few who gave all other bikers a bad name. The Hell's Angels had been founded by disgruntled ex-servicemen in California in the 1940s. Most of them had joined the gangs because it gave them the sense of being able to thumb their noses at society. The association label stuck, bikies liking the idea of being the one per cent who 'don't fit and don't care'.

The Australian bikies were heavily influenced by the bikie culture in the United States. Journalists, Sandra Harvey and Lindsay Simpson, in their book, *Brothers in Arms: The Inside Story of Two Bikie Gangs*, wrote of the inspiration of Anthony Mark 'Snodgrass' Spencer, a member of another outlaw gang, the Commancheros. Snodgrass visited the United States and was enormously impressed by the Bandido Motor Cycle Club, also known as the Bandido Nation, which had formed in Texas in 1966. Snodgrass had been inspired to form an Australian chapter of the Bandidos, and as Harvey and Simpson wrote: 'Snodgrass saw an Australian courtesy card in his mind's eye. It would be the new club's calling card: "1%er" in the left-hand corner in red print – signifying the new Bandidos were the 1 per cent of the motorcycling public who were not law abiding citizens..." revving their motor cycles up while old ladies are on pedestrian crossings,' a former member of another outlaw club, the Nomads, said. 'But most of them don't do that. The nerds, well it's like this, you are following someone in a 100 km zone and they are doing 60 and then you get to a double lane and suddenly they accelerate to 100. They are the nerds, you know what I mean?'

A person wanting to join a club became a nominee, and had to do the menial tasks, such as collecting the wood for a barbecue. Then they got their colours, progressing to probationary status, then full membership. Some women were attracted to them, probably liking the macho feeling, the 'free spirit' mentality. To some women of feminist persuasion, the bikies were misogynists, with wives referred to often as 'old ladies', their t-shirts emblazoned with the words, 'property of', or the same words tattooed on their bodies. The girlfriends, called 'mamas', were passed around as general property. When a former Nomad was asked about this, his best answer was: 'Well, bikies tend to treat women like their motorbikes. They're something you ride around on, you know?'

Within their own ranks, the bikies had certain admirable qualities, including intense loyalty and courage. The Bandidos had as their mottos: 'These colours don't run', and 'I AM my brother's keeper'. They were known to join other motorcycle clubs in such socially beneficial activities as Christmas pickups of presents for handicapped children. The Hell's Angels had annual music festivals at Broadford in Victoria. Many bikies were married. Many had ordinary jobs and were only involved in their bikie activities after hours. As clubs, they used various money-making methods. They provided security services, including protection for tow-truck operators, and bought into businesses, including nightclubs.

But many of them were also heavily into crime, particularly drug dealing, using their mobility, secretiveness and capacity for violence to evade the law. The dealers specialised in amphetamines, sometimes manufacturing as well as supplying, and other drugs, such as cocaine. As well, they or other bikies participated in stolen car rackets, money laundering and prostitution. They were ferociously territorial, whether the territory was geographical or related to their share of a market. Territorial violence was often related to the control of drug distribution. The saving grace for the general community was that when violence broke out, they usually fought among themselves.

The formation of the Australian chapter of the Bandidos in 1983 by disaffected members of the Commancheros produced conflict which escalated into all-out war between the Bandidos and Commancheros, culminating in the Father's Day Massacre on 2 September, 1984, at Milperra in Sydney's outer south-west. Six bikies died in the gun battle and one teenage girl was caught in the crossfire. Thirty-one bikies were convicted and sentenced – and Snodgrass committed suicide.

There was much talk and discussion about the bikies, but none of this put them out of existence. The groups operating in Australia include the Commancheros, Bandidos, Rebels, Hell's Angels, Life and Death, Outcasts, Nomads, Black Uhlans, Gypsy Jokers, Highway 61, Finks and Outlaws.

There were periodic crackdowns by police. In dawn raids in Sydney's outer west on 27 July, 1995, four people were arrested and charged with offences involving cannabis, amphetamines and firearms. Police had intelligence that bikie gangs were amassing huge arsenals of weapons, including hand grenades, rocket-launchers, land mines and machine-guns. The intelligence indicated that there were plans by the bikie clubs to rationalise, to reduce the number of clubs from 22 to six by the year 2000 and have clear areas of demarcation. And linked almost inextricably with the power struggle was the question of drugs.

But it is Western Australia, and the activities of the bikie gangs there, that we must turn our attention.

In Perth, it was understood, by the 1990s, that the Coffin Cheaters were in control of the city's amphetamines and high-quality cannabis markets. They also owned legitimate businesses, such as metal and timber shops, taverns, and nightclubs with skimpily dressed barmaids and strippers. They denied any involvement in drugs, though many had numerous drug convictions. They normally denied that the number 13 on their jackets indicated that they were dealers.

Mick Woodhouse had been a prospective Club Deroes member, and a good one, meting out punishment to bikies who deserted the club. His doing such jobs accorded with the bikie custom of getting prospectives and associates to carry out crimes for members, thus keeping the members' hands clean. In 1993, Woodhouse and three other Deroes had charged into a home in Pinjelly in the south-west of Western Australia, and dealt retribution to Martin Devaney, a one-legged man who had deserted Club Deroes. They had tied up Devaney with cord and adhesive, restrained his distraught wife and daughter in a bedroom, and bashed him mercilessly, kicking and beating him with batons and fists, deliberately breaking his leg.

Devaney should have known that to take bikie club colours was to take on a commitment for life. There was no acceptable way out of the brotherhood. It demanded loyalty beyond family and the law, even beyond members' own safety and wellbeing. Disloyalty deserved the most vicious reprisal. Devaney knew at least that much. Who could forget the thrashing of a disloyal Gypsy Joker to within inches of his life? The Deroes took their colours very seriously. They retained the Hell's Angels initiation ceremony of dirtying their first leathers – members urinating and defecating into a bucket, the contents thrown over the initiate in his new jeans and jacket. His clothes were never to be washed – and it would be 'the last time anyone shits on his colours'.

Woodhouse, however, had made two errors. The first was doing this work on behalf of his brothers in the deserter's home, flouting a strict rule that families are not involved in punishments and pay-backs. His second was to do with the court proceedings. Woodhouse was charged with assault as a result of the beating of Devaney, and because he was deemed to have copped the charge in the line of duty, the Deroes paid $10,000 towards his legal costs. But the night before the case was due to begin, Woodhouse changed his plea from not guilty to guilty, a plea which was to earn him a six-year sentence. The bikies had a rule in keeping with their disdain for the law: they would not plead guilty on any occasion. Not only had Woodhouse broken that rule, but the Deroes had just blown $10,000 and they wanted that back. So Woodhouse, still a Deroes probationary and now a Deroes 'dog', was thrown out of the club. The Coffin Cheaters took him in. To the Deroes, it was not right for another club to take 'their dog'. Someone not worthy of their black and white patch – a raven on a set of pistons – should not be wearing the Cheaters' red and white skull with wings either. Especially when they were owed $10,000. The Cheaters had to be taught a lesson.

But the feud really went beyond Woodhouse. It went far beyond one man; it became another example of the suspicion and hostility rife among the bikie gangs all over the world. While all this had been kept in check in Western Australia through an accepted four-club policy, which restricted the number of major outlaw gangs in the State to four, the deep-seated need to stake out their territory and protect their turf and their profitable drug trade was at the core of much of the violence. The drug trade – hydroponically grown cannabis and amphetamines for long-distance drivers – was too valuable. Others were not to be allowed to muscle in on it.

The Western Australian bikie clubs had cohabited peacefully since the 1970s, their mutual distrust contained by the four-club policy. The Cheaters were by far the biggest and oldest club, followed by the Gypsy Jokers. The Cheaters were known for dealing drugs, the Jokers for random acts of violence, including bashings and rapes. The Club Deroes, the Cheaters' main rival for the drug market – and, due to their initiation ceremony, the dirtiest – had about half the Cheaters' numbers.

While there was an uneasy peace, there was no collaboration. In 1997, the Cheaters banned the Deroes and the Jokers from Australia's biggest bikie gathering, the South West Tattoo at Brusselton. They did invite Western Australia's fourth club, God's Garbage, who certainly had done nothing to clean up the bikies' image. Based in Manjimup in the south-west, this club was notorious for being pack-rapists. In one incident, a 31 year-old mother of three had drunk with members of the club in a local tavern, then endured a 16-hour ordeal of rape and abuse at the gang's clubhouse. Days later, she hanged herself. Club members, maintaining their code of silence, had refused to answer questions at the inquest.

The peace deal between the clubs was matched by the police, who maintained a type of 'containment policy'. If members were caught breaking the law, they were charged, but they were not constantly watched. The police policy was that they would intervene in bikie affairs only if called upon, the hope no doubt being that if police accorded the gangs a certain amount of respect and did not harass them, the gangs would respond by adopting a more responsible attitude. But of course situations arose when police had to intervene. In March 1997, about 300 bikies disrupted family enjoyment of a rhythm and blues festival at Lake Clifton. The police closed it down.

Then the testy relationship changed dramatically. On Sunday, 13 April 1997, a dozen Coffin Cheaters were letting their hair down, grossly misbehaving, at Jarrah Jack's nightclub in Bunbury. An off-duty Aboriginal police aide showed his ID and called them to order. He was knocked out. So was the patron who went to his aid. Police were called. Half a dozen police officers attended, and were set upon by the gang. The police were brutally attacked, their lives threatened. One officer ended up in hospital.

The assaulted policemen's commander, who was in charge of policing in the south-west region, was Superintendent John Watson. If they wanted a fight, the bikies had chosen a man who would give them one. Watson was a big man with a similar background to many of the bikies. He had been raised through the school of hard knocks and the university of life. A professionally trained boxer, martial-arts expert and nightclub bouncer before joining the police, he was strong and tough, standing at 183 cm and weighing 99 kg. Watson had served in the Western Australian Police counter-terrorist team and was the obvious choice to head protective services when such personages as members of the Royal Family and the Pope chose to visit the State.

Watson responded to the bikie challenge by initiating 'Operation No-Tolerance', marching in with the slogan that 'one per cent of nothing is nothing'. He ordered his man to put an end to bikie excesses. The antisocial minority was to be targeted in a proactive operation. In keeping with this policy, police raided bikie headquarters and homes, kicking in doors if they had to, and set up checkpoints on roads. They did a lot of intelligence work, casing the clubhouses, learning numbers of bikies, who their leaders were, the location of safe houses and the general modus operandi.

Watson's senior detective sergeant, George Loverock, based at Bunbury, was also a match for the bikies. Like Watson, had Loverock chosen a different path in life, he might have been one of them. In his early forties, clean-cut and good-looking, he was a ruckman, 190 cm and 104 kg. Raised in Kalgoorlie, he played hard in the ruck for the Aussie Rules club, the Kangas. He tackled his job as if it were a footie match, using footie terms and footie tactics, and saw bikie clubs as operating in much the same way as footie clubs. He rode a Harley and wore a heavy gold phantom ring on one hand and a silver Harley ring on the other. Loverock had previously served in the consorting squad and the drug squad. He knew bikies' business and 'where they were coming from'. He could talk their language. Telling them that his uniform was his colours, he was prepared to front them and take them on.

On the national scale, Operation No-Tolerance was supported by the National Crime Authority (NCA), which in 1995 had launched Operation Panza, a national investigation into bikies' organised crime. In two years, it had managed to have 175 people arrested on 456 charges for offences such as possession of illegal drugs, weapons and counterfeit money. More than $3 million in proceeds of crime had been seized. But there was no cause for thinking the problems of gang lawlessness had been beaten – not with the spectacle of the Blackmarket nightclub shootout in Sydney in November 1997, which wiped out the senior hierarchy of the Bandidos. Killed in the shootout, in the club basement, were Bandido sergeant-at-arms Sasha Milenkovic and club nominee Rick Raymond Destoop. The national president, Michael Alexander Kulakowski, was mortally wounded. Members of the Rebel Motor Cycle Club were seen fleeing the scene, but soon arrests were to follow.

On 10 December 1997, police launched a series of dawn raids nationally, based on intelligence gathered by three police officers, in an undercover operation which would probably rank as the most dangerous ever undertaken. The three had been members of the Bandidos for 12 months. Victorian police arrested 14 gang members after raiding Bandido club houses in Ballarat and Geelong and the houses of gang members in Shepparton and Bendigo. New South Wales police arrested two after raiding houses at Toongabbie and North Parramatta. South Australian police made one arrest, and in Perth, police arrested three Bandidos. In this operation police seized heroin and amphetamines with a street value of more than $1 million, firearms (including an AK-47 assault rifle, sawn-off shotguns and pen guns) and a Harley-Davidson motorcycle suspected of having been stolen. Western Australia might be separated by a desert or two from the populous east, but it hardly existed in a cocoon. The State's bikie clubs were feeling the heat, both from the police and from intruders.

Eastern States gangs were wanting to come into Western Australia. The Rebels, Hell's Angels and Bandidos were all eyeing the west. Challenges from outside clubs were not new. There had been an attempt in the late 1980s, which had been fought off. A major battle with the New Zealand-based Mongrel Mob had been won, and it helped ward off the Hell's Angels and Rebels at that time. The State's police were concerned with the new thrust. Faced with growing numbers of clubs and members, they saw an increased risk of violence, possibly a repetition of the Father's Day Massacre. The new no-tolerance policy in the south-west was extended to cover the whole State. Loverock, transferred to Perth, was put in charge of organised crime. As such, he tackled the bikies statewide in the same way that Watson did.

The harmony that had existed between the four Western Australian bikie gangs under their four-club policy collapsed. The local clubs responded to the challenge from the east by having membership drives, seeking numbers to 'heavy' the eastern States mobs from their 'turf'. The Cheaters smartly doubled their numbers from 50 to 100, aided by enlisting rural groups such as South-West Riders. This club, which had about 20 members and owned a tavern, quickly accepted the Cheaters' invitation to become their south-west chapter. Earlier, they had seen the forced disbandment of the Pannawonica Riders in the north-west, when that club had been refused the right to fly their own colours and had also declined the offer to become the Cheaters' north-west chapter. The Jokers also went on a successful membership drive, growing five-fold. They had to protect themselves from Australia's biggest gang, the Rebels, whose motif was the flag of the US Confederacy, and who boasted 500 members nationwide.

The Cheaters believed that if they ended the four-club policy for the west, thus opening the door for the eastern States clubs, it would diffuse the situation and take police attention off them. The Club Deroes did not want to remove the policy. But it was not long before the Rebels and Bandidos took hold anyway. Now there were six clubs in Western Australia. The Rebels set up a base at Busselton, a coastal town just south of Bunbury, and quickly recruited 45 members. They did not take long to expand to a Perth chapter, and then to a total of five chapters in just two years. Soon the Rebels were second in size only to the Cheaters. The menace was growing.

Coffin Cheater Eddie Withnell had been renowned for protecting the home turf. He had made his mark by fighting off the Mongrel Mob, publicly denouncing them as soldiers of terror and merchants of crime. But he was hardly an innocent himself. He had spent years in gaol for participating in a gang rape in 1974 and a violent bank robbery in 1977. The man who had done the bank robbery with him, Archie Butterly, had also been gaoled and had died in a hail of bullets during an escape attempt. In gaol, Withnell had taken the opportunity to improve himself, obtaining a Bachelor of Arts degree with Honours from the University of Western Australia. With that qualification, he could have joined the 99 per cent and made a life for himself in mainstream society. Instead, he remained a Coffin Cheater, and a powerful one. The Cheaters considered themselves a democracy and had no designated leader. With his education, Withnell became their spokesman, and as such, their most public figure.

In May 1998, Withnell was at the Broken Hill Hotel in Victoria Park, close to the city. He could easily be recognised as a bikie. He was very much part of the bikie culture, bearing scars that had come from his violent lifestyle. But on this occasion he was not wearing his colours, was not engaged in bikie business, and was not at one of the Cheaters' regular hangouts. He had gone especially to see the sexy show staged by the 'Living Dolls', scantily clad girls who titillated the crowd with erotic come-ons of their almost-naked gyrating. His girlfriend, Paris, was one of them and he was there to see the last show for the evening.

If Withnell was not on bikie business, six other bikies were. They were out to get him, and they had made detailed plans to attack him, altering the number plates of their cars and removing the plates from their bikes. Launching their attack, the six tore round the corner and screeched to a halt at the door. Physically huge and determined, clad in black leather, they marched into the hotel armed with telescopic batons and a cut-throat razor. As the girls froze, they opened up their batons and strode through a group of horrified patrons, who made way for them, until they reached Withnell. A flurry of hard-hitting blows from the batons brought him down. Several of them held him down while their leader, producing a razor, hacked at his ear. They could have sliced the ear off and perhaps retained it as a trophy for the mantelpiece. Instead, they left it hanging by a piece of skin. As suddenly as it began, it was over. The six assailants left, mounted their motorbikes, and roared away.

True to the bikies' masochistic code of manliness, Withnell did not go to hospital and refused to talk to the police about the attack. Withnell knew that if he lived by violence, he was to suffer the repercussions silently. But the other part of the code required a payback on the people who had assaulted Withnell. And everyone knew about the attack. Despite his silence when questioned by police, the attack made headlines. There had been too many witnesses to it. The Perth population, which had seen violence between the bikie gangs a decade earlier, knew it was on again.

Four days later, another Cheater, Darren Whittaker, was targeted by assailants. An ambush was planned for him at 6 am. But Whittaker got wind of it and went after the would-be assailants. In the melee, he was shot in the leg, a bullet entering his left calf and exiting beside the knee. During his hospital treatment, he maintained silence on the matter of a shot being fired at him, avoiding any mention of bikies and score-settling, saying he had injured himself with a stake. But the bullet wound was too obvious: he changed his story to say that he had shot himself accidentally. Nobody could get any more out of him. Shot by the retreating rivals or shot by himself through dropping his gun while running? Word spread around the gangs, who decided, with some contempt, that it was the latter.

Three weeks later, the Coffin Cheaters started their reprisals against the identified assailants, the Club Deroes. The first was a two-pronged operation. In one prong, nine Coffin Cheaters, wearing overalls and balaclavas and armed with a baseball bat, went out to get Club Deroes member Brian Edhouse, 32, in his workplace at Bayswater. In the second, Coffin Cheater Jeffrey Fowler, masked in a balaclava, waited outside the house of Club Deroe Nathan Piggott in Balga. At 6 am, the Gang of Nine stormed a rolling stock factory in Raymond Avenue, Bayswater, and made a beeline for their victim. Ordering other staff to lie on the ground, they launched into Edhouse in a swift and brutal attack, nine against one, bearing down on him mercilessly and breaking both his legs. Their speedy getaway was brought to a halt when their Mazda stalled after reversing into a powerpole, but they escaped on foot.

The other prong was potentially more lethal. Fowler was armed with a semi-automatic shotgun, commonly called a 'streetsweeper' – an apt enough name because of the damage it could do. It was loaded with 16 rounds. The Coffin Cheater had driven to Piggott's home in a Holden Rodeo utility with false number plates. He lay in the front seat of the ute, parked in Piggott's driveway, his streetsweeper loaded. It could easily have done away with Piggott and anyone else in the street. But a resident, suspicious of the vehicle and thinking a burglary might have been in progress, called the police. At 6.50 am, two constables surprised Fowler at the wheel. The suburban street, which could have been swept by shotgun blasts, was instead suddenly full of roaring engines and squealing tyres as Fowler took off, pursued by the constables. Blocked at the back of the local high school, he tried to escape on foot but was caught, seized by the officers and demasked.

The law won this round. Fowler, 45, was convicted of possessing an unlicensed firearm and ammunition, reckless driving, driving a vehicle with false plates, and failing to stop. He was fined $2850 and he lost his licence for six months. In court, supporting him, was Eddie Withnell.

The feud had been taken into suburban streets, with illegal killer weapons. Loverock's organised crime team swung into action. The next day, members of the Tactical Response Group (TRG) and other police mounted a series of lightning raids all around Perth. They raided the Cheaters' headquarters, their homes and their properties. If the Cheaters had one streetsweeper, what else did they have? The police had to find and confiscate any more weapons. The raids uncovered a huge arsenal, which indicated that there had been preparations for gang warfare. They found a military assault rifle, a loaded revolver, a .303 calibre repeater rifle and a .22 calibre pump-action rifle, together with thousands of rounds of ammunition, batons, swords, machetes, knuckledusters and baseball bats. And they found tablets of LSD, amphetamines, cannabis and smoking implements.

George Loverock tried another approach to end the feud. As head of the organised crime policing, he approached both clubs personally in an effort to broker a peace. Despite being more than their equal in size and muscle, Loverock knew it would take only a few to set upon him and only one to put a bullet into him. Yet he walked into both clubhouses and fronted the members. He persuaded the Club Deroes' leaders, Philip Rowles and George Mijatow, to put a stop to the feud. They agreed to Loverock's suggestion of a meeting between the two clubs, four members from each with Loverock and an offsider as mediators, at a venue to be advised only half an hour before. But nothing could get the Cheaters to agree, not even the man-to-man talk of Loverock, or the respect he showed in paying to fix damage caused to the clubhouse during a police raid. The Cheaters refused to take part in the meeting on the grounds that they had no argument with the Deroes. It was the Deroes' feud, not theirs.

They still wanted to settle old scores, though. A month later, on 15 July 1998, the Cheaters managed to evade the close police watch over them and made another payback. Four masked and armed men lay in wait for Deroe member Ian Gangell to open the front door of his South Guildford home to go to work. Gangell came out at 7 am and the gang jumped on him, beating him repeatedly with clubs and iron bars. They left the 43-year-old a mangled mess on his front lawn. His skull was fractured and both of his legs and an arm broken.

The feud was well and truly still on. The police could see the risk of homicide. The group of police who had been assigned to deal with the bikie problem was strengthened and used as the basis for a task force. The bikie campaign, Operation Gallipoli, which had been going almost a year, was made up of 15 highly trained squad officers. Loverock was the obvious choice to head it. Gallipoli increased police presence around the bikies' operations, again boosting the pressure on them. Part of the strategy had been suggested by the FBI in the United States – destroy the gangs by targeting their cash flow and sending them broke.

In the meantime, Loverock went to the Cheaters and confronted them about the bashing of Gangell. At first they denied any involvement, then admitted it had been wrong to do their business in front of the family. Loverock put it straight to them. He knew they were out to get rid of the Deroes. But if they were going to continue to fight and stand over people, they would have the police on their backs.

The Deroes decided that, as a reprisal for the attack on Gangell, they would seek out their 'dog', Woodhouse. At 8.45 am on 28 July 1998, a gang of Deroes came across him by chance, visiting a house in Rosemead Avenue, Bechboro. They parked their brown Cortina on the verge near a primary school. When Woodhouse came out and drove by in a brown Falcon, they sprayed his car with bullets, hitting Woodhouse in the face and wrist. With blood gushing from his wounds, Woodhouse slammed on his brakes and wheeled into reverse. Doing a U-turn on the verge, he drove off and managed to get to the Cheaters clubhouse, where two members took him to hospital in a car containing two loaded weapons, a .22 calibre pistol and a .38 revolver. Woodhouse recovered from his wounds but remained silent, refusing to cooperate with the police.

Shooting Woodhouse showed that the Deroes had firearms stashed away. Three days later, the police orchestrated a series of early morning raids on Deroes' properties in various suburbs, netting a haul of firearms and ammunition which prompted the assistant commissioner for crime, Tim Atherton, to call on the Government to outlaw bikie gangs by making it illegal for them to associate. The police kept up the pressure. The gangs did not know where or when they would be hit next. On 6 August the raids netted more drugs, and formidable weapons: 15 firearms, including a Mossberg pump-action shotgun, a 7.62 mm Lithgow self-loading rifle, a .223 Ruger Mini-14 and a .22 Ruger repeating rifle. They seized more than 6500 rounds of ammunition. They also found a 1978 brown Cortina, partly burnt-out, most likely the one used in the Woodhouse shooting.

A month later, the Cheaters' feelings spilled into the public gallery of the Perth Magistrate's Court. The magistrate was about to hear drugs and firearms charges against bikie member Michael Heaton, 40, who was waiting in court with his girlfriend. A member of the Cheaters, who was also facing charges and had been remanded to that day, saw Heaton and yelled abuse at him. He strode up to Heaton, called him a 'f***ing dog' who should 'come outside', and punched him in the face while another Cheater waited by the door. As Heaton's 27-year-old girlfriend screamed, both Cheaters strode out and raced away in a Nissan Bluebird with tinted windows. Heaton's girlfriend burst into tears. The public in the gallery sat stunned. Again, no complaint was laid. Heaton warned the local newspaper against describing him as a Club Deroe member or associate. But Deroes leader, Philip Rowles, was facing similar charges at that time. Heaton, who was fined $1900 for the drugs and firearms offences, denied having been punched, though it happened in the courtroom, in full view of the magistrate.

The preparations continued, weapons being moved around the State to boost the collections of arsenals and to stay one step ahead of the police. A month after Heaton was punched, a Browning 7 mm pistol with magazine and ammunition was found in a passenger's luggage on a flight from Perth to Kalgoorlie. Heaton was charged over the find and ordered to stand trial.

As well as fighting the Cheaters, the Deroes were still paying out their own deserters, although not all attempts were successful. In the early hours of one morning in early 1998, two Club Deroes members had sneaked into the home of Club Deroes deserter Glenn English in Forrestfield. One, a probationary member, had been armed with a knife, and had climbed over the fence. The other keeping lookout from a nearby alleyway. The probationer had unscrewed the security light and thrown a rock through a bedroom window. The response from inside the house had been a gunshot, and the probationer and his companion, who were not carrying firearms, had fled, at least as far as a vacant block where police found them hiding.

On 23 September 1998, three armed and masked Deroes were marginally more successful, driving their Falcon sedan past the home of Deroes deserter, Raymond Washer, in Lion Street, Carlisle, and firing, blasting the house with at least 20 rounds before speeding off. Bullets went through the front windows and hit a car parked in a neighbour's driveway, puncturing a tyre. Washer, 38, and by then a member of the Rebels, was not hit, and in fact had been ready for an attack. Police searching his house in the aftermath of the attack found a loaded Colt revolver, a loaded Winchester and more than 100 rounds of ammunition. This arsenal was in a wardrobe and hidden in the roof cavity. Washer was charged with possession of unlicensed firearms. Having failed to persuade the court that he had assembled the weapons for killing pigs in the bush, he was fined $1200.

With the Coffin Cheaters still after them, life for loyal Deroes was hardly a bed of roses, as demonstrated by events in October that year, involving Deroes member Mark Doyle, who had joined the club as a youth, finding sanctuary there after escaping from an abusive home.

It is six o'clock in the morning, Tuesday 13 October, and Doyle has just left his wife and three young children for work. He is at the wheel of his Toyota Hilux dual cab. It is his normal route. He has ignored police advice, given regularly to the bikies, that they should vary the routes of their routine travel. Despite being broken a few times, it is bikie code that attacks should not be carried out in the homes or workplaces. That means bikies are most in danger as they leave their homes on routine trips, such as to work. Police had doorknocked up to 200 known bikies and told them to vary their daily routines. George Loverock has personally warned Rowles,

Withnell and Mijatow that they should vary their routes to avoid being caught in an ambush.

As Mark Doyle left home, a lone gunman moved into his hiding place in the bushes by the approach ramp leading to Roe Highway in Maida Vale. As Doyle entered the on-ramp and started to accelerate onto the highway, the gunman broke cover and unleashes a volley of shots from a semi-automatic. A hail of bullets hits the cabin. One pierced the cab, ripped through the back of the driver's seat and hits Doyle in the right kidney region, passing right through his body. Another shot punctured a front tyre, sending the vehicle careering downhill, coming to a halt 200 metres away in Poison Gully.

Critically wounded, in agony, and with no feeling in his legs, Doyle grasped for his mobile phone and managed to dial his wife and an ambulance. Residents, woken by the shots, tended to him until the ambulance arrived 10 minutes later. The officers gave him emergency treatment. The police are there quickly, in force, TRG sharpshooters scouring the area for the gunman, who has managed to escape.

With Doyle severely injured and likely to spend the rest of his life in a wheelchair, the Deroes were outraged and desperate for revenge. The next day they were looking for any Coffin Cheater. Twenty-eight hours after Doyle's shooting, they came across Marc Chabriere and Mick Anderson…

Marc Lucien Raoul Chabriere was cremated at Karrakatta Cemetery after his final ride – a grand display of bikie menace and of the general public's combined fear and fascination with them. Hundreds of people lined the streets to watch the procession of 150 big men in black leathers, their faces covered with black bands and sunglasses, the chrome of their stripped-down Harleys glistening as they rode by at 20 km/h. The Cheaters, Rebels and God's Garbage members moved in procession from the Cheaters' headquarters to the cemetery, bikes three abreast, together with hotted-up American cars. It was wondrous and fearsome.

At the cemetery, a black coffin on the back of a blue utility was opened up to provide beer for the mourners. After downing some

Crown Lager, Emu Bitter and Swan Gold, 30 of Shabs' closest mates went ahead to form a guard of honour and the proceedings began. The Rebels stood outside the crematorium chapel, declining to go in. After the funeral, they took off at a roar, beating the police escort and speeding through red lights. That signalled an end to police tolerance for the funeral. During the wake, more than a dozen police cars created roadblocks outside the Cheaters clubhouse. Right through the night, from 7 pm to 4 am, they stopped and searched cars and bikes as they came and went, breath-testing drivers, charging five men with drink-drive offences.

Then the murder inquiry started. Homicide and the crack tactical response group, 79 Division, joined Operation Gallipoli to solve the crime and do their very best to stop reprisals. In a move to beat the code of silence, the Assistant Commissioner for Crime, Tim Atherton, called on bikies' wives, girlfriends and associates to come forward anonymously. It was hardly a success; the women remained loyal. There were calls to have the NCA hold hearings into the outlaw bikie gangs in Perth. With war declared there, it was time to bring on the NCA's Operation Panzer, with its power to compel people to attend and talk. And Operation Gallipoli continued. The clubs would not know when and where the police would turn up. Home raids included one on a female lawyer who had represented several bikies and who associated with Woodhouse. A Joker, returning with seven colleagues from a tattoo festival in Adelaide, was met by police at Perth Airport and arrested for urinating in a wine glass during the flight and possessing a knuckleduster. He was fined $800 for the first offence and $200 for the second.

The Rebels turned their headquarters in Malaga into a garrison. Members of the TRG surrounded the clubhouse. They stopped and checked anybody moving into or out of the premises. Just after 11 pm, they stopped a green Ford LTD carrying three men. When they tried to breathalyse the driver, a scuffle broke out. Then the bikies barricaded themselves inside the clubhouse, one brandishing a nunchuka as a warning. Police brought in a negotiator. But a night of negotiations failed to extract the Rebels. The siege lasted two hours. At 4 am, the TRG cut their way in, using a circular saw on the roller door. The quiet suburban street was lit up by the bright flash of stun grenades and shock waves spread through the area. The Rebels emerged, yelling abuse. One, in club colours, jumped on his motorbike and screamed off, reaching speeds of 140 km/h before police caught him.

The night resulted in three $500 fines for breaching liquor regulations by selling alcohol, and the one who tried to get away was charged with reckless driving. In criminal terms, it was small stuff. But it was a success in terms of the police tactic of continual harassment, showing the anarchic group that they were not beyond the reach of the law. Now the bikies were being told they would get away with nothing. In another raid on the Deroes headquarters in Coverdale, police confiscated alcohol and a fridge.

In November 1998, the Deroes thought of a new way to stash their weapons and explosives somewhere safe. A car parked at the home of a TV personality should be a safe place shouldn't it? Doug Clegg, a high-profile fisherman with a fishing tackle business, had allowed the navy blue Mercedes to be parked at his home. In the boot were enough explosives to blow up half the street: 22 kg of high-explosive TNT booster, more than 50 sticks of gelignite, plus detonator and fuse. As well, the Mercedes contained a rifle, shotgun and revolver. After police discovered the cache, Clegg said the Mercedes had been left there some time previously and he had not looked inside. His explanation, that he had allowed the car to be parked as a favour and had thought nothing more of it, was accepted by police. But someone had seen strange comings and goings by bikies, involving the car and a key held in the fishing shop, and had reported it. Phillip Rowles was charged with possession of explosives and unlicensed weapons. On 4 February 1999, Operation Gallipoli officers made a series of raids on Deroes strongholds around the metropolitan area, swooping on 19 properties in Perth and two in Kalgoorlie and confiscating more armoury, including a sawn-off shotgun, a bolt-action rifle and 1200 rounds of military-style 7.62 mm ammunition. This haul added to the two loaded military-style automatic firearms and 1800 rounds of ammunition they had taken from a fortified drug factory the previous month, and everything found the previous November.

George Loverock was promoted to inspector and returned to Bunbury, where he again served with Watson. Together they were keeping up the pressure on bikies in the south-west corner. Operation Gallipoli was taken over by Senior Detective Sergeant Steve Cross, previously Loverock's second-in-charge, and he was not going to let up. In March, his officers found ecstasy tablets in a car they stopped on a freeway. Cross ordered a dramatic mid-afternoon raid on the home of a Cheater who two days earlier had been rushed to hospital for a cocaine overdose. Fifteen police cars lined the street, their engines still running, ready to give chase, as masked, gun-toting tactical response officers and police with sniffer dogs stormed the house. They made a detailed search of the house and five cars found on the property. The owner of one of the cars refused to open it for them, so the police smashed the window and jemmied the boot.

More war armoury was found in April. The Australian Customs Service checked a parcel addressed to a member of the Gypsy Jokers, who happened to be a brother of the club's sergeant-at-arms. The customs declaration said the parcel contained toys and clothing. Opening it up, the officers found four flak jackets and a paint-ball gun. Customs officers and TRG men from Operation Gallipoli raided the home of the recipient, in suburban Ballajra, one of a series of early-morning raids on Jokers' properties. The raid uncovered an illegal pistol, a crossbow and more paint-ball guns. This 33-year-old Joker had already served an eight-year gaol sentence for causing an explosion that endangered life. This time he and his brother were fined a total of $6000.

Operation Gallipoli's efforts were paying off with the unrelenting searches and seizure of weapons. In early June, a raid on a Cheater's home in Rockingham uncovered 1100 rounds of 7.62 mm ammunition, a concealable .22 calibre pen gun, two flick knives, three knuckledusters and two expanding batons, along with explosives, cannabis and three balaclavas. In another home, the task force found an electronic stun gun. One raid on Cheater properties in three suburbs found a haul of drugs. The man who had been at the centre of the events that led to the entire confrontation and warfare, Mick Woodhouse, was found with some of the goods. He was charged, along with his mother, 54-year-old Rosemary Woodhouse. By mid-1999, police had made 293 arrests and laid 883 charges to do with the bikie war. The total arsenal seized amounted to 87 firearms, all but 18 of them unlicensed, and more than 18,000 rounds of ammunition – along with flak jackets, paint-ball guns, batons and pepper sprays. They had seized 335 ecstasy tables, 3 kg of amphetamines and 53 ml of amphetamine liquid. They found more than 20 kg of cannabis and cannabis seeds.

Woodhouse became a lone wolf, ditched by then by both the Deroes and the Cheaters. Wisely, he had made a will. For the rest, the police were still right on their backs. They were keeping a lid on the bikie war – finding and confiscating arsenals.

In early 2000, Andrew Wayne Edhouse, 25, younger brother of the assault victim Brian Edhouse, was charged with the wilful murder of Marc Chabriere, the attempted murder of Mick Anderson, and the attempted murder of Kevin Woodhouse in Beechborough in July 1998.

THE ESCAPADE OF
BRENDON ABBOTT

Tempt not a desperate man.

William Shakespeare
Romeo and Juliet

'He was scheming, clever, always planning – never leaving
anything to chance. He'd have made a good copper.' That
was how Detective Sergeant Charlie Barham, a senior Queensland
detective involved in the capture and recapture of Australia's Most
Wanted Man, saw Brendon James Abbott, known as 'The Postcard
Bandit'. It was the ultimate compliment, at least for a criminal.

Abbott, like most criminals who through their daring exploits
build an aura of romance around them, was credited with many
crimes and acts of daring for which he was not responsible. Even
his recognised nickname, 'The Postcard Bandit', which gained
national prominence, arose from a mistake. In 1990, *The West
Australian* had carried a report from police who had seized a
getaway car used by Abbott and an accomplice, and found inside it
several vacation snaps, including one of Abbott posing outside a
police station. Abbott had the photographs taken to send to family
members and criminal associates to show he was enjoying himself
on the run. But the story that Abbott had had photographs taken of
himself taken at easily identifiable locations and then sent them to

police, who were looking for him, gained currency. Abbott did taunt police, but only by his exploits and his uncanny ability to keep one jump ahead of them.

Abbott valued his freedom and his high living and would not have used a prank like that, which carried with it the inherent danger of putting the law within snapping distance of his heels. Through his criminal career, Abbott would be accused of involvement in more than 70 armed robberies, with banks the principal target. Though Abbott did not commit anything like that number of crimes, police still estimated his total haul could have been more than $5 million. Ironically, the cost of tracking, capturing, convicting and imprisoning him, if ever such a figure were calculated – based on a minimum term of imprisonment Abbott was facing in June, 1999 – would likely be double that. He was certainly going to have high security for a long time.

It is possible to see in Abbott's life the same pattern of family instability that marks the early lives of so many criminals. Born in Footscray, Victoria, on 8 May 1962, the third of five children of Brian and Thelma Abbott, Brendon Abbott had a bad start. According to family members who spoke long afterwards, Abbott grew up in difficult family circumstances. The youngsters were exposed to bad influences and as it turned out, Abbott was not the only one of them to go astray. His youngest brother, Glenn, born in 1968, was to follow in his footsteps.

In 1971, the family moved to Alice Springs, but Brian Abbott left the family there, returned to Melbourne, and disappeared from their lives. Thelma Abbott and her children found their way to Perth where Brendon Abbott, having virtually no parental control, was arrested at the age of 11 for striking a girl in the face with a pump. He was taken from his mother and placed for a year in a remand centre and boys' home. At school, he was primarily interested in cricket. In his leisure time, his main interest was in cars and tinkering under their bonnets. His first conviction came at the age of 14 for breaking, entering, and stealing. From there, he went on to acquire a juvenile police record for petty crimes and traffic infringements.

He talked a friend, Raymond Skehan, into stealing fuel from a parked car. Both were caught and charged, but Abbott tried to persuade Skehan to say the petrol was not for him. The police got wind of this and charged Abbott with conspiracy to pervert the course of justice. Abbott moved further up the scale of criminality. He and three accomplices decided to snatch a bank bag containing the daily takings at a Perth restaurant. They got the bag, containing more than $12,000, but were caught. Abbott pleaded guilty and was sentenced to four years' gaol, with a minimum of 22 months to serve.

Abbott did try going straight, working as a builder's labourer for a period, but did not care for it. He wanted the easy life, the relaxation, liquor and prostitutes, none of which came cheaply. He loathed prison. Prison authorities would later testify that he was not considered a tough inmate, but rather one who 'did his time hard', despite acquiring over the years a certain prestige among the inmate community. Abbott escaped from Perth's Nollamara police station in December 1987, and was recaptured at Perth's domestic airport in June 1988. He participated in riots that year in Fremantle Gaol and took prison officers hostage, for which he received a six-year sentence.

In November 1989, Abbott scaled the prison's five-metre wall and escaped. Four days later, he broke into a Fremantle gun shop and stole two firearms. The following day, he dropped through a hole in the roof of a Perth bank, surprised staff, and robbed the bank. On the run, he decided his only option was to live on crime, reap the rewards, and avoid capture. He chose his accomplices carefully. They hit banks in Western Australia, South Australia and Queensland over several years, often by cutting security bars and getting into bank ceilings, choosing the right moment to descend, taking anything up to $80,000 a time. Abbott earned another nickname, 'The Drop-In Bandit'.

Catching Abbott posed a major problem. Queensland police inspector Ray Platz said Abbott had no drug or alcohol problem, and had the knack of adopting the 'average man' attitude. Though at the top of Australia's 'Most Wanted' list, Abbott remained highly mobile. Traversing Australia, flying first-class on commercial airlines, Abbott was just a little cocky. 'Put on a pair of sunglasses and a baseball cap and you can be anywhere in the country,' he said.

In 1995, still on the run after nearly six years, he was on Queensland's Gold Coast, staying in various motels. He rented storage sheds in which he kept his tools of trade, including firearms, photographic gear for manufacturing driver's licences, electronic equipment, clothing, more than $70,000 in cash, plus wigs and false moustaches. He kept on robbing banks, this time in south-east Queensland. He robbed the Commonwealth Bank at the Pacific Fair shopping centre in Broadbeach, Gold Coast, which gained him loot totalling $781,252. He also robbed the Elanora Branch of the Commonwealth Bank (coincidentally, the bank used by this author's father, a one-time police prosecutor).

Arrested in March that year, Abbott was charged with robbing six banks in Queensland between April 1992 and the previous January. He appeared at Southport Magistrate's Court and was remanded in custody. There were constant rumours that Abbott had a plan in which underworld figures would help him break out. It was put about that Abbott had boasted that he had millions of dollars stashed on the 'outside', which would allow him to reward anyone who helped him escape. At his court appearance in May 1996, Abbott had chains on his legs and wrists, and massive courtroom security. Abbott was convicted, and on 6 June 1996, sentenced by Judge Brian Hoath to nine years' imprisonment.

Inside, he was not allowed to forget his nickname. Abbott had been the subject of jibes from prison officers, and Perth police were blamed for sending him several postcards. One said: 'Time waits for no man. Glad to see it's finally caught up with you. This is a dose of your own medicine.' The other read: 'Brendon boy, how are ya? Only one thing to say – gotcha!' The image of Abbott was not helped by sensationalist media coverage.

He was considered dangerous. Around the Arthur Gorrie Correction Centre, where he was being held, word was that he had the money if anybody could help spring him. He was moved to the Sir David Longland (SDL) Correctional Centre at Wacol – an outer south-western suburb of Brisbane – in September 1996. But initially, Abbott was kept in solitary confinement. His solicitor complained that Abbott was receiving 'inhumane treatment'. That issue went before the Brisbane Supreme Court on 19 July 1996. The Arthur Gorrie manager, Greg Howden, told the Queensland Chief Justice, Paul de Jersey, that Abbott's cell at that gaol was three metres square and was surrounded by two six-metre high fences. It was also equipped with electronic security and cameras. Howden said he did not believe that even that degree of security was adequate for Abbott. He had requested Abbott be transferred to the more secure SDL prison. Abbott's counsel, Walter Sofronoff QC, submitted that Abbott's treatment in prison was inappropriate. The court decided in favour of Abbott.

Security around Abbott was relaxed to about the standard applied to other high security prisoners. Abbott was allowed out of his cell for 11 hours a day, was able to mix with other prisoners, had a job in the prison library (which gave him some access to a telephone) and was able to receive visitors. The Brisbane *Sunday Mail* revealed that Abbott's brother, David, had paid all his legal bills – including those of the high-profile Gold Coast solicitor, Chris Nyst, and the various barristers and Queen's Counsel who appeared for him.

In 1997, Abbott pleaded guilty to two more robberies, including that at Pacific Fair, and received two, ten-year sentences, to be served concurrently. The time he looked like serving stretched ominously into the distance – some 34 years of it. Abbott, with his newly-acquired freedom within the prison, set about planning an escape. He struck up a friendship with a 20-year-old petty criminal and convicted armed robber, Brendan Luke Berichon, who was serving a two-year sentence for armed robbery.

Berichon's attitude to Abbott became a form of hero-worship. Abbott spent a lot of time speaking with the impressionable young man, plotting, planning and organising. Berichon agreed that when he got his parole he would help Abbott escape. The parole came on 17 September 1997, and Berichon, true to his word, started to put Abbott's plan into action, drawing several of Abbott's mates into it.

But to spring Abbott from gaol they needed equipment; not just for the escape but to allow Abbott to make his way afterwards. Berichon found the semi-automatic .22 calibre pistol, fitted with silencer, which Abbott took to bank jobs to shoot out lights in camera areas. Other equipment put together included clothing, cash, a stolen car, and an AK-47 military-style semi-automatic rifle. For the escape itself, the team acquired bolt cutters, one with handles more than a metre in length, the other, smaller but still very large, to be used to cut through perimeter fencing.

For his own part, Abbott decided to recruit a team from within the gaol. He did not want to break out on his own. Probably he felt that the more who got out, the more there would be for prison officers and police to worry about and the greater chance he, himself, would have of getting away. As his escape companions he selected three convicted murderers and a convicted rapist.

Andrew John Jeffrey, 20, had joined three other youths two years previously in setting upon a frail man on the Sunshine Coast, whom they accused of welshing on a deal to supply them with cannabis. They had kicked and punched him brutally and dumped him on the side of a deserted road. The man died and, on 19 June 1996, Jeffrey was sentenced to imprisonment for life.

Oliver Alincic, on a February night in 1987, entered a newsagency in the Brisbane suburb of Morayfield with the intention of robbing it. A petite shop assistant, Sandra Leanne Mackay, was counting the day's takings. She had left the door open because it was so hot and humid. Alincic, then aged 21, and already with a long record for stealing, bludgeoned her to death with a wheel brace and took the $1500 from the till. Alincic was questioned as a suspect but let go. He was arrested months later, after telling another prisoner in a New South Wales gaol what he had done and confiding to his girlfriend of terrible nightmares he had, of seeing Sandra Mackay dressed in white clothes, walking towards him with her arms outstretched.

Jason John Nixon, 37, while serving a seven-year sentence for armed robbery, killed a fellow inmate, Bart Voxsmaer, at the SDL gymnasium in March 1993, by smashing his head with a barbell weight. Peter Thomas Stirling was serving 13 years for kidnapping and raping a girl.

In SDL, Abbott had inveigled other prisoners, on the promise of cash payment, to supply him with wire cutters, scissors and tin snips. Natalie Anne Hunter, girlfriend of Garry Merrick, the prisoner who was the cook where Abbott was housed, smuggled in angel wire – hardened wire encrusted with diamonds which, when used in a sawing fashion, could cut metal. She had wrapped the angel wire in gladwrap and inserted it in her vagina, then removed it during a visit and threaded it through a hole that had been drilled in a perspex barrier between herself and Merrick. Hunter was later to plead guilty in the Brisbane District Court to assisting prisoners escape, receiving a two-year prison sentence for her trouble. The method of smuggling in the wire in, she confessed later to police, had been 'uncomfortable'.

In the meantime, Abbott was working with his fellow inmates in the high-security Unit 4B on the details of his escape. Several plastic chairs were available in the cellblock kitchen. The backs of the chairs were removed using a heated knife blade. They were then joined together so that they could be thrown over the perimeter razor wire fence. Now it was possible for the prisoners to get over without cutting themselves to ribbons. An experienced outback traveller and camper, Abbott told the others how to make a 'Spanish windlass' – a contraption used to pull bogged vehicles free by winding a rope. Bunks were to be pulled apart to make it. The angel wire was to be used to virtually sever the cell bars. Then bed sheets were to be tied together and attached to the bars, to be wound on the windlass.

In early November 1997, the escape was on. On the night of 4 November 1997, Abbott was alone in Cell 12, Alincic and Nixon were together in Cell 14, and Jeffrey and Stirling were in Cell 10. These were adjoining cells. Abbott, through his unsupervised use of prison telephones, had arranged for the outside team to be in place. Berichon was driving a powerful white Ford Fairlane sedan. Another car, driven by a person whose identity has never been revealed, pulled up nearby.

Abbott chose the half-hour before midnight, when he knew prison officers took a meal, to make the break. The five – Abbott, Jeffrey, Alincic, Nixon and Stirling – having sawed through the bars of their cells, went to work with their sheets and windlasses. The bars came off, with such a clang that, as Abbott later said, he thought they would attract the attention of the entire prison. But things were sleepy. The minds of many were probably on the big event of the next day – the Melbourne Cup. The five got out their cell windows and sprinted to the inside perimeter fence.

It was a brightly illuminated area, and Abbott had expected Berichon, on seeing him, to throw his pistol over the fence so that he could shoot out the light. Guards patrolling in a vehicle saw them. Berichon, watching from the outside, shot at its engine and immobilised it. The prison officers had their own firearms in the back of the vehicle, but, being under fire, could not get to them.

In a subsequent report, police investigator Carl Mengler said: 'Some short time after midnight on Tuesday, November 5, 1997, an alarm was raised at the prison's security control room that five inmates could be seen at the perimeter fence in Zone 7. It is on the far side of the prison from the prison entrance and adjoins scrub country. Beyond the fence were public roads. The alarm was raised by the security control room and some prison officers then on duty ran towards the stated location of the prisoners, who were still in the compound. These staff were prevented from taking further action due to covering gunfire from outside the prison. Additionally, the perimeter security vehicle proceeded, travelling clockwise towards that position.'

Berichon, a small, lightly built man, tried to throw the large bolt cutters over the first two fences, but was not strong enough, and the cutters caught in the fence wire. He tried with a smaller set of cutters but also failed. He tried throwing Abbott his pistol. But it fell between the fences. The five, making use of the chairs which formed a ladder, got over the interior fence and grabbed a pair of bolt cutters. Abbott saw the pistol but decided not to go for it. As he told police later, he had only planned to use the pistol to shoot out the light; he had not wanted to become involved in a shoot-out.

Using the bolt cutters, the five cut through the outer fence and dashed towards the waiting cars.

Abbott got into the Fairlane while the other four made for the second car. The cars then roared off into the night. Mengler said: 'There was more than one getaway vehicle... in which the escapees finally made their escape, firing at police and others as they approached the scene of these crimes. The armed collaborator assisting at the fence is believed by those officers who viewed him to have been a male person and there are indications that a further person, if not two, was also at the scene assisting and that one may well have been a female.'

Abbott did not want the other four escapees around him, at least for the time being. On the run, he was now somewhat dependent on Berichon. That in itself was out of character for him. Abbott normally trusted nobody, even members of his own family. But, as he was to tell police later, he was indebted to Berichon for his assistance in the escape, and regarded him as his protege.

The escape was front-page news around the nation. It appalled Queensland authorities, who asked Mengler to carry out an investigation immediately. It is trite to say that security at the prison left a lot to be desired. Mengler's 'confidential' report was the hottest item around, but within weeks of its being completed and handed to the Queensland Prisons Minister, Russell Cooper, the author of this chapter received a copy and it was published in full on the front page of the *Courier-Mail*.

Mengler said: 'It is clear that those involved planned the incident quite well and gathered the resources to successfully carry out these crimes. It needs to be said that grave danger confronted prison staff as they proceeded towards apprehending the escaping prisoners as the four projectiles striking the perimeter vehicle only narrowly missed the two occupants, whose lives had then been placed in extreme grave danger.

'It can hardly be said that this was a sophisticated plan for an escape. Two of the inmates had escaped from lawful custody on previous occasions with a third being involved in an attempt to escape. An inspection of the unit, in which Abbott was held at

Arthur Gorrie Correction Centre for approximately 18 months prior to being transferred to SDL, indicated that he had been held in almost identical cell conditions at SDL. During this period he would have had ample time to plan what resources were required to breach first the cell, then the perimeter fence.

'The escapees were able to obtain angel wire with which to cut the bars, through the visits system and through the receipt of prisoner property. They were able to modify plastic chairs in the kitchen of their unit during a lockdown period when they were not observed. They cut through the bars when not under direct supervision. They were able to modify cell fittings to force the severed bars apart. They obtained final resources such as wire cutters, a weapon and assistance from persons outside the prison.

'There were several indicators available to SDL management which should have raised the alarm that Abbott and to a lesser degree Nixon may at least have been planning an escape. However, the breadth of dissemination of this information is not clear due to several factors including the fact that Queensland Corrective Services Commissioner's prisoner information network has only recently been established and is not yet fully operational.

'These indicators were: the reputation of inmate Abbott including his previous escape history in Western Australia together with the information contained in his intelligence profile prepared by the QCSC Intelligence Manager which was forwarded to Arthur Gorrie prison on his induction to that prison. That document was later passed with additions to SDL on his transfer to that centre. However, the document did not contain immediate or reliable intelligence as to any pending escape.'

Mengler said other factors were: the previous escape history of Nixon, and his violent behaviour while in prison, including his involvement in the murder of another inmate; the previous escape history of Alincic and his behaviour while in prison; the involvement of inmates Stirling and Jeffrey in opposition to authority while in prison, for which they were both convicted in 1997. 'Although this was known, Stirling and Jeffrey were permitted to occupy the one cell in Unit 4B at SDL,' Mengler said.

'The information reported dated 25 September 1997, from Townsville, indicated that Abbott and Nixon planned to escape from SDL.'

Although this information was entered onto the Queensland Corrective Services Commission (QCSC) database, it was not processed and converted into useful intelligence, apparently because of a lack of resources. A routine search of Abbott's cell on 7 October,1997, turned up a stereo player with a hole in the back. The prison officers reported that at some time this hole may have contained contraband. An information report dated 22 October, 1997, indicated that Abbott sought to divest himself of the stereo and a TV to another inmate's visitor. It said Abbott might have been in possession of a mobile telephone. Abbott had also made a telephone call, which was monitored, and in the opinion of the part-time intelligence officer, there were indications in it that Abbott was preparing to escape.

'This information was reported in writing to centre management and not entered on the QCSC intelligence database as the part-time intelligence officer had not been granted access to that resource,' Mengler said. 'On November 4, 1997, the intelligence officer at Woodford Prison indicated that she had received information from Redcliffe Police suggesting that the Bandidos motorcycle gang had been paid to assist in the planned escape of Abbott should he be transferred to Woodford. However, it needs to be made clear that the nature of this information received at Woodford did not require significant immediate action as the information related to a future event.'

Again, Mengler commented on the failure to have this information converted into useful intelligence. As can be seen from these sections of the Mengler report, security at the prison, and the immediate reaction to the actual escape, were vastly inadequate. The government of the day responded with mass sackings of correction services executive staff. And Abbott, ever arrogant, had had the final laugh, at least for the time being. Prison officers searching Abbott's cell the day after his escape found an application for transfer, filled in by Abbott and describing himself as the 'approving officer'. The form had a 'smiley face' sticker attached.

For law enforcement authorities, it was all hands on deck. They had reports that the prisoners had been spotted in inner Brisbane. Hundreds of police were thrown together in a special task force to recapture them. Police expected that the escapees would have to commit robberies to survive, and given their records, predicted that at least some would not be taken alive.

There were plenty of rumours about. Police intelligence picked up a story that Abbott and the three prisoners who had escaped with him were going to Sydney to assassinate a businessman, and to carry out robberies. Another was that Abbott and others would make an assault on Woodford prison, north of Brisbane, by helicopter and by ground, to free a large number of prisoners and that there was to be a similar attack, using explosives, on SDL.

As it turned out, and as so often happens, the end for the inmates who had made such a spectacular escape was far more mundane. Two nights after his escape, Stirling booked into a Tweed Head brothel, collected a prostitute and drove her to her house at Mermaid Beach on the Gold Coast. The prostitute's colleagues recognised him and were concerned for the welfare of the woman. They called police, who surrounded the house at Mermaid Beach. A phone call was made to the house just after dawn. Stirling surrendered without resistance. Alincic travelled into the Northern Rivers district of New South Wales, to the hippie township of Nimbin, where he approached a woman, asking for drugs and sex. While in the back of a Volkswagen sedan, he grabbed the woman by the breast. The woman protested and Alincic hastily departed. Police were called and he was cornered in a Nimbin service station.

On 13 November, Abbott and Nixon joined forces to rob a branch of the Commonwealth Bank at Palm Beach on the Gold Coast. Abbott, armed with a revolver, and Nixon, with a tomahawk, burst in shortly before closing time. Abbott leapt over the counter and demanded that staff, including a pregnant woman, pack plastic bags with cash. Collecting it, he fled with Nixon through the back door with $17,210. But he had left a fingerprint, on the perspex shield which separated the public from the service desk staff. The next day, Nixon's 28-year-old girlfriend attracted attention by trying to exchange $7000 old one hundred dollar bills for new ones at a bank in Coffs Harbour.

Nixon and his girlfriend booked into the Netanya Resort on Queensland's Gold Coast, arriving with their possessions in sheets stolen from the motel they had just left and the girlfriend flashing wads of cash. Nixon had now been on the run for 16 days. The two went to a luxury unit. Police were tipped off that the two might be dealing drugs. Detectives Gary Kruger and Paul Zohn arrived to execute a search warrant. When they entered Nixon's room, he dived for a shotgun beside his bed, raised it and fired one shot, which went into the ceiling. Kruger and Zohn overpowered him. Then they discovered who'd they had caught. Nixon was charged with attempted murder, resisting arrest, receiving, serious assault, dangerous conduct with a weapon, stating a false name, wilful damage, stealing, unlawful use of a motor vehicle and armed robbery.

For the police, that was three down, three to go, including Berichon. There was never any doubt in the mind of the police that the last fox they would run to ground would be Abbott. Barham said later: 'Abbott was not a particularly violent man. He was always armed and I knew that, if confronted by a police officer, he would not shoot it out if there was another avenue of escape. He had said to me that if he got the drop on a police officer, he would disable him and go. There was never any intention on his part to shoot first if it could be avoided.'

Andrew Jeffrey, the third of those still at large, had gone south. He had made his way to Melbourne and booked into a hotel in the suburb of Footscray. On the night of 30 November, drinking heavily in Footscray's Royal Hotel, he began loudly boasting about his criminal exploits, claiming to have committed murders and robberies. He boasted he had once kicked a man to death, and was one of five escapees who had led police on Australia's biggest manhunt. He offered patrons $15,000 to steal a car for him. One of the patrons indicated he did not believe him, so Jeffrey attacked him.

The two fought, left the hotel and kept fighting on the footpath.

Constable Andrew Logan, a traffic policeman driving home early because he was suffering from flu, saw them and pulled up to investigate. By that time, Jeffrey had knocked his opponent down. Logan arrested Jeffrey. Getting up, the patron told Logan what Jeffrey had been saying. Logan took Jeffrey to a police station where Jeffrey's identity was confirmed. Jeffrey was returned to Queensland. He now has to serve the remainder of his life sentence plus an additional six years for escaping.

By this time, police knew for certain that Abbott and Berichon were travelling together, but there was no trace of either of them. Speculation was rife that Abbott had used cash he had had stashed to buy a boat in Darwin so that he could sail to Indonesia. Another was that the underworld was hiding him. Neither was true. Abbott kept well away from underworld figures, knowing that they would be interested in the money he was rumoured to have as they would likely apply 'toe cutter' techniques to find out where his money was. He divided his time between the Gold Coast and Melbourne, flying without concern using a variety of disguises, usually topping them off with dark glasses and a baseball cap. As time went by, and Abbott remained at large, the Australian Bankers Association offered $100,000 reward for information leading to his arrest. The Queensland Government offered another $50,000.

On 19 December, Abbott went back to his home town of Perth and held up the Mirrabooka branch of the Commonwealth Bank, escaping with more than $320,000. He then dropped his disguise material in a briefcase into an industrial bin, from which all items were later removed by police. Police found the briefcase and in it discovered 52 rounds of .45 calibre ammunition, a bank cash bag, a tie, false moustache and wig. The wig contained enough DNA material, mainly hair follicles, to confirm Abbott's identity. Word went out that Abbott and Berichon could strike anywhere. Banks were on red alert in Western Australia, Victoria and Queensland.

In Melbourne, Abbott and Berichon took up residence in Nicholson Street, Carlton. Berichon had with him a Thai prostitute named Ruang Khiankham, known as Michelle, whom he had picked up in Sydney. He was paying her $500 a day to stay with him. She was an illegal immigrant who had overstayed a five-day visitor visa in 1995. Abbott and Berichon hoped to fade away into the background. In criminal folklore, it was not a bad city to do it in. The feared Melbourne painter and docker and underworld figure, Billy 'The Texan' Longley, said that while he was on the run in Melbourne, he had lived in a number of houses and occasionally played a game of golf. He said Sydney was the place for money, Melbourne for '(reliable) blokes'. He said that in Sydney, criminals had a tendency to invest in their own 'insurance' by ringing the Criminal Investigation Branch and telling their detective friends a certain person was in town.

But any criminal on the run has to be aware of the limitations of his travelling companions. In Berichon, Abbott had chosen poorly. Berichon was a heavy heroin user. On 20 April 1998, Berichon approached a youth dealing drugs in the Melbourne suburb of Box Hill and asked for some caps. Police happened at that time to be campaigning against drug dealing on the streets. Two transit police officers, Senior Constable Peter Baltas and Sergeant Scott Roberts, in an unmarked police car, saw Berichon and the youth talking and drove towards them. Berichon and the youth ran, pursued by Baltas and Roberts, to Surrey Drive, a short distance away.

Baltas started questioning Berichon, and Roberts, on the other side of the car, questioned the youth. Berichon reached into his small bag, pulled out a 9 mm pistol and fired, hitting Baltas in the leg and hip, then turned and fired at Roberts, hitting Roberts in the upper right arm. 'He made absolutely no threats, gave no warning,' Baltas later said. 'He just pulled the gun out, cocked it, pointed it at me and began to fire.' With the youth sprinting for cover, Berichon kept firing, getting away 15 shots, then made off. Baltas and Roberts drew their own pistols. Baltas did not fire but Roberts got off four shots. Berichon, not hit, leapt over several fences and found a woman, Lynette May Bodilly, 56, standing at her front door. He pointed his pistol at her, told her to go to her car and drive him to Carlton. Later, she said Berichon had chatted during the trip about football, his family, and the slow traffic.

Shooting a police officer was not a great career move. From the police point of view, shooting a police officer was personal. Abbott was appalled when he learnt what had happened. He knew the hunt would be on in earnest now. The pair decided to bolt, along with Khiankham. It was a wise move, from their point of view. Shortly afterwards, police raided their flat. Airports were put on 24-hour alert, and cars were being stopped and searched at roadblocks on trunk roads near major population centres. The police did not stop every car, but they stopped vehicles on the flimsiest of suspicions.

Abbott was particularly good with motor vehicles. He was a more than capable motor mechanic and his preference was for older Holdens or Toyota Landcruiser four-wheel drives. Most purchases were made in response to classified advertisements in metropolitan newspapers lodged by private sellers. Abbott seldom paid more than $7000 for a vehicle, and always paid cash. He had a multitude of driver's licences and other forms of identification he could use for registration transfers and other such details. As well, vehicles in this price and model range were inconspicuous. Because of all this, the three evaded the searchers and made it to Adelaide.

Abbott was living it up as best he could. He was never 'flashy', although Charlie Barham, leading the Queensland police team, said Abbott preferred a particular brand of whisky that cost more than $100 a bottle. Abbott enjoyed the company of top-of-the-range prostitutes, women for whom $2000 a night was the base fee. In Adelaide, he and Berichon decided it would be best to split up. Berichon and Khiankam were to travel to Broome in Western Australia and rendezvous with Abbott in Darwin the following April. Abbott had plans for them to drop out of sight for a long time. The imperative was to stay one step ahead of the police.

Berichon and Khiankham travelled to Broome where they booked into the Roebuck Bay Motel. A wild, multicultural town, Broome was an ideal stopover for anyone not wanting to stand out in the crowd. Then the pair made their way to Darwin.

Queensland Police became aware that Abbott was in their jurisdiction. They had information that he was driving one of his favoured Toyotas, a green Landcruiser he had stolen in Western Australia a year before. Banks were on the alert. Information flowing to Queensland Police was complemented by information from Victorian Police that Berichon and Khiankham were in Darwin and that Abbott would be going there too. Abbott obliged by driving his Landcruiser to Darwin. Police had reports that he had been sighted on the Queensland/Northern Territory border.

Leaving aside the fact that he was driving into a trap, Abbott could have picked a better place than Darwin. Once it was known he was there, it was going to be very difficult to get away. It was an isolated area – there were thousands of kilometres of empty highway to the next major settlement – and the Northern Territory police had arranged to check every hotel, motel and caravan park, paying particular attention to young males with an Asian female partner. Of course, they wanted Abbott. They knew Abbott was an expert in disguise, but at least they had narrowed down the search.

On the afternoon of Friday 2 May, a surveillance policeman, Senior Constable Michael Dennien, watched a Landcruiser driven by a lone, strongly built man pull up behind the Top End Hotel in Darwin. The driver was casually dressed in normal Territorian garb – T-shirt and shorts. Dennien was sure it was Abbott. He radioed his superiors and a discussion ensued as to how they were to proceed, given that shops and offices were almost ready to empty at 5 pm and the streets would be full of people. Seven armed detectives got together to make the arrest.

Just after 5 pm that man, who was indeed Abbott, drove his Landcruiser to a supermarket. He alighted and took a basket of laundry to a laundromat, put his clothes into the washer and then went out to get some takeaway food. After walking several paces, he heard the words he had been most dreading: 'Police! Get down on the ground. Now!'

Abbott did not have to look to confirm that he was, at that moment, the target of at least one loaded gun. Even the slightest move, particularly anything threatening, was likely to provoke a lethal response. Within seconds, he felt a knee in the small of his back. His wrists were whipped together and handcuffed behind him. Then he was rolled over. This time, there was none of the bravado that marked his arrest on the Gold Coast. He said: 'Yeah,

I'm Brendon Abbott. I suppose this will make you blokes famous!'

Abbott was taken immediately to police headquarters and put under guard in a holding cell. The wires ran hot informing police around Australia of the capture, and local police chiefs and politicians could not get themselves in front of television cameras quickly enough to have their smiling faces associated with the success of the Northern Territory Police Service. Police searching Abbott's Landcruiser found a virtual treasure trove of criminal accoutrements – firearms, ammunition, a police scanner, false licences, wigs, cash and a supply of marijuana, a product for which Abbott had a particular liking.

Charlie Barham was notified of the arrest and immediately booked a flight to Darwin. A trained analyst and computer expert, he probably knew Abbott as well as anybody outside Abbott's own family. He had interviewed Abbott and had headed the team which spent months compiling a master profile of Abbott. He knew what to expect in the interview. He said later: 'Abbott would answer questions we asked, but never on the record. He would most often answer with another question, because he was always intrigued about the sources of our information. He desperately wanted to know always where he had slipped up, what he did wrong. But Brendon was not prepared for these particular circumstances. His ego had not allowed him to have a plan which included him being captured before Berichon. He had particular concern – and I have not the slightest doubt that his concern was genuine – that no police, member of the public, or Berichon or Michelle get injured when [Abbott] was finally cornered.

'He would not give us any information on where we could find him [Berichon]. What we were trying to get from Abbott was the instructions he had given his willing pupil-in-crime about how to handle a situation such as the one that confronted him now. Did he tell him to shoot it out? We doubted that. What about taking hostages? Or did he advise him to recognise when the game was up, the smart thing to do was to go quietly, and live to fight another day? Abbott would not help, except to say there was no need to hurt anybody.' But police knew Berichon was not far away. 'We knew all there was to know about Berichon, everything from his childhood, the names of his girlfriends, his sporting achievements, even his pets when he was a little boy,' said Barham. 'We had to, because we felt the final showdown would involve a negotiator, and we needed to know the messages that would touch buttons with this bloke.' Police were most concerned that, given his explosive nature, the confrontation could involve firearms, a siege and even hostages.

Then came the break. A Bureau of Criminal Intelligence officer picked up a brown leather wallet. He noticed what appeared to be numbers scratched into the outer leather. Examining them closely under the lights on the fingerprint, he was able to discern what he guessed was a telephone number. The number was checked. It turned out to be the same as the telephone number for Luma Luma Apartments – a multi-storey accommodation block in Darwin, near the city centre.

Although these premises had been checked previously, police were despatched again to have a closer look. Sergeant Les Chapman noted a client registration card stating that a Jason Parker, of Miller Street, Kirwan, Queensland, had booked in, had been allocated Room 608, and had paid cash. Police showed the receptionist the photograph of Berichon. She was not at all sure whether 'Mr Parker' matched the photograph police had of Berichon. But she thought that the female accompanying him might have been Asian. 'Mr Parker's' Kirwan address fuelled interest. It was a Townsville suburb where Berichon had once lived.

Berichon was known to be armed, and if this mystery resident was indeed the fugitive, police could expect trouble. And what about Khiankham? Would Berichon, when cornered, use her as a hostage or shield? It was Sunday, 4 May, and news of Abbott's arrest had been widely circulated. Berichon's mother had gone public pleading with him to 'come to [his] senses mate', and give himself up. Berichon knew he was trapped. When he received a phone call from the police in the hotel foyer, he appeared to have been expecting it. He let Khiankham leave the room and then walked out, offering no resistance and allowing himself to be handcuffed.

Berichon was flown to Melbourne, where police were keen to

enlist his help in their inquiries into the shooting of Roberts and Baltas. Khiankham was deported to Thailand. The Queensland Special Response Group flew to Darwin to help bring Abbott back. Abbott was housed in Darwin's Berrimah prison, a modern establishment in the swampy flatlands south of the city. The commercial airlines said they would not take him, so the Queensland Government had to charter a private jet. Abbott was flown back on 6 May.

Abbott appeared briefly in Brisbane Magistrate's Court. He contacted Nyst and asked him to release a press statement in Abbott's name, denying any involvement in the stories that had got about. 'I've never thought about killing Cooper or anyone else,' Abbott told Nyst. 'That sort of thing is just not my go.' He also denied being part of the helicopter rumour. He said: 'The only bloke I've ever planned to spring out of gaol is Brendon Abbott.'

Aged 36, Abbott faced up to 32 more years in gaol on current charges, leaving aside the possibility of prosecution for bank robbery in Western Australia. It was a natural expectation that he would try to bust out again if he could. Before he appeared in Brisbane Magistrate's Court on 15 June 1998, members of the Queensland Police Special Emergency Response Team had arrived early. Charged with escaping from lawful custody and with four counts of intending to prevent arrest by striking with a projectile, Abbott appeared with chained ankles and hands shackled to a belt.

Nyst said Abbott would not contest the charge of escaping but would contest the charges relating to the projectiles. He was contending that he had not been party to any plan to shoot during the breakout. On 29 June, prosecutor Maria Zappala had the charges relaced with four of assaulting prison officers with intent to resist arrest. Further charges of armed robbery and unlawful use of a motor vehicle were adjourned. Abbott said he was pleading guilty to all charges. Nyst said outside court that Abbott was prepared to 'cop what was coming to him', and might take up some study.

For good measure, Abbott's brother, Glenn Norman Salmon, appeared in the Western Australian Supreme Court on 10 August 1998, charged with the attempted murder of a police officer in

September 1996. Salmon said he had been tormented by being known as Abbott's brother. He had received a telephone call from an anonymous person asking where he was and what his family connections were. He feared criminals might be chasing him in order to get access to the loot they thought Brendon Abbott had accumulated. The younger Abbott was sentenced to eight years' gaol without parole, and at the time of writing was an inmate of Casuarina Prison.

Nixon appeared in Brisbane Magistrate's Court on 27 May 1998, his hands and feet manacled. He was behind a caged security dock, with police standing by. In the Queensland District Court on 24 September, Nixon pleaded guilty to bank robbery. He would not admit that Abbott had been with him. He pleaded guilty to one count of escaping from lawful custody, four of aggravated assault, two of armed robbery and one of unlawful use of a motor vehicle. Judge Fred McGuire sentenced Nixon to 12 years' gaol for robbery and six for the escape, to be served concurrently. Nixon pleaded guilty in the Queensland Supreme Court to attempting to murder Kruger and seriously assaulting Zohn. Justice John Helman gave him 14 years. Together with his life sentence for murder, Nixon would not be able to apply for parole until 23 November 2014. Had he not escaped from gaol, his parole would have been in 2007.

In Melbourne Magistrate's Court on 29 September, Berichon admitted shooting police officers Roberts and Baltas, but pleaded not guilty to attempted murder and intentionally causing serious injury, saying his actions were reckless rather than intentional. On 25 June 1999, he was found guilty on two counts of attempted murder.

Abbott, even in maximum security, was unable to stay out of the news. In December 1998, his lawyers argued that he was being held in inhumane conditions in solitary confinement at Queensland's most secure gaol, Woodford, as a punishment. He had minimal contact with prison guards, who gave him his food through a slot. He had no television set; he had to watch the one outside his cell through a perspex screen. He did not see the sun and, it was claimed, could not even go to the toilet without being watched. His lawyers said they would appeal to human rights groups such as

Amnesty International.

His charisma and charm, such as it was, attracted women admirers. In March 1999, a 46-year-old mother of six, who professed love for Abbott, exposed herself to Abbott during a contact visit. That was spotted by a prison officer. She was banned from visiting him. A month later, after being banned, she said she had done it 'to put something into Brendon's life, to give him something nice to think about'. The next month, Abbott was convicted and sentenced for the Palm Beach robbery and for stealing a car to commit the crime. He issued a plea to the public to stop treating him like a hero and to stop sending him fan mail.

Barham said of Abbott: 'He is intellectually clever, and obviously enjoyed the thrill of the challenge and the chase. His big mistake was sticking with the inexperienced Berichon. If Berichon had not shot the police in Melbourne, they were in a situation where, if they had kept their heads down, they could have lived quietly for years. As smart as Abbott was, he was not clever enough to move with the new wave of technology. In the old days, when we circulated a photograph of a wanted criminal throughout Australia, it was done by post. Now with Internet and e-mail, every police station in Australia can have the latest information and photographs in seconds, including any alteration to a person's appearance. It is available in brilliant colour.

'As well, I do not believe Brendon Abbott acted alone. He has been given the credit for disarming alarms and other electronic surveillance equipment in jobs he did. But he did not have that experience, and never had the opportunity to learn it. No, it was not Abbott who did that. He had somebody working with him, and that person is still out there. I don't know who it is, but one day we will learn. Abbott will serve out his time in prison until he is an old man. He hates the confinement and restriction of prison because he craves challenge and stimulation. He will do his time hard.'

GANGS,
ASIAN STYLE

The rotten apple spoils its companions.

Benjamin Franklin

Nghai Minh Hong, 18, was an unsettled Vietnamese youth who had become used to the streets of Cabramatta in Sydney's outer west, in the late 1980s. He had arrived two years earlier, in 1986, with his sister, who became his guardian. Sydney's outer west was, to a Vietnamese migrant with little or no command of English, a harsh, alienating environment. Hong had learnt some English, but his education had been patchy. He was now in a society which, by and large, did not welcome him enthusiastically. Inevitably, he turned to his own kind, to other unemployed youths. He joined them in the streets and the pool halls, in particular in Cabramatta's Quoc Tien Club. He became a member of a gang called the Tuong Hai, a rival of the more numerous 5T gang.

Vietnamese had begun settling in Cabramatta, and other parts of Sydney, including Bankstown and Dulwich Hill, from 1976, the year after the Communist takeover of their country. The pace of migration had increased. The industriousness of those who had come from a strife-ridden, poor country and had seen prospects in Australia was remarkable, particularly the way the students applied themselves to their studies. It was also noticeable how well so many of the students did. Names such as Nguyen and Minh started appearing in the state's top Higher School Certificate places.

But sadly, Hong joined the group who opted out. Groups who might initially have got together for mutual protection and support, as indeed was the case of the Italian Mafia in its early history, then became corrupted by criminal elements. Crime became endemic. Gang members turned on their own countrymen, extorting and robbing them, as well as other Indochinese. A Vietnamese jeweller was shot dead during an attempted robbery.

There was also incipient gang warfare: a shootout in 1986 in Cabramatta's Belvedere Arcade; the attempted murder of Johnsonny Bo Dinh outside Bankstown's Quoc Tien Club in April 1987; the fatal stabbing of Minh Hoang Nguyen, 20, outside the same club in June 1987, when two shots were fired; and a shoot-out in the upper-floor Barluck Restaurant in John Street, Cabramatta, in December 1987, when Dinh Ngo was killed and three wounded.

At first, conscious of the criticism that they might be singling people out on a racial basis, police treated the incidents as part of normal policing. But they were obviously not just part of the normal pattern. In May 1988, a ten-man task force was established at Cabramatta police station. The task force included ethnic liaison officers, one of whom was Vietnamese. The Cabramatta police station was to be upgraded and there were to be foot patrols from dawn to dusk. There were sceptics, including a former policeman, Michael Tharme, who had worked with the Federal Bureau of Criminal Intelligence (FBCI). He shook his head. The cultural difference was so vast that the police were really boxing at shadows, he said. They did not really understand what it was all about.

In October 1988, rival gangs met outside Sweethearts Restaurant in Cabramatta. A shot was fired and one gang member was wounded. Hong was said to have been involved. Shortly afterwards, he got out of town. He went to Perth, returning on about 23 October, when he thought things had settled down. At 3 am on the morning of 30 October, Hong was inside the Beyond 2000 Disco in Cabramatta. Another row erupted and the participants spilled out into the street. Two shots rang out, one bullet smashing the window of Vallore Cellars liquor store. Hong, knowing that he was the one being shot at, took to his heels, running to the corner of Park Road, where he paused, hoping he was far enough away to be out of trouble. He heard an engine roar and tyres squeal, and took off again, sprinting down Park Road.

Pursuing him in the car were three Vietnamese men and a 14-year-old boy, Tri Minh Tran, who, despite his youth, had acquired a rather serious gangster profile. The occupants of the car blazed away with firearms, including, it was thought, a high-powered rifle and a .38 calibre pistol. The noise sounded like a machine-gun, said Greg Reid, a long-time Cabramatta resident woken from his sleep by the noise. One bullet hit a shutter in Kim's Pharmacy as Hong ducked across the street towards the Quoc Tien Club. Hong would have known the club was closed, but in his desperation, he associated it with friends and safety. The door at the top of the steps was locked. A passageway down another flight of stairs was blocked by an iron gate. There was a space at the top of the gate but it was awkward, and it was dark, and behind him he could hear the pounding of his pursuers' feet. Hong sank into the shadows outside the club door and his pursuers dispatched him with three or four shots.

Several days later, I was sent to Cabramatta to find out what was going on. I had lunch with the then State Australian Labor Party member for Cabramatta, John Newman, a passionate advocate for the Vietnamese people, who were striving at that time to counter the view that Cabramatta was crime-ridden. It was, he said, a great place. His secretary agreed as we tucked into a magnificent crab dinner in one of Cabramatta's sumptuous Asian restaurants. But what about the bullet holes? And the bodies? No amount of gladhanding could gloss over that.

It was easy to sympathise with those wanting to give the majority of decent, hard-working Asian immigrants a fair go. But there was simply too much evidence that things were going bad with the minority. Part of that evidence was a lengthy surgical scar on the abdomen of a then 15-year-old youth, Simon Bull, a student at Canley Vale High, near Cabramatta, which had at the time an 'ethnic' component of about 85 per cent of its student body. Gangs had formed there, ethnically based, and they were warring, some emulating the standover tactics of their older colleagues on the streets. Bull, a stockily built lad, had become involved in a gang war with 'Russian Chinese', people of Eurasian origin. A group of these saw Bull and a friend at Cabramatta railway station and made for them. Bull's friend took off along the railway tracks while Bull tried vainly to get through a rotating gate which would only turn the wrong way. Surrounded, Bull tried to fight his opponents, but received a knife thrust that ruptured his spleen and came within a centimetre of his heart.

I used that story, and others, in an article for *The Sydney Morning Herald*, headlined 'The Wild West', highlighting law and order problems. Newman rounded on me in Parliament. 'I am ashamed of the article,' he said. Newman and I nevertheless became friends. He saw me in Cabramatta one day, swerved and had his secretary pass me an invitation to his next political rally, which I attended. He knew there were crime problems. A karate champion, he had confidence in himself. As he changed tack and started calling for more police resources for Cabramatta, he attracted adverse attention from some quarters, and was perhaps less cautious about his personal safety than others might have been.

Crime has been associated with many immigrant communities, including the English and Irish who arrived from 1788 onwards. Some of them got up to much mischief. While wave after wave of immigrants from various parts of the world worked hard and built up the country, criminal elements always came with them. That included the 'Ndrangheta, which came with the Italians and focused initially on Italian migrants, taking advantage of their insularity within the larger community. And the Chinese brought the triads, who engaged in illegal gambling, loansharking, prostitution and extortion.

One of the biggest reputed illegal gaming operators in Sydney's Chinatown, based in Dixon Street in the inner city, was Frank Hing, reputedly a leader of the 14K triad. In the 1980s, he was owner of the Goulburn Club, which was home to a huge gaming operation. On 12 April 1987, police arrested 45 people, including Hing, and charged them with gaming offences.

The New South Wales Police Service entrusted the policing of illegal gambling to its Gaming Squad, but on evidence later presented to the New South Wales Independent Commission Against Corruption (ICAC), that was not terribly effective. In its 'Operation Milloo' inquiry, ICAC took evidence about the possible involvement of former bookmaker Bruce Galea, son of the well-known consort of premiers, Perc Galea, in an illegal gambling operation in Chinatown. Galea, represented in typically vigorous style by lawyer Chris Murphy, denied involvement. He was merely running an 'entertainment' club, he said, and if people paid $5 for a cup of coffee and $7 for a sandwich, that was what they chose to pay. It did not represent a hidden charge. Galea said it was nonsense to suggest that Asian high-rollers had come to the club and blown $600,000 in a week. Had that happened, everyone in town would have known about it.

The ICAC investigated an alleged tip-off arrangement with some members of the Gaming Squad, but whether or not that was true, illegal gaming was notoriously difficult to police. Some Chinese loved to gamble, and they were well versed in having 'cockatoos' placed to warn of police raids, and in the art of destroying any evidence that gaming was taking place. Hing's reputed success as an illegal gaming operator was not appreciated by everybody. He was attacked and badly wounded by underworld figures who, it was said, were anxious to muscle in on his operation. Sydney identities George Freeman, Branko Balic and Tony Torok were charged with malicious wounding, but the case was dismissed when no witnesses were able to identify the assailants.

Despite the undercurrent of violence, illegal gambling was what it has always been in Australian folklore – a cat-and-mouse game with the police. But once the criminals became established, they were able to turn their attention to other things. Such as drugs.

Stanley Wong, a much-admired Chinese businessman, the unofficial 'mayor of Chinatown', born in China, 1912, had fled the

Communist regime and arrived in Australia in his thirties. He had opened his first yum-cha restaurant in 1961 and gone on to make a fortune. He had bought racehorses, hobnobbed with politicians and had been awarded the honour of Member of the British Empire for his work in developing the inner city and for his community activities. By the mid-1980s, he owned the Tai Yuen, New Tai Yuen and Tai Yuen Palace restaurants. In the latter, he entertained the Premier of China, Zhao Ziyang, in 1983. But he was to become a victim of the drug scourge.

Tina Wong, one of his four daughters, was also doing well in the restaurant business. But she became mixed up in a serious drug allegation through her association with David Yung Chow, an Adelaide restaurateur. As was later to be alleged, Chow conspired between 1 March and 30 April 1984, with Charoen Rirastik, a Bangkok jeweller, and others to import heroin. On 19 April 1984, a suitcase containing 27.9 kg of heroin, divided into 69 blocks wrapped in brown paper, with an estimated street value of between $70 and $90 million, arrived by air from Bangkok. Police, tipped off, were waiting. They intercepted the shipment and a Thai, Kitti Komthacrue, who had arrived on the flight. Komthacrue agreed to cooperate, plaster of Paris was substituted for the heroin, and the consignment was followed to where it was apparently intended to go. It ended up in Tina Wong's bedroom.

Police raided the home in Linden Way, Castlecrag, northern Sydney, and charged Wong with being knowingly concerned in the importation of a prohibited drug. She told police she had no knowledge of what had been in the parcel. When she appeared in court, Crown prosecutor Ian Barker QC said the deal was that Chow had borrowed $68,000 from Tina Wong to pay a drug courier and in return, he was to have paid her $225,000 bail, with conditions. She is said to have raised that money, that night, in $50 bills. Word might have gone round the criminal fraternity operating in Chinatown that Stanley Wong was loaded with cash.

Just after 10 pm on 2 January 1985, Stanley Wong and his wife, Lung Po Chun, arrived home in Mons Avenue, Maroubra, in Sydney's east, after dining at the South Sydney Junior Leagues

Club, to be greeted by their maid, Ah Lin Wong. Waiting in the shadows were illegal immigrants Wee Lam Choo and Kwang Lum Cheung, 17. Armed with knives and a pistol, they approached the Wongs and Choo and said in Cantonese: 'Don't say anything. I need some money to leave here.' The two took the Wongs into the house and tied them up. For 15 minutes, they demanded to know where Stanley Wong kept his money. Choo then gave Cheung the pistol while he searched the house. Returning, he cut Wong's throat, leaving him to bleed to death while he and Cheung made off with five gold figurines and $1000 in cash.

Tina Wong and her family went to Stanley Wong's funeral. At Rookwood cemetery, Tina cried bitterly. But she was not long for this world herself. Electing to give evidence in her committal proceedings, she repeated that she had no knowledge of what had been in the parcel. The following morning, she collapsed with a brain haemorrhage and went into a coma. On 21 March 1985, magistrate John Williams said that he could not rule out the possibility that Tina Wong was telling the truth and dismissed the information. Two days later, Tina Wong died. Choo sent flowers to her funeral. They were picked up by a family member and angrily flung aside, an understandable protest.

Chow and Rirastik were charged over the drug importation. Chow made a number of allegations in court implicating both Stanley and Tina Wong in drug trafficking. He claimed to have had a love affair with Tina Wong and that during this affair she had got him to do things related to drug trafficking. The allegations had to be measured against the man making them, and nothing was substantiated, though there were suggestions emanating from the Customs Service that Stanley Wong was trafficking duty-free items.

On 2 October 1985, Chow and Rirastik were found guilty of being knowingly involved in the importation of heroin and Chow was found guilty of conspiring to supply the drug. Both received 20 years' imprisonment, with Chow getting six years, to be served concurrently, for conspiracy. In the murder case, Wee Lam Choo pleaded guilty and was gaoled for life. Cheung pleaded not guilty and received a 14-year sentence for assault with intent to rob and eight years for manslaughter, the sentences to be served concurrently. He appealed his conviction and was granted a new trial before Justice James Wood. Again found guilty, he received a heavier sentence.

Many people have not been overly zealous in declaring everything they have earned to the Taxation Commissioner and sadly this has applied to at least some members of the Chinese community. At the time in question, some kept their wealth at home, others put it into bank security boxes. Regardless of where it was, the criminals wanted it. Between New Year's Eve, 1987, and 6 January 1988, thieves took advantage of a weakness in the security system of the National Australia Bank's Haymarket branch, backing onto Chinatown. A building behind the bank had been demolished, leaving an empty space and an exposed flank of the bank building. Using explosives and blowtorches, they got right inside, spent possibly 24 hours in the bank and removed the contents of up to 80 safety deposit boxes. These had contained, it was said, cash, jewellery and share certificates, of total value up to $20 million. They tried without success to get into the bank's main vault. When they left, they abandoned their equipment on site.

The customers, predominantly Chinese, were less than forthcoming when interviewed by police. They knew that the Taxation Commissioner would also be interested in what had been in those boxes. Henry Ming Lai, who had replaced Stanley Wong as a spokesman for the Dixon Street Chinese community, said there was 'no information or knowledge of how many Chinese had boxes or the contents of them'. In January 1991, thieves made a similar raid on a branch of the Westpac Bank at the corner of Liverpool and Castlereagh streets, Sydney, a bank also heavily used by Chinese, and took an unknown number of security envelopes, a haul that might have come to millions of dollars. The then Detective Sergeant of the City of Sydney Police, Ian Teasdale, expressed surprise at the failure of customers to come forward and declare what they had lost.

If money and valuables were not always taken directly from banks, there were certainly other ways of getting them. In March

1991, police, disturbed by complaints that a restaurateur in Sydney's northern suburbs was being extorted, formed Task Force Oak, with an initial brief to operate for three years to deal with Asian crime. They followed the model of Victoria Police, who had in 1985 received complaints from Vietnamese in Springfield, in Melbourne's suburbia, about extortion, and had formed the Bao Ve Investigation Group.

Not all the crime was being perpetrated by professionals, or with professionalism. Chiew Seng Liew, aka Ah Sung, 48 years old in 1991, a Malaysian national, thought he might join the band of desperados preying on the rich. Liew had a serious enough criminal record in his own country, having been gaoled in 1969 for armed robbery and robbery with a deadly weapon. In Australia, he went back into crime, looking at a list of prominent Asians who might be robbed. He decided that the heart-transplant pioneer, Dr Victor Chang, was a good target. Liew got together a team, including Lim Choon Tee, aka Phillip Lim, a Malaysian national with no criminal record and permanent residency status in Australia, and Lim's one-time flatmate and brother-in-law, Tiong Ha (Stanley) Ng.

Liew, Lim and Ng moved into a flat in Summer Hill, in Sydney's inner west, and carried out surveillance on Chang's home at Clontarf on Sydney's northern beaches, and his place of work, St Vincent's Hospital in Sydney's inner east. They might have noted that Chang had made a marvellous contribution to medical knowledge, having revived the heart transplant program after the medical establishment had lost enthusiasm for it. As far as the gang was concerned, Chang represented money only. One of their plans was to invade the Chang household and tie up the family – Chang, his wife, Anne, and children Vanessa, Matthew and Mark. They would then demand millions of dollars. Another was to stage a car accident as Chang was driving to work, and when he got out, demand money from him. Lim provided four pistols and two silencers and they decided on the car-crash plan.

It was a naive, amateurish ploy, and because they would be armed, a particularly dangerous one. The gang made their first move on 26 June, but they could see that someone else was in the car and Ng did not want to proceed. Ng, who had earned a living in Melbourne as a part-time waiter, then got cold feet, withdrew from the enterprise and travelled back to Melbourne on 3 July 1991. On 4 July, Liew and Lim made their move. They collided with Chang's $250,000 Mercedes in Military Road, Mosman, and as he turned into Lang Street to stop and find out what the damage was, they confronted him with firearms. David Goff, a passer-by, heard Chang call out: 'Call the police. They have got guns.' Two shots rang out. Chang fell, one bullet through his temple and another through his right cheek. Liew and Lim got away, and made their way to Victoria. But they did leave behind some evidence, too, with Liew's wallet, which was dropped at the scene of the crime. For a while, Liew stayed on a farm at West Daylesford. The farm's owner asked him whether he had shot Chang and Liew replied: 'No, not me. The other man did.'

In Melbourne, police placed Liew and Lim under surveillance. On 1 October, Liew and Ng met at the back of a restaurant. Liew said it had been 'mucked up'. Liew told Jimmy Tan, a restaurateur from Sunbury, an outer suburb of Melbourne: 'He [Dr Chang] loves his money more than his life.' He also said: 'We hit the doctor's car and when he got out of his car, we extort $3 million. The doctor did not want to pay and he took out his wallet. There were only a few $10 notes. I did not want that. I wanted millions of dollars. I then banged the doctor's head on the windscreen of the car... I said to the doctor, "Don't do any tricks or I will harm you!". Then I fired.'

Police arrested Liew at Melbourne Airport. He had earlier tried to disguise himself and had booked a flight to Malaysia. They charged him with murder, feloniously slaying, demanding money with menace, with intent to steal money, and detaining Chang with intent to hold him for an advantage. They arrested Ng and charged him with having conspired, between 18 and 28 June 1991, to detain Chang and hold him for advantage, and being an accessory after the fact. Jimmy Tan was also charged with being an accessory. Somehow, Lim slipped through the net, and got out of the country on either 11 or 12 July. He was at large until 13 November that year, when Malaysian police received a tip-off that Lim's girlfriend was in Ipoh State. Intercepted at a bus terminal, Lim was extradited to Australia on 12 December, 1991, and charged over the killing.

Liew and Lim were committed for trial at Sydney's Central Criminal Court on 19 October, 1992, and on that day Liew pleaded guilty. Ng and Tan, given indemnity from prosecution, gave evidence. On 22 December 1992, acting Justice Slattery sentenced Liew to 26 years' imprisonment with a non-parole period of 20 years. He gave Lim 24 years' gaol with a minimum of 18. On 14 December 1993, both failed in their appeals.

In the meantime, the crime situation in Cabramatta and other areas of Indochinese settlement had scarcely improved since the night in 1988 when Nghia Minh Hong made his last, despairing rush to what he had hoped was safety. By the early 1990s, there was a vast racial and cultural swimming pool in Sydney's outer west. For the criminals, the new arrivals provided a smorgasbord of potential victims. Between 1986 and 1991, the Vietnamese population of Australia had increased by 47.3 per cent to 160,000 Australia-wide, including 70,000 in New South Wales. In Cabramatta, the Vietnamese started displacing the Italian and Yugoslav communities as the dominant group.

The gangs were young people who had been educated in Australia. Having a command of English and an understanding of Australian ways, they were able to straddle both worlds. Because their parents had not had an Australian schooling, and had devoted so much time and effort to setting themselves up in their new country, the youngsters were freed from the sort of parental and community control they would have had in their own country. The youthful criminals were able to move into the breach. They could instil fear into their own countrymen by carrying out acts of revenge, targeting anybody who cooperated with police. In 1992, 200 people saw a 22-year-old Vietnamese man, Duong Van Chu, gunned down – and nobody came forward to give evidence.

The death of Laotian-born Thi Inthasan, 17 years old, Year 11 student at Canley Vale High, was another outrage. According to his school principal, Geoffrey Garland, he had been 'a youth of promise, a quiet boy, well liked by all', a quiet achiever. The trouble Inthasan became involved in did not start with him. In December 1992, his friend, aged 16, became involved in an altercation with another boy on the school bus about a girl. The other boy had a relative in the 5T gang, and apparently went to that relative suggesting the 16-year-old be dealt with. The 16-year-old and Inthasan were at the crowded Barluck Restaurant in Cabramatta on 8 December that year, celebrating the end of their school exams. Twenty members of the 5T gang came in and started assaulting the 16-year-old. Inthasan rushed to his friend's aid and the gang turned on him, violently assaulting him, dragging him downstairs and bashing him in John Street, fracturing his skull. A schoolmate said later: 'Thi was unconscious but they still kept kicking him and kicking him. They just did not stop.'

The gang fled the scene, shooting a 20-year-old woman who happened to be walking along the street in the leg – a warning to more than 100 witnesses that anybody who said anything would be killed. Inthasan was pronounced dead a few hours later. Investigating police arrested three Vietnamese youths, charged them with murder, and arrested a fourth as an accessory. But the committal proceedings became a fiasco. Twenty-four witnesses ignored subpoenas to attend court. Of the few who did turn up, one did not recognise his own photo and another did not know where Cabramatta was. The police prosecutor, Sergeant Col Kennedy, told magistrate Bill Gilbert that it was understood the 5T gang had put the word out that anyone who gave evidence would be killed. Gilbert had no choice but to dismiss the defendants. The then Senior Constable Brett Poultney said Cabramatta was getting 'the justice it deserves' by not standing up to the street gangs. He added: 'Poor old Thi Inthasan, you can only conclude that he must have committed suicide.'

The terror visited on the witnesses of Inthasan's demise continued to be visited on Asian people in the privacy of their own homes, even in areas where Indochinese were not concentrated. So came the 'home invasion', where a gang of robbers brushed aside the ethic that a man's home is his castle and burst in on occupants.

By May 1994, the situation looked desperate. There had been a been a spate of assaults and some murders. Bankstown business people were complaining of systematic extortion, and had resorted to hiring a private security firm. John Newman had by then long abandoned his protests about Cabramatta's innocence and had called for more police resources. He had been to Los Angeles to study how police dealt with Asian crime there and brought home the message that vastly enhanced witness security was the only way police could get evidence. I spoke to John Newman in May 1994. He was clearly a worried man. 'Out in the streets of Cabramatta now, not even a knife is used,' he said. 'Those fellows get firearms so quickly it is not funny.' On 5 September 1994, while putting a cover over his car to protect it from paint bomb attacks, Newman was gunned down in his driveway. Because at the time of writing court proceedings are in progress, we will leave further discussion of circumstances surrounding the shooting. But the shooting had profound repercussions. And whether it had anything to do with the killing or not, the drug trade involving Asian traffickers was more entrenched than ever.

In Australia, between 85 and 90 per cent of the heroin was at that time controlled by Chinese syndicates, who had changed the method of importation. Instead of being brought in one or two kilogram lots by couriers, it was being shipped in 30 kg lots. Police had made significant arrests from time to time. One man, Chai Nan-Yung, who had run a gambling club, had been gaoled for 24 years for importation of 152 kg of heroin valued at $4 million. By December 1996, triad societies with names such as See Yee Oh, 4K, Wo Hop and Wo Yee Tong had been identified as being involved in large-scale heroin trafficking. A restaurateur who reputedly made his fortune by importing 'China White' was implicated in one of the country's biggest seizures, of 78 kilograms of heroin. Police estimated that he had been involved in the importation of nearly half a tonne of China White, with a street value of nearly $1 billion. Ia Van Duong, a Cabramatta businessman, was named as one of the country's biggest heroin distributors, with a distribution network outstripping even that of the 5T gang.

Despite the arrests, and the public identification of the traffickers, the heroin kept coming – a vast, unmanageable flood. In 1997, the Australian Federal Police Commissioner, Mick Palmer, estimated that between two and three tonnes of heroin, valued at up to $3 billion, entered Australia each year, and of this, police and customs seized only about ten per cent.

One of the effects of the drug trade was that it created an endless demand for cash. And one way to get it was to take it from people – brutally, directly, blatantly.

Home invasion came to be described as a 'specifically Asian' crime, although that is not quite true. It had happened in Australia before. On one notable occasion in June 1977, home invaders rushed in on Sydney bookmaker Lloyd Tidmarsh. When Tidmarsh went to the aid of his son, the robbers killed him. But now, in the Asian community, it was being done repeatedly.

On 13 May 1993, a family of seven were terrorised by three youths wearing balaclavas at their home in Claymore, near Campbelltown in Sydney's far south-west; on 25 May a family was attacked in Summer Hill in Sydney's inner-west by a gang brandishing shotguns and a machete; an Asian family in Chandos Street, Ashfield, were pulled from their beds and tied up at 3.15 am on 29 July 1993. On 10 March 1994, a gang of robbers at Cabramatta cut the throat of the family dog and systematically cut the arms of their victim, including his wrists. In another case, a father was tied up, his daughter was taken into another room and he heard her screaming. At Bonnyrigg, west of Cabramatta, a gang held a man outside his home at gunpoint and threatened to kill him unless his family let him in. They took $4000 in cash and jewellery.

In October 1994, Edward Chan, 54, a food importer who had migrated from Malaysia to Australia in 1981, answered the doorbell at his home in Waterhouse Avenue, St Ives, on Sydney's North Shore, and was then subjected, with his wife, to assault by a gang brandishing a samurai sword, a dagger and an electric cattle prod. They demanded that he open his safe. When he refused, they hit him over the head with a truncheon, splitting his scalp, then kicked and punched him. That same month, a gang raided a house in

Cabramatta and stabbed a 14-year-old boy in his bed before escaping with electrical goods and cash, the haul valued at $6000.

The New South Wales Government, confronted at that time with the fact that there had been of the order of 265 reported home invasions in Sydney in three years (and more that had gone unreported), announced that it was doubling gaol terms for those who caused serious injury during home invasions. Task Force Oak was given a three-year extension and another task force, Acacia, was formed to deal specifically with the home invasion problem. There was evidence that people from other ethnic backgrounds were doing copycat home invasions, and because the perpetrators were often masked, it was sometimes difficult to tell who the offenders actually were.

On 29 November 1994, a 21-year-old man was pistol-whipped with an automatic handgun after two men wearing balaclavas crashed through the window of his home in Braemer Street in Smithfield, which is near Fairfield in Sydney's south-west. On 26 December, a Fairfield couple and their 17-year-old daughter were woken at knifepoint by four men wearing balaclavas demanding money. Their hands and feet were bound (by torn bedsheets) for six hours. The robbers tore a ring off the woman's finger and kicked and bashed the man in the head.

There was a lot of talk about why ordinary Australians should put up with this imported violence at all. Why not send the perpetuators back to their own country? was one cry. Dr Rod Milton, a forensic psychiatrist, suggested that Vietnamese had come from a violent culture and that was just the way they were. A counter view was put by Dr Don Weatherburn, Director of the New South Wales Bureau of Crime Statistics and Research, who said that, in time, immigrant communities fitted into the patterns of their host communities. But in the meantime, there would be more knifings, more shootings, more extortion, and more robbery.

One of the characteristics of criminal groupings, however they were described – secret societies, perhaps – was that apart from existing along broadly ethnic lines, they also carved up the spectrum of illegal activity, so that they did not have to compete.

A Commonwealth report in 1994 said that the Hong Kong triads specialised in gambling and protection rackets, the 'Ndrangheta in cultivation of marijuana, money laundering, distribution of drugs and protection rackets. Lebanese tended towards importation of heroin and trafficking. The Vietnamese gangs specialised in heroin distribution, systematic extortion and home invasion. Other groups had carved out areas for themselves, the Romanians dealing in heroin and social security, insurance and other frauds, Colombians doing large drug importations and the Japanese Yakuza specialising in money laundering, drugs, prostitution and standover tactics.

In 1994, six Asian heroin smugglers were sentenced to a total of 105 years' gaol in the Melbourne County Court. Posing as tourists, they had tried to bring heroin with a street value of between $20 and $30 million into Australia. One of the convicted, Yoshio Katsuno, 35, was a former member of the Yakuza. Katsuno had enlisted the help of two brothers, one of them a former Japanese police officer, two other Japanese and a Malaysian, Fong Huat Su.

In politically correct Australia, mentioning ethnicity in relation to crime was still frowned upon, as the New South Wales Police Commissioner, Peter Ryan, quickly discovered when he made a public statement linking crime with ethnicity. But in no way could ethnicity be overlooked if any law enforcement agency wished to grapple with the problems. Nor could the particular cultural mores of the gangs they were confronting. Cabramatta's 5T gang had got its name from the Vietnamese words *tinh* (meaning love and sex), *tien* (money), *tu* (gaol), *toi* (criminal conviction or charge), and *tu* (death of a friend, family member or gang member). A gang member was entitled to have a 't' tatooed on his body for each of those five items achieved.

The gangs in Cabramatta, most of them Vietnamese-based, acquired heroin, high-grade, and lots of it, which they sold cheaply, for as little as $35 a cap. In Kings Cross, it was sometimes more than twice as much. The gangs started strutting their authority. On 14 April 1994, two police officers patrolling Cabramatta had been assaulted by a gang of four youths, including, it was later alleged, two members of the 5T gang, and one officer was bashed unconscious. The next month, a Liverpool man visiting Cabramatta with his girlfriend told a Vietnamese youth who was hassling him to go away and for that he was set upon, stabbed, and ended up losing a kidney and his spleen.

One of the toughest and most ruthless gang leaders was Tri Minh Tran, who started very young – he was picked up by the police at the age of 11 carrying a shortened firearm, for which he spent six months in a juvenile institution. He was 12 when he threatened a teacher with a machete, and 13 when he was present at the murder of Phuy Thuan Nguyen, 27, a member of a rival gang, hacked 11 times on Cabramatta Road with machetes. Tran was 14 when he was in the car pursuing the hapless Nghia Ninh Hong through Cabramatta. On 6 November 1991, Tran was found not guilty of the murder of Hong. In 1992, probably because of the difficulties with evidence, he was no-billed over the Nguyen murder.

But the 5T gang, which at its peak had up to 200 members, had a factional falling-out, and in 1995 the decision was taken to wipe out Tran. On the night of 7 August 1995, members of the rival faction burst into the flat in McBurney Road, Cabramatta, occupied by Tran and two colleagues and opened fire. Tran put up his hands to fend off the bullets. The bullets went through them, hitting him twice in the head. His lieutenant, Than Hao Nguyen, 18, was fatally wounded in the head and stomach and a determined attempted was made to kill another of Tran's associates, Hieu Dinh Trinh; he was shot in the leg but was saved when another bullet bounced off his thick belt buckle. He told the police nothing. Huong Tran, sister of Tri Minh Tran, said she believed Tran had been killed because of rivalry for leadership of the 5T gang. 'I know deep down that someone has betrayed him,' she said.

On 9 August, the New South Wales Police Minister, Paul Whelan, paid a visit to Cabramatta and stressed that policing in Cabramatta was effective. He said that in the previous 12 months there had been 620 arrests and 897 indictable charges laid. He said pressure would continue to be applied until the streets of Cabramatta were free of crime. But journalists accompanying him saw drug dealing taking place in front of them. At one hotel, two minutes after a police drug sniffer dog had climbed up a ramp, four drug dealers were back in business.

The traditional gangland ethic is to catch and kill your own. For the 5T gang, if one of their number was attacked, there would be retribution. Failure to take action handed political and psychological victory to the other side. On 30 September 1995, the end of a 48-day mourning period which in Buddhist tradition was the time allowed for the souls of the dead to make their transition to heaven, the mainstream 5T gang was ready to teach the rebel faction a lesson. They chose an occasion when a Vietnamese entrepreneur had hired the Croatian Jadran Hadjuk Club in Edensor Road, Bonnyrigg, for a fashion show. More than 270 people attended, including, it appeared, several members of the rebel faction.

At 11.30 pm, members of the 5T mainstream, waiting in the darkness across the road, saw a group of at least seven men they identified as the rebels and opened fire with semi-automatic rifles, shotguns and pistols. In the fusillade of at least 30 shots, four men fell to the ground, wounded in the legs and thighs. They were then stabbed and slashed as they lay on the ground. One, hit in the groin with a shotgun blast, staggered into the club's foyer and his assailants got to him there. Police investigating recovered an abandoned M1 carbine, machetes, meat cleavers and a sawn-off shotgun. Then they sought out witnesses. But everybody, it quickly became apparent, had been in the toilet at the time. The club had only had four toilets, but at the critical time all 279 people at the club, from the accounts police received, had had occasion to go there. The result, said the then patrol commander at Wetherill Park, Inspector Malcolm Cox, was that the police got nothing.

In the meantime, the home invasions continued, sometimes with dreadful results for the victims. On 28 November 1995, when two sisters were bound by home invaders, a woman suffered a miscarriage. In July 1996, four youths raided a home in Canley Vale and threatened to kill an 11-year-old girl unless a $50,000 ransom was paid, then took $2000 in cash and a mobile phone before taking off with the girl in the family's Suzuki car. The girl managed to get a note to staff at the hotel in Bonnyrigg where she was held, and four youths, aged 16 to 18, were arrested.

It would be possible to cite many more instances of violence. The courts have been filled with accused people. New South Wales Police Commissioner Ryan complained that too much police time was being taken up attending to the formalities of court proceedings. This civilised, time-honoured system, ensuring that all accused people had rights granted them in accordance with proper procedure, has always been open to abuse and exploitation by criminals, who pleaded not guilty, hired lawyers, and did anything they could to obstruct justice. But what is the alternative?

The next group to come to the attention of the police and public were the Koreans. From 1992, Kings Cross had become a mecca for Sydney's Korean community after the conversion of the former Crest Hotel in Darlinghurst Road into the Capitol Hotel, a Korean establishment with a bath house. From then on, many Korean restaurants and bars sprang up in Kings Cross to service an influx of Korean businessmen and tourists. Three gangs started operating, running protection rackets and moving into the vacuum in the drug trade created by the New South Wales Police Royal Commission clean-out of the Lebanese heroin connection in Kings Cross. One Korean gang was based in Korea, two were based in Sydney. Korean prostitutes were recruited to come to Australia and work in brothels and karaoke bars. Korean criminals were recruited to come to Australia to do a particular piece of dirty work. They stayed freelancing.

The Korean problem came into the open in the Christmas period of 1996, when 'enforcers' started carrying out their version of discipline on erring Koreans. On Boxing Day, a resident at Kings Cross videotaped the actions of an enforcer in Llanelly Place as he bashed and lectured a Korean victim kneeling before him. Another enforcer assaulted a woman and took her wallet. Police were called and the assailants lined up beside the victim for questioning. And nobody complained, which restricted the police in what they could do, even when handed the video. On 7 January 1997, a group of four Korean gangsters bashed staff at the Bee Won restaurant in

Kings Cross. Two men, Duk Soo Kim, 31, and Duk Hwan Kim, 27, who had arrived in Australia on a tourist visa, were apparently involved. Police were concerned about all these incidents. There had been reports that prostitutes in an apartment block in Macleay Street, Kings Cross, were screaming as they were being assaulted by enforcers from rival gangs. Two days after the Bee Won incident, police and migration officers raided the apartment block.

On 31 January 1997, Duk Soo Kim and Duk Hwan Kim arrived at the Namkang Restaurant and Ewah karaoke bar in Earl Place, Kings Cross, and were turned away. They were still in their car when they were attacked, dragged from their car and taken into a garage. A former flatmate of the Kims, Jin Hun Jang, arrived at the garage and saw the Kims stripped to their waists and being dragged along the floor, with boots smashing down on their skulls. The assailants ordered Jang to drive to the front of the Namkang restaurant and take away his friends. When the Kims were delivered to him, they were badly injured, their heads pulverised beyond recognition. He rushed them to the nearby St Vincent's Hospital but both died.

The bashings brought the whole issue of Korean crime into the open. Korean criminals had come into Sydney to exploit their countrymen, particularly over casino operations. Losing gamblers were given loans, and when they could not repay them they were bashed and their wives were often forced into prostitution. In the 12 months to June 1997, dozens of Korean men were treated in hospital for injuries sustained in the bashings. But they refused to cooperate with police.

The extortion was wide-ranging. Koreans anywhere, even English-language students at Eastwood in Sydney's north-west, were targeted by extortionists. As with all other Asian crime, it was a dreadful blight on a newly arrived ethnic group seeking acceptance. There was visible evidence that the arrivals had been highly beneficial to the wider community. In Eastwood, for example, the older shops, which had lost ground to the huge retailing complexes at Parramatta, North Ryde, West Ryde and Carlingford and had become 'el cheapo' alternatives, were transformed by the investment of Asian money into places that were often chic and sophisticated. The Korean Christian churches were active, reaching out evangelically to all Australians. They had no more time for criminals than anyone else. As the Rev Mark Fairhurst, Rector of St Philips Anglican Church, Eastwood, said as he launched his multicultural outreach, the migrant communities stood to enrich not only the economy but also the culture and spirituality of their new home.

But always the bad pennies arrived with the others. Korean gangs came to the attention of the National Crime Authority and the New South Wales Police. Several Korean gangs were identified. One was the 'Casino Gang', which did loansharking at Sydney Harbour Casino. One major loan shark, Tae Il Kang, was reported to have visited Sydney Harbour Casino 111 times between January and July 1997, reportedly threatening Korean gamblers and conducting business in casino lounges. Another outfit, the Tae Kun Oh gang, located at North Sydney, Kings Cross and Campsie in Sydney's south-west, busied itself with extortion, particularly in the karaoke bars in Kings Cross, and standing over tour operators.

The White Hawk gang, based at Sydney Harbour Casino, North Sydney and Campsie, tried to muscle in on the Casino Gang's operations, but its members were bashed. It was not slow to turn its attention elsewhere. At the Unicorn Karaoke Club in North Sydney, the manager, Earl Yang, and staff were allegedly assaulted by members of the White Hawks, one of them wielding a tomahawk. Police arrested several people, including Jae Oh Soh, reputedly a member of the White Hawk gang. On 8 February 1996, Soh was walking home in Campsie with his friend when a car containing six men pulled up. They viciously assaulted him, knocking him to the ground, hitting him with a lump of wood and an iron bar, and stabbing him 21 times. Despite suffering terribly, sustaining a ruptured spleen and a cut hamstring, Soh declined to assist police in their inquiries. A reputed key figure in the Kings Cross gang, Chong Mun Chai, manager of the Ewah karaoke bar, was arrested, along with an employee, Sang Hyun Bae, for the murders of the two Kims. Two others, Ba Da La, a student, and Sang Hoon Lee, were also arrested. On 22 July 1998, Chai was acquitted of murder but convicted on two charges of manslaughter. Bae was convicted on two charges of inflicting grievous bodily harm.

So why should such people be allowed into the country? A Federal political row erupted over suggestions that potential visitors be screened for criminal convictions. For non-Australian adults who were serious offenders, it was possibly a reasonable suggestion. But what about the case of Minh Duc Hong, a Vietnamese who had come to Australia in March 1995 as a 12-year-old, settled in Cabramatta, become a drug addict and acquired a criminal record? At the age of 22, not having been naturalised and with a string of drug-related convictions stretching back to the Children's Court, he was convicted on two counts each of supplying and possessing a prohibited drug and two of goods in custody.

That prompted moves to have him deported, and in fact that order was made by a representative of the Minister for Immigration and upheld by Dr Paul Gerber, deputy president of the Commonwealth Administrative Appeals Tribunal. The case went on appeal to Justice Rodney Madgwick in the Australian Federal Court in November 1999. Madgwick went along with a plea by the ultimate battler's lawyer, Bruce Miles, that Hong had been accepted into Australia as a child and had fallen victim to the particular local community into which he had been thrust. It was Australia's duty, he said, to look after someone so young and to accept some responsibility for the boy's descent into drugs and crime. Madgwick stayed the deportation until the case could be reconsidered and at the time of writing, that reconsideration was still pending.

At Dulwich Hill, Tuan Than (Peter) Ho, who had given evidence before Gerber that Hong was capable of rehabilitation, said: 'Hong grew up in the culture of Cabramatta by accident. The bucket became dirty here. Why send it to Vietnam?' And that would seem to be the final word. Australia must take its dirty buckets, accept responsibility for them, and clean them up. If one

Nghia Minh Hong lost his life in a hail of bullets in a Cabramatta stairway, perhaps Minh Duc Hong, 11 years later, could be given a chance, along with so many others who had erred. But there is a lot of cleaning to be done.

CONCLUSION

Everyone is entitled to their brief moment of 'retreat' from a competitive and at times hostile world. For me, it is coffee on a Sunday morning at Eastwood in Sydney's north-west, swapping asides with Pedro Sasso, proprietor of a rather nice little place called Rumbles. I got myself expelled from bible study at the local Anglican Church back in 1994, for alleged irreverence. I could have made a stand, but all I wanted was a chin-wag and a chance to raise a laugh, and I must agree that people are entitled to study the Word in a serious vein. With my youngest child in Sunday School, the elder children looking after themselves, and work another 24 hours away, it is an hour of peace.

But even that involves a degree of shutting one's mind off.

Across the road from Rumbles, on West Parade, stands a palm tree, and beneath it is the spot where, on a Sunday morning in June 1992, a jogger found the body of Joseph John Attard. Attard, 38, had been drinking at the Eastwood Hotel and had walked through the railway tunnel on his way home. He had been killed by Wayne Allan McGarritty, 27, and Rowan Andrew Clark, 31, who had followed him from the hotel with the intention of robbing him. Further on, about a block away in First Avenue, is the Eastwood Baptist Church, a worthy institution which provided a playschool attended by the children of Korean housewife, Sue Park, for two years before she, and they, disappeared. Her body, and those of her children, aged three and two, were found in suitcases in bushland in August 1997. On 7 March 2000, her husband, Sung Eun (Nick) Park, 29, was found guilty of their murders.

Behind me is Windborne Street, West Ryde, where Reynette June Holford, asleep in her own home in January 1987, was woken by a burglar. She took action to repel the intruder and paid with her life. Her elderly, stroke-ridden husband, Bill Graf, who came under suspicion for involvement in some way in the death, died before the coroner's inquest was held in 1988.

Moving in the other direction, towards North Ryde, at the corner of Blaxland Road and Edgar Street is a house once occupied by a former milkman, Edward 'Ted' Victorsen, whose battered body was discovered just inside his back door in November 1987. Victorsen's son, William, told police he found the body at 5 am after he returned home from a night out. There was something odd about the story, and in fact William was ultimately charged with his father's murder. On 13 August 1999, he was sentenced by Justice Peter Hidden in the Supreme Court of New South Wales to 18 years' gaol, with 13 still to be served.

On such balmy Sunday mornings, if I am able to cast such dark thoughts aside, I say to Pedro that I would like to stay forever in my spot outside his establishment, thinking only good thoughts. But on Monday morning, I will pass the spot where Attard breathed his last, and get onto that train and into work, and it all starts again. I will pass Strathfield station and see the shopping centre where Wade Frankum cut loose, and North Strathfield station, which he might have chosen for his massacre.

There have in recent times been studies of conflict resolution; entire university departments have been given over to peace studies. All manner of people have had a go at this subject, from Jesus onwards. Modern psychology has looked at personality types, geneticists at genetic makeup, sociologists at environment. Government policy towards law and punishment swings in an endless pendulum pattern between 'toughening up' and humanitarian outrage. Nobody has yet come up with anything that is guaranteed to work.

Professor Charles Birch, Emeritus Professor of Biology at Sydney University, now in his 1980s, has devoted his remaining years to a study of how the universe can restore tranquillity to its soul. His latest attempt to grapple with this subject, *Biology and the Riddle of Life*, was published in 1999 by the University of New South Wales Press. Birch's thesis is that people must rediscover compassion, not only for each other, but for all things, compassion for animals and insects and other organisms which, having subjective experiences of life, also have rights. Perhaps the answer lies somewhere there.

Had the mass killers paused to consider the feelings of the people whose lives they were to so brutally disrupt, the serial killers to consider the feelings of the hapless hitchhikers, the bank robbers to consider the innocent staff going about their work, making an honest living, they might have restrained themselves. With crime, there is a dislocation of that feeling. There is no automatic, intuitive empathy. That, Birch says, is what has been lost.

One of the underlying factors in the spasmodic violence that has afflicted Australian society over the last quarter of the twentieth century is that people have lost that compassion. Instead of projecting themselves, trying to step into the shoes of the other person – the hitchhiker on the Hume Highway, for instance – the predators 'objectify' those other beings and treat them as they have no subjective experience, and no rights.

There is no easy solution to this. It is a matter of dealing with each outrage individually, creating institutions such as the Family Court which, however imperfect, try to combine firmness with compassion, seeking to conciliate matters and looking at the possibilities, taking account of the legal menagerie of early intervention.

No system has yet been devised to accommodate the determined wrongdoer who has no conscience. The individual who becomes deranged and loses control is in a different category. There are often warning signs – a change in a person's demeanour, or lifestyle, a visit to a psychiatrist – things that suggest something ominous is going on in the inner recesses of that person's mind. Perhaps in a society which is more caring, more enlightened, more considerate of those that fall away from the pack, the affected individual might have options other than the road of disaster.

ABOUT
THE
AUTHORS

Malcolm Brown, an author and the contributing editor, started journalism at the *Daily Liberal* newspaper in Dubbo, New South Wales, in 1969 and, following two years national service in the army, he joined *The Sydney Morning Herald* in 1972. He has been a general reporter, covering the courts, royal commissions and coroner's inquests for many years. He has also been an interstate and foreign correspondent. Brown is the co-author of *Justice and Nightmares: Case Studies in Forensic Science* (University of New South Wales Press), and contributing editor of *Australian Crime* and *Rorting: The Great Australian Crime* (both issued by Lansdowne Publishing).

Estelle Blackburn started her career in journalism at *The West Australian* newspaper in 1969, and has since worked for the ABC and as a press secretary to a Western Australian premier. She is the author of the award-winning book *Broken Lives*, about serial killer Eric Edgar Cooke. Estelle has won both the 1999 Perth Press Club Award and the 1999 Clarion Award. She is also the winner of the 1999 Western Australian Premier's Award for non-fiction.

Roderick Campbell has been a legal reporter for *The Canberra*

Times for nearly 20 years. Since 1989, he has covered all the events of the Colin Winchester case. He co-wrote the book *The Winchester Scandal*, published by Random House in 1992, with Brian Toohey.

Les Kennedy is the co-author of two non-fiction Australian crime novels; *Granny Killer: The story of John Glover* (HarperCollins Publishing) and the acclaimed *Sins of the Brother: The Definitive Story of Ivan Milat and the Backpacker Murders* (Pan Macmillan). He was the chief police reporter for the *Daily Telegraph* newspaper in Sydney for 12 years, and since 1997 has been the chief police reporter for *The Sydney Morning Herald*.

Nigel Hunt has been reporting on crime and police related stories for the past 18 years. He was the chief police reporter for the now defunct *Adelaide News* for 10 years before joining *The Advertiser* as police reporter. He is currently assistant editor of *The Advertiser*, but is still involved in crime reporting with the paper and through other projects.

Tony Koch is currently the chief reporter at the *Courier Mail* newspaper in Brisbane. He was formerly a shorthand reporter for the Brisbane courts. He has won the Walkley Award for journalism three times, and is co-author of book *Joh KO* (Boolarong Publishing, 1983), which is about the fall of the Queensland state premier, Joh Bjelke-Petersen.

ACKNOWLEDGMENTS

The authors are indebted to *The Sydney Morning Herald* Library and to the New South Wales Supreme and District Court archives for the assistance both provided. Particular thanks should be given to Kimberley Ashbee, the New South Wales Supreme Court media and information coordinator, and to Peter Symonds, media officer for the New South Wales Director of Public Prosecutions and the New South Wales Police Integrity Commission. Thanks should also go to journalists Stephen Gibbs, Mark Whittaker and Kate McClymont. Special cooperation was received from Task Force Yandee, in particular Detective Inspector Rod Baker and Detective Sergeant Matt Appleton, and from former Detective Inspector Aarne Tees. The authors would also like to thank the following for their permission to use the pictures that appear in this book:

Garbage Truck (Ric Stevens/The Fairfax Photo Library)

Emergency services (The Fairfax Photo Library)

Evan Pederick (Dean Sewell/*Sydney Morning Herald*/The Fairfax Photo Library)

Aarne Tees (George Fetting/*Sydney Morning Herald*/The Fairfax Photo Library)

Tim Anderson (News Limited)

Dean and Cecil Waters 1 (News Limited)

Dean and Cecil Waters 2 (News Limited)

Judge Ray Watson press conference (Peter Morris/*Sydney Morning Herald*/The Fairfax Photo Library)

Hoss Majdalawi (Dean Sewell/*Sydney Morning Herald*/The Fairfax Photo Library)

NCA building (*The Advertiser* - Adelaide)

Domenic Perre (Chris Mangan/*The Advertiser* - Adelaide)

Peter Wallis (*The Advertiser* - Adelaide)

Hieu Duy Dinh and Angela Sinclair (*The Advertiser* - Adelaide)

Angela Sinclair (Michael Milnes/*The Advertiser* - Adelaide)

Frank Mercuri (Michael Milnes/*The Advertiser* - Adelaide)

Gerald Preston (Chris Mangan/*The Advertiser* - Adelaide)

Julian Knight (News Limited)

Frank Vitkovic (News Limited)

Martin Bryant (News Limited)

Seascape guest house (News Limited)

Lindsay Becketts (Mike Bowers/*The Age*/The Fairfax Photo Library)

Leslie Camilleri (Simon O'Dwyer/*The Age*/The Fairfax Photo Library)

Parents of Bega schoolgirls (News Limited)

Michael Murphy (News Limited)

Ivan Milat 1 (News Limited)

Challinder Hughes (News Limited)

Ivan Milat's prison cell (News Limited)

Ivan Milat 2 (Nick Moir/*The Sydney Morning Herald*/The Fairfax Photo Library)

Winchester funeral (Richard Briggs/*Canberra Times*)

Police searching Winchester car (Jon Beale/*Canberra Times*)

Arrest of David Eastman (Richard Briggs/*Canberra Times*)

Gwen and Peter Winchester (Graham Tidy/*Canberra Times*)

Ric Ninness (Richard Briggs/*Canberra Times*)

Jaidyn Leskie (News Limited)

Greg Domaszewicz (Joe Castro/*The Age*/The Fairfax Photo Library)

Bilynda Murphy (Sebastian Costanzo/*The Age*/The Fairfax Photo Library)

Jaidyn Leskie's funeral (News Limited)

Brett Leskie (News Limited)

Kadee Leskie (News Limited)

Eddie Withnell (Greg Burke/*The West Australian*)

Gun and mask (Greg Burke/*The West Australian*)

Maida Vale shooting (Nic Ellis/*The West Australian*)

Operation Gallipoli poster (Rod Taylor/*The West Australian*)

Bikie funeral procession (*The West Australian*)

Body in car (John Mokrzycki/*The West Australian*)

John Watson and Richard Court (John Evans/*The West Australian*)

Brendon Abbott and two detectives (Queensland Police)

Brendon Berichon (Jason South/*The Age*/The Fairfax Photo Library)

John Newman (Simon Alekna/*The Sun-Herald*/The Fairfax Photo Library)

Tu Quang Dao (News Limited)

Man stabbed in Cabramatta (News Limited)

Dr Victor Chang (The Fairfax Photo Library)

index